DIGITAL SAT

MATH PREP WORKBOOK

AMERICAN MATH ACADEMY

By H. TONG, M.Ed.

Math Instructor & Olympiad Coach
www.americanmathacademy.com

AMERICAN MATH ACADEMY

DIGITAL SAT
MATH PREP WORKBOOK

TABLE OF CONTENTS

CHAPTER 3: Advanced Math (35% 13–15 Questions)

CHAPTER 4: Geometry and Trigonometry (15%. 5–7 Questions)

CHAPTER 5: Review Tests

About the Author

Mr. Tong teaches at various private and public schools in both New York and New Jersey. In conjunction with his teaching, Mr. Tong developed his own private tutoring company. His company developed a unique way of ensuring their students' success on the math section of the SAT. Over the years his students, have been able to apply the knowledge and skills they've learned during their tutoring sessions in college and beyond. Mr. Tong's academic accolades make him the best candidate to teach SAT Math. He received his Master's Degree in Math Education. He has won several national and state championships in various math competitions and has taken his team to victory in the Olympiads. He has trained students for Math Counts, American Math Competition (AMC), Harvard MIT Math Tournament, Princeton Math Contest, and the National Math League, and many other events. His teaching style ensures student success. He puts great effort, and time into his students. He uses different teaching strategies to help struggling students. His dedication towards his students is evident through his student's achievements.

Acknowledgements

I would like to take the time to acknowledge the help and support of my beloved wife, my colleagues, and my students–their feedback on my book was invaluable. I would like to say an additional thank you to my dear friend Robert for his assistance in making this book complete. Without everyone's help, this book would not be the same. I dedicate this book to my precious daughter Vera and Nora who were my inspiration to take on this project.

Digital SAT Math Sample Test

1

If $4x - (2x - 3) = 10$, what is the value of $2^{(2x)}$?

A) 2^5

B) 3^6

C) 2^7

D) 2^8

Hard

2

$$0.12x + 0.15y = 0.14(x + y)$$

In a chemistry experiment, Mia will mix x milliliters of a 12% by volume ethanol solution with y milliliters of a 15% by volume ethanol solution to create a 14% by volume ethanol solution. The equation above represents this situation. If Mia uses 80 milliliters of the 15% by volume ethanol solution, how many milliliters of the 12% by volume ethanol solution must she use?

A) 20

B) 40

C) 60

D) 80

Easy

3

A car rental company charges a flat fee of $50 plus $20 per day for renting a car.

Let's represent the number of days as x and the total cost as C(x).

Which of the following equations represents the total cost C(x) in terms of the number of days?

A) $C(x) = 50x + 20$

B) $C(x) = 50 + 20x$

C) $C(x) = 20x - 50$

D) $C(x) = 20 - 50x$

Medium

4

A car rental company charges a flat fee of $50 per day plus an additional $0.25 per mile driven.

Let's say x represents the number of days a customer rents the car, and y represents the total number of miles driven. Which of the following inequalities represent the condition where the total cost of renting the car is at most $150?

A) $50x + 0.25y \leq 150$

B) $0.25x + 50y > 150$

C) $50x + 0.25y < 150$

D) $0.25x + 50y \geq 150$

5

Which of the following expressions is equivalent to $4(x^2 - 2x + 3) + 2(x^2 - 5x + 2) - (3x^2 - 4x + 1)$?

A) $-4x^2 + 9x + 7$

B) $-7x^2 + 7x + 5$

C) $3x^2 - 14x + 15$

D) $-x^2 + 9x + 7$

7

In a right triangle, one angle measures $x°$, where $\cos x° = \dfrac{5}{13}$.

What is $\tan(90° - x°)$?

A) $\dfrac{12}{13}$

B) $\dfrac{5}{12}$

C) $\dfrac{7}{12}$

D) $\dfrac{13}{12}$

6

Line p contains the point $(5, -2)$ and $(4, k)$. If line p is parallel to line q, whose equation is $x - 2y = 6$, what is the value of k?

A) $k = 5$

B) $k = -5$

C) $k = -\dfrac{5}{2}$

D) $k = \dfrac{5}{2}$

8

In a 30° -60° -90° degrees special triangle, if the shorter leg measures 6 units, what are the lengths of the other two sides?

A) Shorter leg: 6 units, longer leg: 12 units, hypotenuse: $6\sqrt{3}$ units

B) Shorter leg: 6 units, longer leg: $6\sqrt{3}$ units, hypotenuse: 12 units

C) Shorter leg: 6 units, longer leg: $3\sqrt{3}$ units, hypotenuse: 6 units

D) Shorter leg: 6 units, longer leg: 3 units, hypotenuse: $3\sqrt{3}$ units

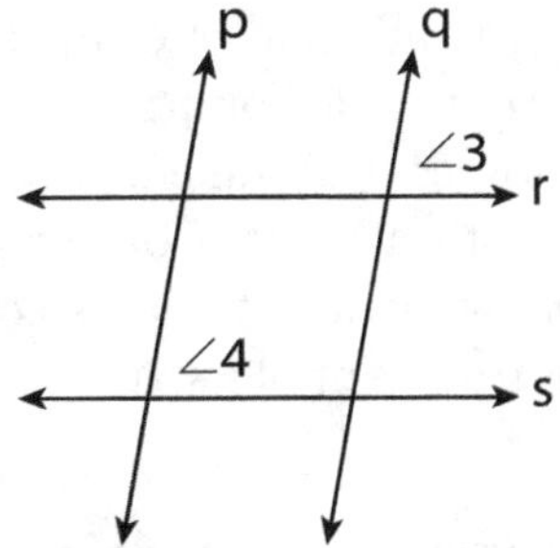

In the given figure, lines p and q are parallel, and lines r and s are parallel.

If the measure of $\angle 3$ is 70°, what is the measure of $\angle 4$?

A) 35°

B) 70°

C) 105°

D) 140°

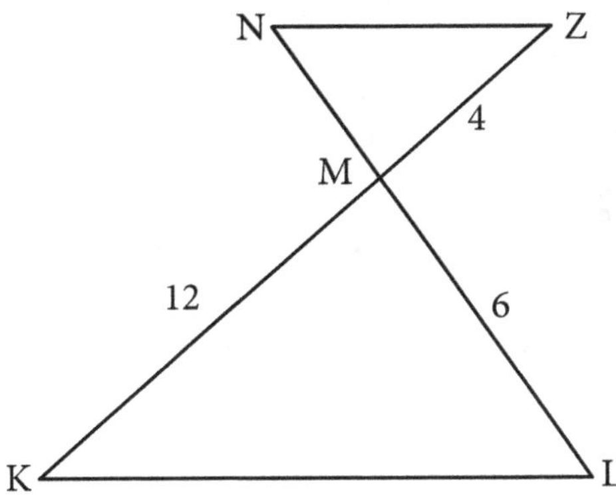

In the figure above, KL || NZ and segment, KZ intersects segment NL at M.

What is the length of segment NM?

A) 1

B) 2

C) 3

D) 4

An object is launched from the ground and reaches a maximum height of 100 meters in 5 seconds after launch.

A quadratic function can be used to model the height, in meters, of the object above the ground in terms of time, in seconds, after launch.

Based on this model, what is the height of the object 2.5 seconds after launch?

A) 60 meters

B) 75 meters

C) 80 meters

D) 90 meters

$$x^2 + 12x + y^2 - 6y = 25$$

The equation above defines a circle in the xy-plane.

What are the coordinates of the center of the circle?

A) (-6, 3)

B) (-6, -3)

C) (-12, 6)

D) (-12, -6)

Hard

13

A cylindrical tank has a diameter of 10 meters and a height of 6 meters.

It is filled to 80% of its capacity. What is the volume of the water in the tank, in cubic meters?

A) 18π cubic meters

B) 30π cubic meters

C) 36π cubic meters

D) 120π cubic meters

Medium

14

$$\frac{3x+5}{2x-1} = \frac{7}{4}$$

Which of the following represents all the possible values of x that satisfy the equation above.

A) $\dfrac{-27}{2}$

B) 2

C) 27

D) $\dfrac{27}{2}$

Medium

15

In a survey conducted to estimate the average salary of employees in a company, a random sample of 100 employees was taken. The sample mean was $50,000 with a margin of error of $2,000. Which of the following statements is correct regarding the inference from sample statistics and the margin of error?

A) The true average salary of all employees falls between $48,000 and $52,000.

B) The sample mean is exactly $50,000.

C) The margin of error represents the variability in the sample mean.

D) The sample size should have been larger to reduce the margin of error.

Hard

16

Which of the following values of x satisfies the equation

$$\sqrt{2x-1} = x-1?$$

A) $x = 1 \pm \sqrt{2}$

B) $x = 2 \pm \sqrt{2}$

C) $x = \pm \sqrt{2}$

D) $x = 2 \pm \sqrt{3}$

Simplify the following expression using rational exponents:

$$\left(\frac{4}{9}\right)^{\frac{3}{2}} \cdot \left(\frac{9}{16}\right)^{\frac{1}{2}}$$

A) $\frac{1}{9}$

B) $\frac{2}{3}$

C) $\frac{2}{9}$

D) $\frac{4}{9}$

In the xy-plane, the point (5, 3) lies on the graph of the function $f(x) = 2x^2 + bx + 10$.

What is the value of b?

A) 11

B) -11.4

C) -12.4

D) -14

If $(6x + 5)(6x + 4) = 36x^2 + cx + 20$ for all values of x, what is the value of c?

A) 12

B) 24

C) 30

D) 54

If $\frac{1 + 4i}{2 - 3i} = a + bi$, what is the value of a+b?

A) $\frac{1}{13}$

B) $-\frac{1}{13}$

C) $\frac{3}{13}$

D) $\frac{4}{13}$

Easy

21

$6x - ay + 12 = 0$. If the slope of the equation is $\frac{1}{3}$, what is the value of $a = ?$

Easy

22

If 4 is one of the solutions of the equation

$x^2 - 4ax - 12 = 0$, what is the value of a?

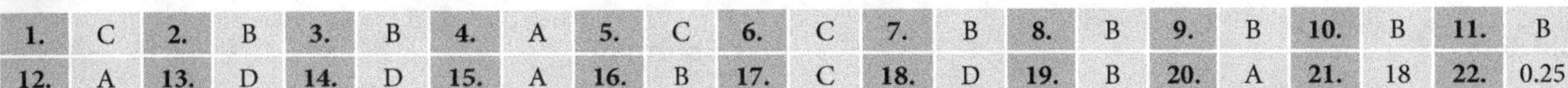

Digital SAT Math Sample Test Solution

1.	C	2.	B	3.	B	4.	A	5.	C	6.	C	7.	B	8.	B	9.	B	10.	B	11.	B
12.	A	13.	D	14.	D	15.	A	16.	B	17.	C	18.	D	19.	B	20.	A	21.	18	22.	0.25

1. Solution:

To find the value of 2^{2x}, we first need to solve the given equation $4x - (2x - 3) = 10$.

Let's simplify the equation step by step:

$4x - (2x - 3) = 10$

Distribute the negative sign inside the parentheses:

$4x - 2x + 3 = 10$

Combine like terms:

$2x + 3 = 10$

Subtract 3 from both sides:

$2x = 7$

Divide both sides by 2:

$x = \dfrac{7}{2}$

Now that we have found the value of x, we can substitute it into 2^{2x}:

$2^{2x} = 2^{\frac{2 \times 7}{2}} = 2^7$

Correct Answer is C

2. Solution:

To find the number of milliliters of the 12% ethanol solution Mia must use, we can substitute the given value of y into the equation and solve for x.

$0.12x + 0.15(80) = 0.14(x + 80)$

Simplifying the equation:

$0.12x + 12 = 0.14x + 11.2$

Subtracting 0.12x from both sides:

$12 = 0.02x + 11.2$

Subtracting 11.2 from both sides:

$0.8 = 0.02x$

Dividing both sides by 0.02:

$x = 40$

Correct Answer is B

3. Solution:

Let's break down the equation step by step:

- The flat fee of $50 is constant and does not change with the number of days. This can be represented as 50.
- The additional cost per day is $20, and it is multiplied by the number of days. This can be represented as 20x.

Combining both parts, we get:

$C(x) = 50 + 20x$

Correct Answer is B

4. Solution:

The correct answer is option A) $50x + 0.25y \le 150$.

To understand why, let's break down the equation:

The flat fee charged per day is $50, so the cost for x days is 50x.

The additional cost per mile driven is $0.25, so the cost for y miles is 0.25y.

To find the total cost, we add the flat fee and the additional cost:

Total cost = 50x + 0.25y

The inequality states that the total cost should be at most $150.

$50x + 0.25y \le 150$

This represents the condition where the total cost of renting the car is at most $150.

Correct Answer is A

5. Solution:

To simplify the expression, we can distribute and combine like terms:

$4(x^2 - 2x + 3) + 2(x^2 - 5x + 2) - (3x^2 - 4x + 1)$

$= 4x^2 - 8x + 12 + 2x^2 - 10x + 4 - 3x^2 + 4x - 1$

$= (4x^2 + 2x^2 - 3x^2) + (-8x - 10x + 4x) + (12 + 4 - 1)$

$= 3x^2 - 14 + 15$

Correct Answer is C

6. Solution:

The equation of line q is x - 2y = 10. We can rewrite this equation

in slope-intercept form (y = mx + b) by isolating y:

$-2y = -x + 10$ $y = \frac{1}{2} x - 5$

The slope of line q is $\frac{1}{2}$.

Since line p is parallel to line q, the slopes of the two lines will be equal.

Therefore, the slope of line p is also $\frac{1}{2}$.

Use the two-point slope formula to find k:

(5, -2) and (4, k).

$$m_p = \frac{y_2 - y_1}{x_2 - x_1},$$

$$\frac{1}{2} \cdot = \frac{k-(-2)}{4-5}$$

$$\frac{1}{2} \cdot == \frac{k+2}{-1} \text{ cross multiply}$$

$-1 = 2k + 4$, then $2k = -5$

$$k = -\frac{5}{2}$$

Correct answer is C

7. Solution:

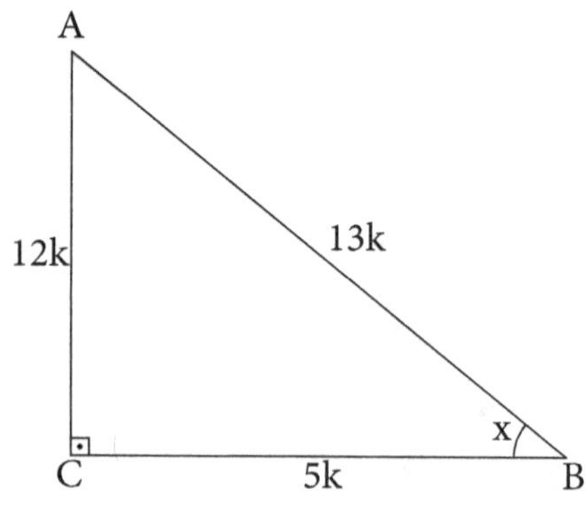

$$\tan(90 - x°) = \cot x° = \frac{5k}{12k} = \frac{5}{12}$$

Correct Answer is B

8. Solution:

In a 30° -60° -90° degrees special triangle, the relationship between the sides is as follows:

Shorter leg: Longer leg: Hypotenuse = $1 : \sqrt{3} : 2$

Given that the shorter leg measures 6 units,

we can determine the lengths of the other two sides:

Shorter leg = 6 units Longer leg = $6\sqrt{3}$ units

Hypotenuse = 2 x 6 = 12 units

Correct Answer is B

9. Solution:

If lines p and q are parallel and lines r and s are parallel,

we can determine the measure of $\angle$ 4 based on the given information that $\angle$ 3 measures 70°.

$\angle$ 3 and $\angle$ 4 are corresponding angles since they are on the same side of the transversal line and parallel lines. Corresponding angles are congruent when the transversal intersects parallel lines.

Therefore, the measure of $\angle$ 4 is also 70°

Correct Answer is B

10. Solution:

Segment KZ intersects segment NL at M.

First, let's observe triangle KLM and triangle MNZ.

Triangle KLM and triangle MNZ are similar triangles

because KL is parallel to NZ, and segment KZ intersects segment NL at M.

Similarity of the triangles:

$$\frac{KM}{ML} = \frac{MZ}{MN}$$

Plugging in the given values, we have:

$$\frac{12}{6} = \frac{4}{MN}$$

2 = MN

Correct Answer is B

11. Solution:

To model the height of the object above the ground as a quadratic function, we can use the standard form of a quadratic equation:

$h(t) = at^2 + bt + c$

Where: $h(t)$ is the height of the object at time t (in seconds) after launch. a, b, and c are constants.

Given that the object reaches a maximum height of 100 meters in 5 seconds after launch, we can determine the values of a, b, and c.

At the maximum height, the object's velocity is zero.

This means that the first derivative of the height function with respect to time is zero.

Taking the derivative of the quadratic function:

$h'(t) = 2at + b$

Setting $h'(t)$ equal to zero: $2a(5) + b = 0$

$10a + b = 0$ ...(Equation 1)

At $t = 0$, the object's height is 0 meters.

Plugging these values into the quadratic function:

$h(0) = 0$

$a(0)^2 + b(0) + c = 0$

$c = 0$ ...(Equation 2)

Substituting Equation 2 into the quadratic function:

$h(t) = at^2 + bt$

Using the fact that the maximum height is 100 meters at $t = 5$:

$h(5) = a(5)^2 + b(5) = 100$

$25a + 5b = 100$ ...(Equation 3)

Now, we have three equations with three unknowns (a, b, c).

Solving this system of equations will give us the values of a, b, and c.

From Equation 1, we can rewrite b in terms of a: $b = -10a$

Substituting $b = -10a$ into Equation 3:

$25a + 5(-10a) = 100$

$25a - 50a = 100$

$-25a = 100$

$a = -4$

Using the value of a in Equation 1:

$10(-4) + b = 0$

$-40 + b = 0$

$b = 40$

Thus, the quadratic function that models the height of the object above the ground is:

$h(t) = -4t^2 + 40t$

To find the height of the object 2.5 seconds after launch,

we can substitute $t = 2.5$ into the height function:

$h(2.5) = -4(2.5)^2 + 40(2.5)$

$h(2.5) = -4(6.25) + 100$

$h(2.5) = -25 + 100$

$h(2.5) = 75$

Therefore, the height of the object 2.5 seconds after launch is 75 meters

Correct Answer is B

12. Solution:

Equation in the standard form of a circle:

$(x - h)^2 + (y - k)^2 = r^2$

where (h, k) represents the center of the circle, and r represents the radius. Let's rearrange the given equation to match the standard form:

$x^2 + 12x + y^2 - 6y = 25$

To complete the square for the x terms,

we add $\left(\dfrac{12}{2}\right)^2 = 36$ to both sides:

$x^2 + 12x + 36 + y^2 - 6y = 25 + 36$

Simplifying further: $(x + 6)^2 + y^2 - 6y = 61$

Now, we need to complete the square for the y terms. To do that,

we add $\left(\dfrac{6}{2}\right)^2 = 9$ to both sides: $(x + 6)^2 + y^2 - 6y + 9 = 61 + 9$

Simplifying further: $(x + 6)^2 + (y - 3)^2 = 70$

Now, the equation is in the standard form of a circle.

The center of the circle is (-6, 3).

Correct Answer is A

13. Solution:

The formula to calculate the volume of a cylinder is given by: Volume $= \pi \cdot r^2 \cdot h$

In this case, the diameter of the cylinder is given as 10 meters, which means the radius r is half of that 5meters.

The height (h) of the cylinder is 6 meters. Let's calculate the volume of the cylinder:

Volume $= \pi \cdot 5^2 \cdot h \cdot 6 = 25\pi \cdot 6 = 150\pi$ cubic meters

Now, to find the volume of the water in the tank, we multiply the volume of the cylinder by the percentage filled, which is 80% or 0.8: Volume of water $= 150\pi \cdot 0.8 = 120\pi$ cubic meters

Therefore, the volume of the water in the tank is 120π cubic meters.

Correct Answer is D

14. Solution:

To solve this proportion equation, we can cross-multiply and simplify:

$$\frac{3x + 5}{2x - 1} = \frac{7}{4}$$

$12x + 20 = 14x - 7$

$12x - 14x = -7 - 20$

$-2x = -27$

$$x = \frac{27}{2}$$

Correct Answer is D

15. Solution:

The margin of error represents the range within which the true population parameter is likely to fall. In this case, with a sample mean of $50,000 and a margin of error of $2,000, we can infer that the true average salary of all employees in the company is likely to be between $48,000 and $52,000.

Correct Answer is A

16. Solution:

To find the value of x that satisfies the equation, we need to isolate the square root term and solve for x.

$$\sqrt{2x - 1} = (x - 1)^2$$

Squaring both sides of the equation, we have:

$2x - 1 = (x - 1)^2$

$2x - 1 = x^2 - 2x + 1$

Rearranging the equation, we get: $x^2 - 4x + 2 = 0$

In this case, a = 1, b = -4, and c = 2.

Substituting these values into the quadratic formula:

$$\frac{-b \pm \sqrt{b^2 - 4ac}}{2a}$$

$$= \frac{-(-4) \pm \sqrt{(-4)^2 - 4(1)(2)}}{2(1)}$$

$$= \frac{4 \pm \sqrt{16 - 8}}{2}$$

$$= 2 \pm \sqrt{2}$$

Correct Answer is B

17. Solution:

Simplify the following expression using rational exponents:

$$\left(\frac{4}{9}\right)^{\frac{3}{2}} \cdot \left(\frac{9}{16}\right)^{\frac{1}{2}}$$

To simplify the expression, we can evaluate each part separately and then multiply the results together.

Let's start with

$$\left(\frac{4}{9}\right)^{\frac{3}{2}} = \left(\frac{2^2}{3^2}\right)^{\frac{3}{2}} = \frac{2^3}{3^3} = \frac{8}{27}$$

$$\left(\frac{9}{16}\right)^{\frac{1}{2}} = \left(\frac{3^2}{4^2}\right)^{\frac{1}{2}} = \left(\frac{3}{4}\right)^1 = \frac{3}{4}$$

The simplified expression is:

$$\frac{8}{27} \cdot \frac{3}{4} = \frac{2}{9}$$

Correct Answer is C

18. Solution:

Expanding the left side of the equation, we have:

$(6x+5)(6x+4) = 36x^2 + (24x + 30x) + 20$

$= 6x^2 + 54x + 20$

Comparing this with the given quadratic equation,

$36x^2 + cx + 20 = 6x^2 + 54x + 20$

$cx = 54x$

$c = 54$

Correct Answer is D

19. Solution:

Substituting $x = 5$ and $y = 3$ into the function f(x), we have:

$3 = 2(5)^2 + b(5) + 10$

Simplifying the equation, we get:

$3 = 2(25) + 5b + 10$

Further simplifying, we have:

$3 = 50 + 5b + 10$

Combining like terms, we have:

$3 = 60 + 5b$

$-57 = 5b, \quad b = -11.4$

Correct Answer is B

20. Solution:

Multiplying both the numerator and denominator by the conjugate of the denominator. The conjugate of 2 - 3i is 2 + 3i.

So, we have:

$$\frac{1 + 4i}{2 - 3i} \cdot \frac{2 + 3i}{2 + 3i}$$

Expanding the numerator and denominator:

$$\frac{(1 + 4i)(2 + 3i)}{(2 - 3i)(2 + 3i)}$$

Simplifying each term:

$$\frac{(1 \cdot 2) + (1 \cdot 3i) + (4i \cdot 2) + (4i \cdot 3i)}{(2 \cdot 2) + (2 \cdot 3i) + (-3i \cdot 2) + (-3i) \cdot 3i}$$

$$= \frac{2 + 3i + 8i + 12i^2}{4 + 6i - 6i - 9i^2}$$

Since i^2 is defined as -1:

$$= \frac{2 + 3i + 8i - 12}{4 + 6i - 6i + 9}$$

$$= \frac{-10 + 11i}{13}$$

Comparing this with a+bi, we can see that

$$a = \frac{-10}{13} \qquad b = \frac{11}{13}$$

Therefore, $a + b = \dfrac{-10}{13} + \dfrac{11}{13} = \dfrac{1}{13}$

Correct Answer is A

21. Solution:

$6x - ay + 12 = 0$

Equation Slope $= \dfrac{6}{a}$

$\dfrac{6}{a} = \dfrac{1}{3}, \quad a = 18$

Correct answer is 18

22. Solution:

$x^2 - 4ax - 12 = 0$

$16 - 4 \cdot 4a - 12 = 0$

$16 - 16a - 12 = 0$

$4 - 16a = 0$

$4 = 16a$

$\dfrac{1}{4} = a = 0.25$

Correct answer is 0.25

CHAPTER 1
ALGEBRA
(35%. 13–15 Questions)

- ➡ Linear Equations in One Variable & Two Variables

- ➡ System of Two Linear Equations

- ➡ Linear Functions

- ➡ Linear Inequalities

- ➡ Equivalent Expressions

- ➡ Slopes of Parallel Lines and Perpendicular Lines

- Linear equations in one variable they can be written in the form ax + b = 0, where a and b are constants.
- Linear equations in two variables they can be written in the form ax + by = c, where a and b and c are constants.

Example 1:

Solve the equation 3x - 7 = 8.

Solution:

Step 1: Simplify the equation if necessary. The equation 3x - 7 = 8 is already simplified.

Step 2: Use addition or subtraction to move the constant term to the opposite side of the equation. To isolate the variable term, we can add 7 to both sides of the equation: 3x - 7 + 7 = 8 + 7

This simplifies to: 3x = 15.

Step 3: Use multiplication or division to isolate the variable term on one side of the equation. Since the variable term is currently multiplied by 3, we can divide both sides of the equation by 3 to solve for x: $\frac{3x}{3} = \frac{15}{3}$

This simplifies to x = 5.

Therefore, the solution to the equation is x = 5.

Example 2:

Solve the equation 3x + 2y = 10, when x = 2. Find the value of y.

Solution:

To solve this equation, we will substitute the known value of x into the equation and solve for y.

Given equation: 3x + 2y = 10

Substitute x = 2 into the equation:

3(2) + 2y = 10 6 + 2y = 10

Next, isolate the term with y by subtracting 6 from both sides:

2y = 10 - 6, 2y = 4 then y=2.

Therefore, when x = 2, the value of y is 2.

Digital SAT Sample Question:

If 3x + 2 = 8. What is the value of 2^x?

A) 4

B) 5

C) 6

D) 7

Solution:

Let's solve the equation step by step to find the value of x: 3x + 2 = 8

Step 1: Subtract 2 from both sides of the equation: 3x + 2 - 2 = 8 – 2, then 3x = 6

Step 2: Divide both sides of the equation by 3 to isolate the term with x: $\frac{3x}{3} = \frac{6}{3}$, x = 2

Now that we have the value of x, we can substitute it into the expression 2^x to find its value:

$2^2 = 4$

Therefore, the value of 2^x, where x = 2, is 4.

Correct answer is A

Linear Equations in One Variable & Two Variables Test

If $4x - (2x - 3) = 10$, what is the value of 2^{2x}?

A) 2^5

B) 2^6

C) 2^7

D) 2^8

The y-intercept of the graph of $y = 2x - 11$ in the xy-plane is $(0, y)$. What is the value of y?

A) -5

B) -11

C) 11/2

D) 11

$$(x - 2)^2 = -9$$

How many distinct real solutions does the given equation have?

A) Exactly one

B) Exactly two

C) Infinitely many

D) Zero

Solve the equation $4(x + 3) - 2(x - 1) = 6$.

A) $x = -1$

B) $x = 0$

C) $x = 1$

D) $x = -4$

Easy

5

Solve the equation $3(2x - 1) = 9x + 6$.

A) $x = -3$

B) $x = -2$

C) $x = 1$

D) $x = 2$

Easy

6

When $\frac{3}{5}x + 2 = 4y$ and $x = 10$, what is the value of y?

A) 1

B) 2

C) 3

D) 4

Easy

7

In the equation $y = -0.8x + 12$, what are the coordinates of the y-intercept?

A) (0, 12)

B) (12, 0)

C) (0, -0.8)

D) (-0.8, 0)

Easy

8

The sum of twice a number and 5 is equal to 17. What is the number?

A) 5

B) 6

C) 7

D) 8

Easy

9

The sum of two numbers is 12, and their difference is 4. Find the two numbers.

A) (8, 4)

B) (6, 6)

C) (7, 5)

D) (9, 3)

Medium

10

Convert a temperature of 15 degrees Celsius to Fahrenheit.

Use the formula $F = \frac{9}{5} C + 32$, where F represents the temperature in Fahrenheit and C represents the temperature in Celsius.

A) 32°F

B) 45°F

C) 59°F

D) 68°F

Medium

11

If $\frac{x + 3}{4} = y$ and $y = 7$, what is the value of x - 2?

A) 20

B) 21

C) 23

D) 25

Medium

12

On Friday, Ayra sent m text messages each hour for 8 hours, and John sent p text messages each hour for 6 hours. Which of the following expressions represents the total number of messages sent by Ayra and John on Friday?

A) 8m + 6p

B) 6m + 8p

C) 14m + 6p

D) m + 6p

Linear Equations in One Variable & Two Variables Test Solution

1. Solution:

To find the value of 2^{2x}, we first need to solve the given equation 4x - (2x - 3) = 10.

Let's simplify the equation step by step:

4x - (2x - 3) = 10

Distribute the negative sign inside the parentheses:

4x - 2x + 3 = 10

Combine like terms:

2x + 3 = 10

Subtract 3 from both sides:

2x = 7

Divide both sides by 2:

$x = \dfrac{7}{2}$

Now that we have found the value of x, we can substitute it into 2^{2x}:

$$2^{2x} = 2^{\frac{2 \times 7}{2}} = 2^7$$

Correct Answer is C

2. Solution:

To find the y-intercept of the graph, we need to determine the value of y when x is 0.

Given the equation: y = 2x - 11

Substitute x = 0 into the equation: y = 2(0) - 11, then

y = 0 - 11, y = -11

Correct Answer is B

3. Solution:

To solve the equation $(x - 2)^2 = -9$, we can start by taking the square root of both sides:

$$\left(\sqrt{(x-2)}\right)^2 = \pm\sqrt{-9}$$

Simplifying the left side:

x - 2 = ± 3i

There are no real values for x that satisfy the equation

x - 2 = ±3i. Thus, there are no real solutions to the given equation.

Correct Answer is D

4. Solution:

Expanding both sides of the equation, we get

4x + 12 - 2x + 2 = 6.

Combining like terms, we have 2x + 14 = 6.

Subtracting 14 from both sides, we find 2x = -8.

Dividing both sides by 2, we obtain x = -4.

Correct Answer is D

5. Solution:

Distributing the 3 to the terms inside the parentheses gives us 6x - 3 = 9x + 6.

Next, subtracting 6x from both sides gives us -3 = 3x + 6.

Then, subtracting 6 from both sides, we get -9 = 3x.

Dividing both sides by 3, we find x = -3.

Correct Answer is A

6. Solution:

To find the value of y, we can substitute

the given value of x into the equation $\frac{3}{5}x + 2 = 4y$ and solve for y.

Let's substitute x = 10 into the equation:

$\frac{3(10)}{5} + 2 = 4y$ Simplifying:

$\frac{30}{5} + 2 = 4y$, then 6 + 2 = 4y

8 = 4y

Dividing both sides by 4:

$\frac{8}{4} = y$

2 = y

Therefore, when x = 10, the value of y is 2.

Correct Answer is B

7. Solution:

In the given equation, the y-intercept represents the point where the line crosses the y-axis.

To find the coordinates of the y-intercept, we can set x to 0 and solve for y.

Let's substitute x = 0 into the equation:

y = -0.8(0) + 12

Simplifying:

y = 0 + 12

y = 12

Therefore, the coordinates of the y-intercept are (0, 12).

Correct Answer is A

8. Solution:

Let's represent the unknown number as x.

The given information can be written as the equation:

2x + 5 = 17.

First, let's subtract 5 from both sides of the equation:

2x + 5 - 5 = 17 - 5

Simplifying:

2x = 12

x = 6

Correct Answer is B

9. Solution:

Let's represent the first number as x and the second number as y.

x + y = 12

x - y = 4

To eliminate one variable, let's add the two equations together:

(x + y) + (x - y) = 12 + 4

Simplifying:

2x = 16

x = 8

Now, substitute the value of x back into one of the original equations to find y:

8 + y = 12

y = 4

Correct Answer is A

10. Solution:

To convert Celsius to Fahrenheit, we can use the formula $F = \frac{9}{5}C + 32$. Let's substitute C = 15 into the formula:

$F = \frac{9(15)}{5} + 32$, Simplifying:

$F = 27 + 32$

$F = 59$

Correct Answer is C

11. Solution:

To find the value of x - 2,

we need to substitute the given equations into the expression.

Given: $\frac{x+3}{4} = y$ and $y = 7$

Let's substitute y = 7 into the equation to solve for x:

$\frac{x+3}{4} = 7$

Multiplying both sides of the equation by 4:

x + 3 = 7 * 4

x + 3 = 28

x = 25

x - 2 = 25 - 2

x - 2 = 23

Correct Answer is C

12. Solution:

Ayra sent m text messages each hour for 8 hours, so the total number of messages sent by Ayra is 8m.

John sent p text messages each hour for 6 hours, so the total number of messages sent by John is 6p.

To find the total number of messages sent by Ayra and John, we need to add their individual totals.

The correct expression representing the total number of messages sent by Ayra and John on Friday is 8m + 6p.

Correct Answer is A

System of Two Linear Equations

A system of two linear equations involves two equations with two variables, typically represented by x and y. The general form of a linear equation in two variables is:

ax + by = c

A system of two linear equations can be written as:

ax + by = c, dx + ey = f

The goal of solving a system of two linear equations is to find the values of x and y that satisfy both equations simultaneously.

The solution to the system is the set of values (x, y) that make both equations true.

There are three possible types of solutions for a system of two linear equations:

- **One Solution:** The system has a one solution where the two lines representing the equations intersect at a one point.

- **No Solution:** The system has no solution, meaning the lines representing the equations are parallel and never intersect.

- **Infinite Solutions:** The system has infinitely many solutions, meaning the two lines representing the equations are coincident or overlapping.

To solve a system of two linear equations, substitution or elimination methods can be used.

Substitution Method: Solve one equation for one variable and substitute that expression into the other equation.

Then solve for the remaining variable and find the value of the other variable using substitution.

Example:

Solve the system of equations using the Substitution Method:

3x + 2y = 8,

2x - y = 1

Solution:

Step 1:

Solve one equation for one variable. Let's solve the second equation, 2x - y = 1, for y: y = 2x - 1.

Step 2:

Substitute the expression for y into the other equation. Substitute y = 2x - 1 into the first equation,

3x + 2y = 8: 3x + 2(2x - 1) = 8.

Step 3:

Simplify and solve for x. Expand and simplify the equation:

3x + 4x - 2 = 8, 7x - 2 = 8, 7x = 10, x = 10/7.

Step 4:

Substitute the value of x back into one of the original equations to find y.

Substitute x = 10/7 into the second equation,

$$2x - y = 1 : \frac{2(10)}{7} - y = 1$$

$$\frac{20}{7} - y = 1$$

$$\frac{20}{7} - 1 = y$$

$$y = \frac{13}{7}$$

Elimination Method: Add or subtract the two equations to eliminate one variable, creating a new equation with only one variable. Solve for that variable and substitute it back into either of the original equations to find the value of the other variable.

Example :

Solve the system of equations using the Elimination Method:

$2x + 3y = 5$

$4x - 2y = 6$

Solution:

Step 1:

Let's multiply the first equation by 2 and the second equation by 3 to eliminate the x term.

$2(2x + 3y) = 2(5), 3(4x - 2y) = 3(6).$

This simplifies the system to:

$\{4x + 6y = 10, 12x - 6y = 18\}$

Step 2:

Add or subtract the two equations to eliminate one variable.

In this case, adding the two equations eliminates the y term:

$(4x + 6y) + (12x - 6y) = 10 + 18.$

This simplifies to: $16x = 28.$

$x = \dfrac{7}{4}.$

Step 3:

Substitute the value of x back into one of the original equations to find y.

$\dfrac{2(7)}{4} + 3y = 5.$

This simplifies to: $\dfrac{7}{2} + 3y = 5.$

Subtract $\dfrac{7}{2}$ from both sides of the equation:

$3y = 5 - \dfrac{7}{2}$

This simplifies to: $3y = \dfrac{3}{2}$

$y = \dfrac{1}{2}$

System of Two Linear Equations Test

$$4x + 3y = 10$$

$$2x - y = 5$$

What is the value of $3x - 2y$?

A) 3

B) 5

C) 7.5

D) 10

Emma and Liam are selling tickets for a school fundraiser.

Emma sold 3 adult tickets and 2 child tickets for a total of $70.

Liam sold 4 adult tickets and 1 child ticket for a total of $80.

What is the cost of one adult ticket and one child ticket?

A) Adult ticket: $20, Child ticket: $10

B) Adult ticket: $15, Child ticket: $12

C) Adult ticket: $18, Child ticket: $8

D) Adult ticket: $25, Child ticket: $5

John is tracking the growth of a plant over time.

He measures the height of the plant every week and records it in a table.

The height of the plant (h) can be estimated using the equation $h = 12t + 30$, where t represents the number of weeks since John started tracking the plant.

What is the meaning of the value 30 in this equation?

A) The initial height of the plant when John started tracking it.

B) The maximum height that the plant can reach.

C) The rate at which the plant grows per week.

D) The number of weeks it takes for the plant to reach maturity

At a car dealership, the price (in dollars) of a new car and a used car can be estimated using the equations:

New car price: $n = 20{,}000 + 500x$

Used car price: $u = 15{,}000 + 800x$

In the equations above, n represents the price of the new car, u represents the price of the used car, and x represents the number of years since the car was manufactured.

At what year will the price of a used car be equal to the price of a new car?

A) 5 years

B) 8 years

C) 10 years

D) 17 years

System of Two Linear Equations Test

$$0.12x + 0.15y = 0.14(x + y)$$

In a chemistry experiment, Mia will mix x milliliters of a 12% by volume ethanol solution with y milliliters of a 15% by volume ethanol solution to create a 14% by volume ethanol solution. The equation above represents this situation. If Mia uses 80 milliliters of the 15% by volume ethanol solution, how many milliliters of the 12% by volume ethanol solution must she use?

A) 20

B) 40

C) 60

D) 80

$$2x + 3y = 7$$

$$3x - 2y = 4$$

The system of equations above is graphed in the xy-plane.

What is the x-coordinate of the intersection point (x, y) of the system?

A) 1

B) 2

C) 3

D) 4

$$2x + 3y = 10$$

$$4x - y = 8$$

What is the solution (x, y) to the system of equations above?

A) $\left(\frac{7}{17}, \frac{7}{12} \right)$

B) $\left(\frac{18}{5}, \frac{12}{5} \right)$

C) $\left(\frac{17}{7}, \frac{12}{7} \right)$

D) $\left(\frac{17}{7}, \frac{7}{12} \right)$

$$3x - 2y = 6$$

$$2x + 4y = 10$$

What is the solution (x, y) to the system of equations above?

A) $\left(\frac{1}{2}, \frac{3}{4} \right)$

B) (1, 2)

C) $\left(\frac{9}{4}, \frac{11}{4} \right)$

D) $\left(\frac{11}{4}, \frac{9}{8} \right)$

Medium

9

Sam is saving money to buy a new bike. He plans to save a fixed amount of money each week.

The total amount of money he will save after t weeks can be estimated using the equation S = 20t + 50, where S represents the total savings.

What is the meaning of the value 50 in this equation?

A) The cost of the new bike that Sam wants to buy.

B) The initial amount of money Sam had before he started saving.

C) The fixed amount of money Sam saves each week.

D) The number of weeks it will take for Sam to save enough money for the bike.

Easy

10

$$2x + 3y = 10$$

What is the value of y when x = 2?

A) 1

B) 2

C) 3

D) 4

Hard

11

A chemist has a solution that is 25% acid and another solution that is 40% acid. How many liters of each solution should be mixed to obtain 15 liters of a solution that is 30% acid?

A) 8 liters of 25% solution and 7 liters of 40% solution

B) 10 liters of 25% solution and 5 liters of 40% solution

C) 6 liters of 25% solution and 9 liters of 40% solution

D) 7 liters of 25% solution and 8 liters of 40% solution

Medium

12

If the sum of three consecutive odd integers is 39, what is the largest integer?

A) 11

B) 13

C) 15

D) 17

System of Two Linear Equations Test Solution

| 1. C | 2. C | 3. A | 4. D | 5. B | 6. B | 7. C | 8. D | 9. B | 10. B | 11. B | 12. C |

1. Solution:

Let's solve equation 2 for y:

$2x - y = 5$, $y = 2x - 5$

Now substitute the expression for y into equation 1:

$4x + 3(2x - 5) = 10$, then $4x + 6x - 15 = 10$,

$10x - 15 = 10$, $10x = 10 + 15$, then $10x = 25$ and $x = 2.5$

Substitute the value of x back into the expression for y:

$y = 2(2.5) - 5$, then $y = 0$

Now, calculate $3x - 2y$: $3x - 2y = 3(2.5) - 2(0) = 7.5$

Therefore, the value of $3x - 2y$ is 7.5.

Correct Answer is C

2. Solution:

Let x represent the cost of one adult ticket and y represent the cost of one child ticket.

From the information given, we can create the following system of equations:

$3x + 2y = 70$ (Equation 1)

$4x + y = 80$ (Equation 2)

We can use the method of substitution. Let's solve Equation 2 for y:

$y = 80 - 4x$

Now substitute this expression for y into Equation 1:

$3x + 2(80 - 4x) = 70$,

$3x + 160 - 8x = 70$

$-5x = -90$, then $x = 18$

Substitute the value of x back into Equation 2 to solve for y:

$4(18) + y = 80$

$72 + y = 80$, then $y = 8$

Therefore, the cost of one adult ticket is $18, and the cost of one child ticket is $8.

Correct Answer is C

3. Solution:

In the given equation $h = 12t + 30$,

the value 30 represents the initial height of the plant when John started tracking it.

This means that at $t = 0$ (the start of the tracking), the plant's height is 30 units.

As the equation estimates the height of the plant (h) based on the number of weeks (t) since tracking began, the constant term 30 represents the starting point or initial height of the plant.

Correct Answer is A

4. Solution:

To find the year when the price of a used car is equal to the price of a new car, we need to set the equations for the new car price (n) and used car price (u) equal to each other and solve for x (n = u)

$20,000 + 500x = 15,000 + 800x$

To isolate x, we can subtract 500x from both sides and subtract 15,000 from both sides:

$20,000 - 15,000 = 800x - 500x$

$5,000 = 300x$

$x = \dfrac{5,000}{300}$

$x \approx 16.67$

Since x represents the number of years, we can round the value of x.

to the nearest whole number, which is 17.

Correct Answer is D

5. Solution:

To find the number of milliliters of the 12% ethanol solution Mia must use, we can substitute the given value of y into the equation and solve for x.

$0.12x + 0.15(80) = 0.14(x + 80)$

Simplifying the equation:

$0.12x + 12 = 0.14x + 11.2$

Subtracting 0.12x from both sides:

$12 = 0.02x + 11.2$

Subtracting 11.2 from both sides:

$0.8 = 0.02x$

Dividing both sides by 0.02:

$x = 40$

Correct Answer is B

6. Solution:

To find the x-coordinate of the intersection point, we need to solve the system of equations:

$2x + 3y = 7$, $3x - 2y = 4$

We can solve this system by using the method of substitution or elimination.

Multiply the first equation by 2 and the second equation by 3 to eliminate the x term: $4x + 6y = 14$, $9x - 6y = 12$

Add the two equations together: $13x = 26$

$x = 2$

Correct Answer is B

7. Solution:

Multiply the second equation by 3 to make the coefficients of y in both equations the same:

$2x + 3y = 10$

$12x - 3y = 24$

Now, add the two equations together:

$(2x + 3y) + (12x - 3y) = 10 + 24$, then $14x = 34$

$x = \dfrac{34}{14}$ or $x = \dfrac{17}{7}$

Substitute the value of x back into one of the original equations, let's use the first equation:

$2\left(\dfrac{17}{7}\right) + 3y = 10$

$\dfrac{34}{7} + 3y = 10$

$3y = 10 - \dfrac{34}{7}$

$3y = \dfrac{70}{7} - \dfrac{34}{7}$

$3y = \dfrac{36}{7}$

$y = \dfrac{12}{7}$

Correct Answer is C

8. Solution:

To solve the system of equations, let's use the method of elimination. Multiply the first equation by 2 and the second equation by 3 to eliminate the variable x:

$2(3x - 2y) = 2(6) \quad 3(2x + 4y) = 3(10)$

Simplifying, we get:

$6x - 4y = 12$

$6x + 12y = 30$

Subtracting the first equation from the second equation, we eliminate x:

$(6x + 12y) - (6x - 4y) = 30 - 12$

$16y = 18$, then $y = \dfrac{18}{16}$ or $y = \dfrac{9}{8}$

Substitute the value of y back into one of the original equations, let's use the first equation:

$3x - 2\left(\dfrac{9}{8}\right) = 6$

$3x - \dfrac{18}{8} = 6$

$3x - \dfrac{9}{4} = 6$, then $3x = 6 + \dfrac{9}{4}$

$x = \dfrac{33}{12}$ or $x = \dfrac{11}{4}$

Correct Answer is D

9. Solution:

In the given equation S = 20t + 50, the value 50 represents the initial amount of money Sam had before he started saving for the bike. The constant term 50 indicates that Sam already had $50 before he began saving. As the equation estimates the total savings (S) based on the number of weeks (t) since he started saving, the initial amount is represented by the constant term 50.

Correct Answer is B

10. Solution:

To find the value of y when x = 2, we can substitute the value of x into the equation and solve for y:

$2(2) + 3y = 10$

$4 + 3y = 10$

$3y = 10 - 4$

$3y = 6 \quad y = \dfrac{6}{3}$

$y = 2$

Therefore, when x = 2, the value of y is 2.

Correct Answer is B

11. Solution:

Let's assume the chemist mixes x liters of the 25% acid solution and (15 - x) liters of the 40% acid solution.

We can set up the following equation:

$0.25x + 0.40(15 - x) = 0.30(15)$

Simplifying the equation,

we get: $0.25x + 6 - 0.40x = 4.5$

$-0.15x = -1.5$

$x = 10$ Substituting this value of x into the second part,

we get: $15 - x = 15 - 10 = 5$

So, the chemist should mix 10 liters of the 25% acid solution and 5 liters of the 40% acid solution.

Correct Answer is B

12. Solution:

Let's solve the problem step by step.

We are given that the sum of three consecutive odd integers is 39.

Let's assume the first odd integer is x.

Since the integers are consecutive, the second odd integer would be x + 2, and the third odd integer would be x + 4.

The sum of these three integers can be expressed as an equation: x + (x + 2) + (x + 4) = 39

Simplifying the equation, we get: 3x + 6 = 39

Subtracting 6 from both sides of the equation: 3x = 33

Dividing both sides of the equation by 3: x = 11

Now that we have the value of x, we can find the other two consecutive odd integers:

First odd integer: x = 11

Second odd integer: x + 2 = 11 + 2 = 13

Third odd integer: x + 4 = 11 + 4 = 15

Therefore, the three consecutive odd integers are 11, 13, and 15.

The largest integer is 15.

Correct Answer is C

Linear Functions

Linear function is a type of function in mathematics that can be represented by a straight line on a coordinate plane. It follows the form:

$$f(x) = mx + b$$

In this equation, 'm' represents the slope of the line, and 'b' represents the y-intercept, which is the point where the line intersects the y-axis.

Note:

- The y-intercept, indicated by 'b', is the value of 'y' when 'x' is equal to zero.

- Linear functions have one solution.

Digital SAT Sample Question:

If $f(x) = 2x + 3$. Find the value of $f(5)$?

A) 3

B) 5

C) 11

D) 13

Solution:

To find the value of $f(5)$, we substitute $x = 5$ into the function $f(x) = 2x + 3$:

$$f(5) = 2(5) + 3 = 10 + 3 = 13.$$

Therefore, $f(5) = 13$.

Correct Answer is D

Linear Functions Test

If f(x) = 2x + 3. Find the value of x-intercept?

A) 1

B) 3

C) -3

D) $-\dfrac{3}{2}$

$$f(x) = 2x^2 - 5x + 3$$

For the function f defined above, what is the value of f (2)?

A) 1

B) 4

C) 7

D) 11

$$f(x) = (x+2)(x-4)(3x-1)$$

The function is defined above. which of following is not an x- intercept of the graph of the function in the xy plane?

A) x = -2

B) x = 4

C) x = 1/3

D) x = 7

$$f(x) = 2x + 3$$

Which of the following statements is true about this function?

A) The slope of the function is 2.

B) The y-intercept of the function is 2.

C) The x-intercept of the function is 3.

D) The graph of the function is a parabola.

Medium

5

f(x) = 2x - 3

Which of the following options correctly describes the slope and y-intercept of the function?

A) Slope = 2, y-intercept = -3

B) Slope = -3, y-intercept = 2

C) Slope = 2, y-intercept = 3

D) Slope = -2, y-intercept = -3

Medium

6

f(x) = 2x - 3

Which of the following statements is true?

A) The y-intercept of the graph of f(x) is 3.

B) The slope of the graph of f(x) is -2.

C) The x-intercept of the graph of f(x) is 3/2.

D) The function f(x) has a constant value of -3 for all x.

Medium

7

A car rental company charges a flat fee of $50 plus $20 per day for renting a car. Let's represent the number of days as x and the total cost as C(x).

Which of the following equations represents the total cost C(x) in terms of the number of days?

A) C(x) = 50x + 20

B) C(x) = 50 + 20x

C) C(x) = 20x - 50

D) C(x) = 20 - 50x

Hard

8

A bookstore charges a $2 flat fee plus $3 per book for shipping.

Let's represent the total cost, C, as a function of the number of books, n, using the linear function C(n) = 3n + 2.

Based on this information, which of the following statements is false?

A) The flat fee for shipping is $2.

B) The shipping cost per book is $2.

C) The total cost for shipping 2 books is $8.

D) The total cost for shipping 5 books is $17.

Medium
Medium
9

$$f(x) = 3x - 5$$

Which of the following represents the x-intercept of the linear function?

A) $\dfrac{-5}{3}$

B) $\dfrac{-3}{5}$

C) $\dfrac{5}{3}$

D) $\dfrac{3}{5}$

Medium
11

$$f(x) = \frac{3}{2}x - 5?$$

Which of the following is the x-intercept of the line represented by the equation?

A) $(0, -5)$

B) $(2, 0)$

C) $\left(\dfrac{10}{3}, 0\right)$

D) $(-10, 0)$

Easy
10

$P\,(2, 4)$ and $Q\,(6, 10)$

Determine the slope of the line passing through these two points.

A) 2

B) $\dfrac{3}{2}$

C) 3

D) 5

Medium
12

The table below represents a linear function.

What is the value of b in the equation $y = mx + b$?

x	y
2	7
4	13
6	19
8	25

A) -1

B) 0

C) 1

D) 2

Linear Functions Test Solution

1. Solution:

To find the x-intercept, we set f(x) = 0 and solve for x:

2x + 3 = 0.

Subtract 3 from both sides of the equation:

2x = -3.

Divide both sides by 2:

$x = -\dfrac{3}{2}$.

Therefore, the x-intercept is $x = -\dfrac{3}{2}$.

Correct Answer is D

2. Solution:

To find the value of f (2), we substitute x = 2 into the function f(x):

f (2) = 2(2²) - 5(2) + 3

= 2(4) - 10 + 3

= 8 - 10 + 3 = 1

Therefore, the value of f (2) is 1

Correct Answer is A

3. Solution:

To find the x-intercepts of the graph of the function f(x), we need to set f(x) equal to zero and solve for x.

f(x) = (x+2) · (x-4) · (3x-1)

Setting f(x) = 0, we have:

(x+2) · (x-4) · (3x-1) = 0

To determine the x-intercepts, we need to find the values of x that make the expression equal to zero.

Now, let's find the solutions for each factor:

x+2 = 0 --> x = -2

x-4 = 0 --> x = 4

$3x-1 = 0 --> x = \dfrac{1}{3}$

So, the x-intercepts of the graph are x = -2, x = 4, and

$x = \dfrac{1}{3}$.

Correct Answer is D

4. Solution:

In the given linear function, the coefficient of x is 2, which represents the slope of the line.

The slope determines the steepness of the line and is equal to the ratio of the vertical change (rise) to the horizontal change (run).

Therefore, the slope of the function 2.

Correct Answer is A

5. Solution:

The slope-intercept form of a linear function is given by y = mx + b, where m represents the slope and b represents the y-intercept. Comparing this with the given function f(x) = 2x - 3, we can determine that the slope is 2 and the y-intercept is -3.

Correct Answer is A

6. Solution:

The linear function f(x) = 2x - 3 is in the form

y = mx + b, where m represents the slope and b represents the y-intercept.

A) The y-intercept of f(x) is -3, which means the point (0, -3) lies on the graph of the function.

Therefore, statement A is false.

B) The slope of f(x) is 2, Therefore, statement B is false.

C) The x-intercept of f(x) can be found by setting y = 0

In this case, 2x - 3 = 0, which gives $x = \dfrac{3}{2}$. Therefore, statement C is true.

D) The function f(x) is not constant, its value changes as x changes D is false.

Correct Answer is C

7. Solution:

Let's break down the equation step by step:

- The flat fee of $50 is constant and does not change with the number of days. This can be represented as 50.

- The additional cost per day is $20, and it is multiplied by the number of days. This can be represented as 20x.

Combining both parts, we get:

$C(x) = 50 + 20x$

Correct Answer is B

8. Solution:

The linear function $C(n) = 3n + 2$ represents the total cost, C, as a function of the number of books, n.

A) The flat fee for shipping is represented by the constant term in the linear function, which is $2. Therefore, statement A is true.

B) The coefficient of n in the linear function represents the shipping cost per book, which is $3. Therefore, statement B is false.

C) To calculate the total cost for shipping 2 books, we substitute n = 2 into the function:

$C(2) = 3(2) + 2 = 6 + 2 = \$8$. Therefore, statement C is true.

D) To calculate the total cost for shipping 5 books, we substitute n = 5 into the function:

$C(5) = 3(5) + 2 = 15 + 2 = \$17$.

Therefore, statement B is true.

Correct Answer is B

9. Solution:

To find the x-intercept, we set f(x) = 0 and solve for x.

$0 = 3x - 5$

Adding 5 to both sides:

$5 = 3x$

Dividing both sides by 3:

$\frac{5}{3} = x$

Correct Answer is C

10. Solution:

The slope of a line passing through two points (x_1, y_1) and (x_2, y_2) can be calculated using the formula:

$$\text{slope} = \frac{y_2 - y_1}{x_2 - x_1}$$

In this case, the coordinates of point P are (2, 4) and the coordinates of point Q are (6, 10).

Plugging these values into the slope formula,

$$\text{slope} = \frac{10 - 4}{6 - 2} = \frac{3}{2}$$

Correct Answer is B

11. Solution:

To find the x-intercept, we set f(x) = 0 and solve for x.

$0 = \frac{3}{2}x - 5$ Adding 5 to both sides: $5 = \frac{3}{2}x$

$x = \frac{10}{3}$

So, the x-intercept is $x = \frac{10}{3}$

Correct Answer is C

12. Solution:

We can choose any two points from the table and use them to find the slope (m). Let's use the points (2, 7) and (4, 13):

$$m = \frac{(\text{change in } y)}{(\text{change in } x)}$$

$$m = \frac{(13 - 7)}{(4 - 2)} = \frac{6}{2} = 3$$

Now, we can choose one of the points and substitute the slope (m = 3) into the slope-intercept form, y = mx + b.

Let's use the point (2, 7): 7 = 3(2) + b,

$7 = 6 + b$

b = 1 Therefore, the value of b in the equation y = mx + b is 1.

Correct Answer is C

A linear inequality is an inequality involving a linear expression in one or more variables.

It represents a relationship between two expressions, indicating that one expression is greater than, less than, greater than or equal to, or less than or equal to the other expression.

The general form of a linear inequality in one variable 'x' is:

$ax + b < c,$

$ax + b > c,$

$ax + b \leq c,$

$ax + b \geq c.$

Here, 'a', 'b', and 'c' are constants, and 'x' is the variable.

The inequality symbol ($<$, $>$, $\leq$, $\geq$) determines the type of inequality.

To solve a linear inequality, follow these steps:

- Treat the inequality like an equation and simplify if necessary.

- Isolate the variable term on one side of the inequality.

- If the variable is multiplied or divided by a negative number, flip the inequality sign.

- Solve for the variable.

- Write the solution in interval notation or represent it on a number line.

Example:

Solve the inequality $-3x + 5 \geq 10$.

Solution:

1. Subtract 5 from both sides of the inequality to isolate the variable term:

$-3x + 5 - 5 \geq 10 - 5$. Simplifying the equation,

we get: $-3x \geq 5$.

2. Divide both sides of the inequality by -3.

Since we are dividing by a negative number, we need to reverse the inequality sign: $\dfrac{(-3x)}{(-3)} \leq \dfrac{(5)}{(-3)}$

Dividing, we get: $x \leq -\dfrac{5}{3}$.

The solution to the inequality

$-3x + 5 \geq 10$ is $x \leq \dfrac{-5}{3}$.

Digital SAT Sample Question:

The cost of a concert ticket is $50. You want to buy a ticket, but you have a budget constraint. You can spend no more than $100 on the ticket and concessions.

Let's say 'x' represents the amount of money you spend on concessions.

Which of the following inequalities represents the budget constraint?

A) $50x \leq 100$

B) $50x + 100 \geq 100$

C) $50 + x \leq 100$

D $50 + x \geq 100$

Solution:

Let's analyze the problem to find the correct inequality.

The cost of the concert ticket is $50, and you can spend no more than $100 in total, including the ticket and concessions.

If we spend 'x' dollars on concessions, the remaining amount we can spend on the ticket is $100 - 'x' dollars.

To represent the budget constraint, we need to ensure that the total amount spent, including the ticket and concessions, does not exceed $100.

Therefore, the correct inequality is: $50 + x \leq 100$.

Correct Answer is C

Linear Inequalities Test

The cost of a movie ticket is \$12. You want to buy a ticket and some snacks, but you have a budget constraint. You can spend no more than \$25 on the ticket and concessions combined. Let's say 'x' represents the amount of money you spend on concessions.

Which of the following inequalities represents the budget constraint?

A) $12x \leq 25$

B) $12 + x \leq 25$

C) $12 + x < 25$

D) $12 + x \geq 25$

Which of the following numbers is NOT a solution of the inequality $2x + 3 < 7x - 5$?

A) $x = 1$

B) $x = 2$

C) $x = 3$

D) $x = 4$

Which of the following represents the solution to the inequality $-2x + 7 > 15$?

A) $x < -4$

B) $x > -4$

C) $x < 4$

D) $x > 4$

$y \geq ax - b$

$y < bx + a$

In the xy-plane, if (-1, 2) is a solution to the system of inequalities below, which of the following relationships between a and b must be true?

A) $a > b$

B) $b \geq a$

C) $a < b$

D) $a = b$

Linear Inequalities Test

Medium

5

The temperature in a city must remain below 80 degrees Fahrenheit for a marathon race to proceed. The temperature during the race can be represented by the inequality $t < 80$, where t is the temperature in degrees Fahrenheit.

Which of the following temperature ranges represents temperatures that are suitable for the marathon race?

A) $t > 80$

B) $t < 75$

C) $t \geq 80$

D) $t \leq 80$

Hard

6

A worker is packaging items into boxes. Each box can hold a maximum weight of 20 pounds.

The worker has items that weigh either 4 pounds or 6 pounds each.

Let x represent the number of 4-pound items and y represent the number of 6-pound items.

Which of the following systems of inequalities represents the packaging constraint?

A) $4x + 6y \leq 20$
    $x + y \leq 10$

B) $4x + 6y \leq 10$
    $x + y \leq 20$

C) $6x + 4y \leq 20$
    $x + y \leq 10$

D) $6x + 4y \leq 10$
    $x + y \leq 20$

Medium

7

A car rental company charges a flat fee of $50 per day plus an additional $0.25 per mile driven.

Let's say x represents the number of days a customer rents the car, and y represents the total number of miles driven. Which of the following inequalities represent the condition where the total cost of renting the car is at most $150?

A) $50x + 0.25y \leq 150$

B) $0.25x + 50y > 150$

C) $50x + 0.25y < 150$

D) $0.25x + 50y \geq 150$

Hard

8

$y \geq 3x - 5$

$2x + y \leq 10$

In the xy-plane, if a point with coordinates (a, b) lies in the solution set of the system of inequalities above, what is the minimum possible value of b?

A) -5

B) 4

C) 5

D) 10

Linear Inequalities Test

Which of the following expressions is equal to 0 for some value of x?

A) $|2x - 5| - 1$

B) $|2x - 5| + 1$

C) $|3x + 2| + 1$

D) $|3x - 2| + 1$

Let x and y be numbers such that $x > 0$ and $y < 0$.

Which of the following must be true?

A) $x > y$

B) $x < y$

C) $x + y > 0$

D) $x + y < 0$

If $6x - 3y \geq 6$ and $10x + 5y \leq 10$, what is the maximum possible value of $3x + 4y$?

A) 2

B) 3

C) 4

D) 5

The temperature in a room must be kept below 25 degrees Celsius. The current temperature is 22 degrees Celsius. The air conditioner can reduce the temperature by at most 3 degrees Celsius. Which inequality represents the possible temperature range after the air conditioner is turned on?

A) $x > 25$

B) $x \leq 19$

C) $x \leq 22$

D) $x \leq 25$

| 1. | B | 2. | A | 3. | A | 4. | A | 5. | B | 6. | A | 7. | A | 8. | B | 9. | A | 10. | B | 11. | A | 12. | B |

1. Solution:

The budget constraint states that the amount spent on the ticket ($12) plus, the amount spent on concessions (x) should be less than or equal to $25.

Therefore, the correct inequality is $12 + x \leq 25$. Option B is correct.

Option A is incorrect because it only considers the amount spent on concessions and does not include the ticket cost.

Option C is incorrect because it adds the amount spent on concessions twice.

Option D is incorrect because it implies that spending more than $25 satisfies the budget constraint, which is not the case

Correct Answer is B

2. Solution:

To solve the inequality, we need to isolate the variable x.

Step 1: Subtract 7 from both sides of the inequality:

$-2x + 7 - 7 > 15 - 7$

$-2x > 8$

Step 2: Divide both sides of the inequality by -2.

Since we are dividing by a negative number, the inequality sign will flip:

The solution to the inequality is $x < -4$.

Correct Answer is A

3. Solution:

To determine which number is not a solution, we can substitute each value of x into the inequality and check if the inequality holds true.

For option A, x = 1: $2(1) + 3 < 7(1) - 5$ $2 + 3 < 7 - 5$ $5 < 2$ (False)

For option B, x = 2: $2(2) + 3 < 7(2) - 5$ $4 + 3 < 14 - 5$ $7 < 9$ (True)

For option C, x = 3: $2(3) + 3 < 7(3) - 5$ $6 + 3 < 21 - 5$ $9 < 16$ (True)

For option D, x = 4: $2(4) + 3 < 7(4) - 5$ $8 + 3 < 28 - 5$ $11 < 23$ (True)

Based on our calculations, option A does not satisfy the inequality.

Correct Answer is A

4. Solution:

To determine the relationship between "a" and "b" based on the given system of inequalities and the solution (-1, 2), we need to substitute the values of x and y into both inequalities and see which one holds true.

For the first inequality, substituting x = -1 and y = 2, we have:

$2 \geq a(-1) - b$

$2 \geq -a - b$

$-a - b \leq 2$ (Equation 1)

For the second inequality, substituting x = -1 and y = 2, we have:

$2 < b(-1) + a$

$2 < -b + a$

$a - b > 2$ (Equation 2)

Now, let's analyze the possible relationships between "a" and "b" based on Equations 1 and 2.

If Equation 1 holds, then $-a - b \leq 2$, which means that "a" could be greater than or equal to "b" ($a \geq b$), or "a" could be less than or equal to "b" ($a \leq b$).

If Equation 2 holds, then $a - b > 2$, which means that "a" must be greater than "b" ($a > b$).

Since both Equations 1 and 2 need to hold true simultaneously for the given solution to satisfy both inequalities, the only possible relationship between "a" and "b" is: $a > b$

Correct Answer is A

5. Solution:

The given inequality states that the temperature (t) must be less than 80 degrees Fahrenheit for the marathon race to proceed.

To determine the suitable temperature range, we need to find the correct inequality representation.

Since the marathon can proceed when the temperature is below 80 degrees, the correct representation is: $t < 80$

This means that the temperature should be less than 80.

So, any value of t that is less than 80 degrees Fahrenheit would be suitable for the marathon race.

Correct Answer is B

6. Solution:

To determine the packaging constraint, we need to ensure that the total weight of the items in each box does not exceed 20 pounds, and the total number of items in each box does not exceed the box's capacity.

The correct system of inequalities is:

$4x + 6y \leq 20$

$x + y \leq 10$

This system of inequalities ensures that the total weight of the items does not exceed 20 pounds and the total number of items does not exceed 10.

Correct Answer is A

7. Solution:

The correct answer is option A) $50x + 0.25y \leq 150$.

To understand why, let's break down the equation:

The flat fee charged per day is $50, so the cost for x days is $50x$.

The additional cost per mile driven is $0.25, so the cost for y miles is $0.25y$.

To find the total cost, we add the flat fee and the additional cost:

Total cost = $50x + 0.25y$

The inequality states that the total cost should be at most $150.

$50x + 0.25y \leq 150$

This represents the condition where the total cost of renting the car is at most $150.

Correct Answer is A

8. Solution:

To find the minimum possible value of b, we need to consider the inequality that imposes the strictest constraint on the value of y.

In this case, it is the first inequality: $y \geq 3x - 5$.

To minimize the value of b, we want to minimize the value of y while satisfying the given inequalities.

The minimum value of y occurs when $y = 3x - 5$.

Substituting this value of y into the second inequality:

$2x + (3x - 5) \leq 10$

Simplifying the equation: $5x - 5 \leq 10$

$x \leq 3$

So, the minimum possible value of x is 3.

Substituting this value into $y = 3x - 5$:

$y = 3(3) - 5,$

$y = 9 - 5$, then $y = 4$

Therefore, the minimum possible value of b is 4.

Correct Answer is B

9. Solution:

An expression is equal to 0 for some value of x if and only if the expression inside the absolute value bars is equal to 0.

A) $|2x - 5| - 1$ To find the values of x for which this expression equals 0, we set $|2x - 5| = 1$ and solve for x. However, there is value of x that makes the absolute value of $2x - 5$ equal to 1, so option A is correct.

B) $|2x + 5| + 1$ To find the values of x for which this expression equals 0, we set $|2x + 5| = -1$, which is not possible since the absolute value cannot be negative.

C) $|3x + 2| + 1$ To find the values of x for which this expression equals 0 we set $|3x + 2| = -1$, which is not possible since the absolute value cannot be negative.

D) $|3x - 2| + 1$ To find the values of x for which this expression equals 0, we set $|3x - 2| = -1$, which is not possible since the absolute value cannot be negative.

Correct Answer is A

10. Solution:

Given inequalities:

1. $6x - 3y \geq 6$

2. $10x + 5y \leq 10$

To find the maximum possible value of $3x + 4y$, we need to find the feasible region defined by the intersection of these inequalities and evaluate the expression at the boundary points.

1. Solve $6x - 3y \geq 6$ for y:

$-3y \geq -6x + 6$

$y \leq 2x - 2$

2. Solve $10x + 5y \leq 10$ for y:

$5y \leq -10x + 10$

$y \leq -2x + 2$

The feasible region is bounded by the lines $y = 2x - 2$ and $y = -2x + 2$.

The intersection point of these two lines is where $y = 2x - 2$

intersects $y = -2x + 2$

$: 2x - 2 = -2x + 2$

$4x = 4$

$x = 1$

Plugging $x = 1$ into $y = 2x - 2$:

$y = 2(1) - 2 = 0$

So, the intersection point is $(1, 0)$.

Now, calculate the value of $3x + 4y$ at this point:

$3x + 4y = 3(1) + 4(0) = 3$

Correct Answer is B

11. Solution:

To determine which statements must be true, let's analyze each option:

A) x > y Given that x > 0 and y < 0, it is guaranteed that x is greater than y.

Therefore, statement A must be true.

B) x < y Since x is greater than 0 and y is less than 0, it is not possible for x to be less than y.

Therefore, statement B is not true.

C) x + y > 0 Adding a positive value (x) and a negative value (y) will not necessarily result in a sum greater than 0. Therefore, statement C is not necessarily true.

D) x + y < 0 Similarly, the sum of a positive value (x) and a negative value (y) will not necessarily be less than 0. Therefore, statement D is not necessarily true.

Correct Answer is A

12. Solution:

To represent the possible temperature range after the air conditioner is turned on, we need to subtract at most 3 degrees Celsius from the current temperature of 22 degrees Celsius. Therefore, the inequality is $x \leq 22 - 3$, which simplifies to $x \leq 19$.

Correct Answer is B

Equivalent Expressions

Equivalent expressions are algebraic expressions that have the same value for all possible values of the variables involved.

These expressions may look different, but they represent the same mathematical relationship.

To determine if two expressions are equivalent, you can perform various operations such as simplifying, factoring, expanding, or combining like terms.

- **Like Terms:** Like terms have the same variables raised to the same powers.

For example, $3x$ and $5x$ are like terms, but $3x$ and $5x^2$ are not.

To simplify expressions, you can combine like terms by adding or subtracting their coefficients.

- **Distributive Property:** The distributive property allows you to multiply a term outside parentheses by each term inside the parentheses.

For example, $a(b + c) = ab + ac$.

- **Commutative and Associative Properties:** The commutative property states that the order of addition or multiplication does not affect the result.

For example, $a + b = b + a$. The associative property states that the grouping of terms in addition or multiplication does not affect the result.

For example, $(a + b) + c = a + (b + c)$.

- **Factoring:** Factoring involves expressing an expression as a product of its factors.

It can help identify common factors and simplify expressions.

For example, $2x + 4$ can be factored as $2(x + 2)$.

Digital SAT Sample Question:

Which of the following equations is equivalent to $3x - 5 = 7x + 3$?

A) $6x - 10 = 14x + 6$

B) $6x - 5 = 7x + 8$

C) $6x - 3 = 7x - 5$

D) $6x - 8 = 7x + 5$

Solution:

To find the equivalent equation, we need to perform operations to isolate the variable 'x' on one side of the equation.

Starting with the equation $3x - 5 = 7x + 3$,

Step 1: Move the terms with 'x' to one side and the constant terms to the other side. $3x - 7x = 3 + 5$

Simplifying the equation, we get: $-4x = 8$

Step 2: Divide both sides of the equation by -4 to isolate 'x'.

$x = -2$

Now, let's substitute the value of 'x' back into the answer choices to find the equivalent equation:

A) $6x - 10 = 14x + 6$ Substituting $x = -2$, we get:

$6(-2) - 10 = 14(-2) + 6$

$-12 - 10 = -28 + 6$

$-22 = -22$ (equal)

B) $6x - 5 = 7x + 8$ Substituting $x = -2$, we get:

$6(-2) - 5 = 7(-2) + 8$

$-12 - 5 = -14 + 8$

$-17 = -6$ (not equal)

C) $6x - 3 = 7x - 5$ Substituting $x = -2$, we get:

$6(-2) - 3 = 7(-2) - 5$

$-12 - 3 = -14 - 5$

$-15 = -19$ (not equal)

D) $6x - 8 = 7x + 5$ Substituting $x = -2$, we get:

$6(-2) - 8 = 7(-2) + 5$

$-12 - 8 = -14 + 5$

$-20 = -9$ (not equal)

The correct answer is A

Easy

1

Which of the following expressions is equivalent to $3x - 2y + 5x + 3y$?

A) $8x - 5y$

B) $8x + y$

C) $8x + y + 1$

D) $8x + y - 1$

Easy

2

Which of the following expressions is equivalent to $3(x - 2) + 2(4x + 1)$?

A) $5x + 2$

B) $6x + 5$

C) $14x - 4$

D) $11x - 4$

Medium

3

Which of the following expressions is equivalent to $4(x^2 - 2x + 3) + 2(x^2 - 5x + 2) - (3x^2 - 4x + 1)$?

A) $-4x^2 + 9x + 7$

B) $-7x^2 + 7x + 5$

C) $3x^2 - 14x + 15$

D) $-x^2 + 9x + 7$

Medium

4

Simplify the expression:

$2(3x + 5) - 4(2x - 1)$

A) $2x - 14$

B) $2x + 14$

C) $-2x + 14$

D) $4x + 6$

Equivalent Expressions Test

A rectangular garden has a length of 12 meters and a width of 8 meters.

The owner wants to increase both the length and width by the same unknown value, x.

If the area of the new garden is equivalent to 252 square meters, what is the value of x?

A) 4 meters

B) 6 meters

C) 7 meters

D) 9 meters

Which of the following expressions is equivalent to the expression

$(2x + 3)(x - 4) - (3x - 1)(2 - x)$?

A) $5x^2 - 12x - 10$

B) $-5x^2 + 11x - 10$

C) $5x^2 + 10x + 12$

D) $-5x^2 - 10x - 12$

Which of the following expressions is equivalent to $2(x + 3) - 3(2 - x) + 4x$?

A) $3x$

B) $3x + 9$

C) $9x - 9$

D) $9x$

A bookstore offers a discount on the purchase of multiple books.

The regular price of a book is $15, but if you buy 3 or more books, you get a 10% discount on the total purchase. If Jack bought a certain number of books and paid $54 in total after the discount, how many books did Jack buy?

A) 2

B) 3

C) 4

D) 5

Equivalent Expressions Test

A store is offering a sale where customers can buy three items and get the fourth item for free. The regular price of each item is \$20.

If Sarah buys a total of seven items, including the free one, what is the total cost of her purchase?

A) \$80

B) \$100

C) \$120

D) \$140

$(x^3 - 2x^2y + 5xy^2) - (-2x^3 + 3xy^2 - 4y^2)$

Which of the following is equivalent to the expression above?

A) $3x^3 - 2x^2y + 2xy^2 - 4y^2$

B) $-x^3 - 5x^2y + 8xy^2 - 4y^2$

C) $3x^3 - 2x^2y + 2xy^2 + 4y^2$

D) $-x^3 - 2x^2y + 8xy^2 - 4y^2$

Which expression is equivalent to

$(3x^2-8) -(-2x^2+5x-10)$?

A) $5x^2 - 5x + 2$

B) $5x^2 + 5x - 2$

C) $5x^2 - 3x - 2$

D) $5x^2 + 3x - 2$

Which of the following expressions is equivalent to $(a - b)^2 - (a^2 + b^2)$?

A) $2ab$

B) $2b^2$

C) $-2ab$

D) $a^2 - b^2$

Equivalent Expressions Test Solution

1. Solution:

To determine the equivalent expression, we can combine like terms:

$= 3x - 2y + 5x + 3y$

$= (3x + 5x) + (-2y + 3y)$

$= 8x + y$

Correct Answer is B

2. Solution:

To simplify the expression, we can distribute and combine like terms:

$3(x - 2) + 2(4x + 1)$

$= 3x - 6 + 8x + 2$

$= 11x - 4$

Correct Answer is D

3. Solution:

To simplify the expression, we can distribute and combine like terms:

$4(x^2 - 2x + 3) + 2(x^2 - 5x + 2) - (3x^2 - 4x + 1)$

$= 4x^2 - 8x + 12 + 2x^2 - 10x + 4 - 3x^2 + 4x - 1$

$= (4x^2 + 2x^2 - 3x^2) + (-8x - 10x + 4x) + (12 + 4 - 1)$

$= 3x^2 - 14x + 15$

Correct Answer is C

4. Solution:

To simplify the expression, we need to distribute the coefficients:

$2(3x + 5) - 4(2x - 1)$

$= 6x + 10 - 8x + 4$

$= (6x - 8x) + (10 + 4)$

$= -2x + 14$

Correct Answer is C

5. Solution:

To solve the problem, we need to set up an equation using the given information. The area of a rectangle is calculated by multiplying its length and width.

Original area = Length x Width = 12 x 8 = 96 square meters.

The new length will be 12 + x, and the new width will be 8 + x.

The new area is given as 252 square meters.

Equation: $(12 + x) \cdot (8 + x) = 252$

To solve this equation, we can simplify and solve for x:

$96 + 12x + 8x + x^2 = 252$

$x^2 + 20x + 96 = 252$

$x^2 + 20x - 156 = 0$

Factoring or using the quadratic formula, we find that $x = 6$ or $x = -26$.

Since the length and width cannot be negative, we discard the negative value.

Therefore, the value of x is 6 meters.

Correct Answer is B

6. Solution:

To find the equivalent expression, we need to simplify the given expression by performing the necessary operations.

Expanding the expression $2(x + 3) - 3(2 - x) + 4x$,

we get: $2x + 6 - 6 + 3x + 4x = 9x$

Correct Answer is D

"}

7. Solution:

To find the equivalent expression, we need to simplify the given expression by expanding and combining like terms.

Expanding the expression, we get:

$=(2x + 3)(x - 4) - (3x - 1)(2 - x)$

$= 2x^2 - 8x + 3x - 12 - (6x - 3x^2 - 2 + x)$

$= 2x^2 - 8x + 3x - 12 - 6x + 3x^2 + 2 - x$

$= 5x^2 - 12x - 10$

Correct Answer is A

8. Solution:

To solve this problem, let's denote the number of books Jack bought as "n".

If Jack bought n books and received a 10% discount on the total purchase,

the equation for the total cost after the discount can be expressed as:

Total cost = Regular price per book x Number of books x (1 - Discount percentage)

Given that the total cost for Jack was $54, we can set up the equation as follows:

$54 = $15 x n x (1 - 0.10)

Simplifying the equation:

$54 = $15 x n x 0.90

Now, let's solve for "n":

$$\frac{\$54}{(\$15 \ x \ 0.90)} = n$$

$$\frac{\$54}{\$13.50} = n$$

$4 = n$

Therefore, Jack bought 4 books.

Correct Answer is C

9. Solution:

To solve this problem, let's determine how many items

Sarah will pay for and calculate the total cost accordingly.

Since the sale offers the fourth item for free,

Sarah will only pay for six out of the seven items she purchased.

The cost of one item is $20, so the cost of six items will be:

6 x $20 = $120

Therefore, the total cost of Sarah's purchase will be $120.

Correct Answer is C

10. Solution:

To simplify the expression $(3x^2 - 8) - (-2x^2 + 5x - 10)$, we can distribute the negative sign to the terms inside the parentheses:

$(3x^2 - 8) + (2x^2 - 5x + 10)$

Next, we can combine like terms:

$3x^2 + 2x^2 - 8 - 5x + 10$

Combining the x^2 terms and the constant terms:

$5x^2 - 5x + 2$

Correct Answer is A

11. Solution:

The expression by removing the parentheses and combining like terms: $x^3 - 2x^2y + 5xy^2 + 2x^3 - 3xy^2 + 4y^2$

Combining like terms, we get: $3x^3 - 2x^2y + 2xy^2 + 4y^2$

Correct Answer is C

12. Solution:

Let's expand the expressions and simplify: $(a - b)^2 - (a^2 + b^2)$

$= a^2 - 2ab + b^2 - a^2 - b^2$

The simplified expression is -2ab

Correct Answer is C

Parallel Lines:

Parallel lines are lines in a two-dimensional plane that never intersect.

- Parallel lines have the same slope ($m_1 = m_2$).

- Parallel lines have different y-intercepts.

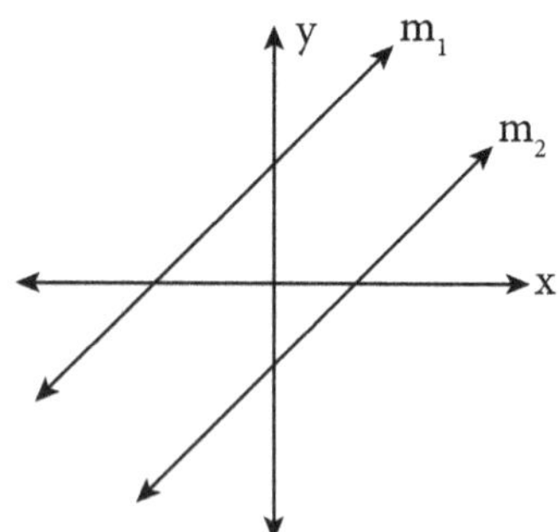

Perpendicular Lines:

- Perpendicular lines are lines that intersect at a right angle (90 degrees).

Perpendicular lines have slopes that are negative reciprocals.

$$m_1 = -\frac{1}{m_2}$$

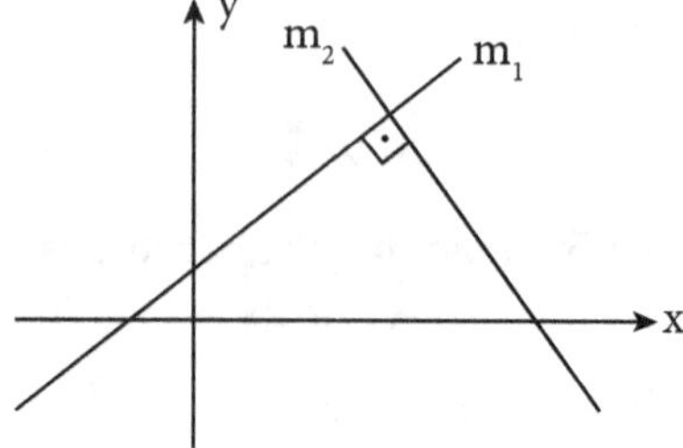

Digital SAT Sample Question:

Line p contains the point (3, -2) and (-5, k).

If line p is parallel to line q, whose equation is

$4x + 2y = 8$, what is the value of k?

A) $k = -4$

B) $k = 4$

C) $k = 14$

D) $k = -14$

Solution:

Since the lines are parallel, they have the same slope.

Given line q: $4x + 2y = 8$

To determine the slope of line q, we can rewrite it in slope-intercept form ($y = mx + b$):

$2y = -4x + 8$, then $y = -2x + 4$

The slope of line q is -2. Since line p is parallel to line q, it will have the same slope.

Use the two-point slope formula to find k:

$$m = \frac{y_2 - y_1}{x_2 - x_1},$$
$$-2 = \frac{k - (-2)}{-5 - 3}$$
$$-2 = \frac{k + 2}{-8} \quad \text{cross multiply}$$

$16 = k + 2$, Therefore, the value of k is 14.

Correct Answer is C

Digital SAT Sample Question:

Line p contains the point (3, -2) and (-5, k).

If line p is perpendicular to line q, whose equation is $4x + 2y = 8$, what is the value of k?

A) $k = 6$

B) $k = -6$

C) $k = -4$

D) $k = 4$

Solution:

To find the value of k, we need to determine the equation of line p and use the fact that it is perpendicular to line q.

Given line q: $4x + 2y = 8$

To determine the slope of line q, we can rewrite it in slope-intercept form ($y = mx + b$): $2y = -4x + 8$

$y = -2x + 4$

Since slope of line q is -2, then the slope of line p will be the negative reciprocal $m_p = \frac{1}{2}$

Use the two-point slope formula to find k:

$$m_p = \frac{(y_2 - y_1)}{(x_2 - x_1)},$$

$$\frac{1}{2} = \frac{k - (-2)}{-5 - 8}$$

$$\frac{1}{2} = \frac{k + 2}{-8} \quad \text{cross multiply}$$

$-4 = k + 2$, Therefore, the value of k is -6.

Correct Answer is B

Slopes of Parallel Lines and Perpendicular Lines Test

Line p contains the point (5, -2) and (-4, k). If line p is perpendicular to line q, whose equation is x - 2y = 6, what is the value of k?

A) k = 8

B) k = 16

C) k = -8

D) k = -16

Which of the following lines is parallel to the line y = 2x + 3?

A) y = 2x + 5

B) y = 3x - 2

C) $y = \frac{1}{2}x - 1$

D) y = -2x + 3

Line p contains the point (5, -2) and (4, k). If line p is parallel to line q, whose equation is x - 2y = 10, what is the value of k?

A) k = 5

B) k = -5

C) $k = \frac{-5}{2}$

D) $k = \frac{5}{2}$

A line in the xy-plane passes through the point (2, 5) and has a slope of $\frac{1}{4}$. Which of the following points lies on the line?

A) (1, 4)

B) (6, 6)

C) (-2, -1)

D) (0, 2)

Slopes of Parallel Lines and Perpendicular Lines Test

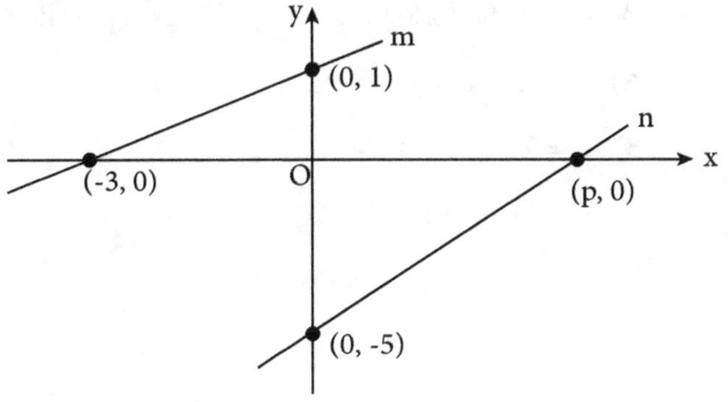

In the xy-plane above, line m is parallel to line n.

What is the value of p?

A) 5

B) 10

C) 15

D) 20

The graph of a line in the xy-plane has a slope of $\frac{1}{2}$ and passes through the point (4, 3). The graph of a second line has a slope of $-\frac{2}{3}$ and passes through the point (2, -5). If the two lines intersect at the point (a, b), what is the value of a + b?

A) -1

B) -3

C) -4

D) -5

Which of the following lines is perpendicular to the line with equation y = 2x + 3?

A) y = -2x + 5

B) y = 3x - 2

C) $y = \frac{-1}{2}x + 1$

D) y = -3x + 4

Which of the following lines is parallel to the line with equation y = 3x + 2?

A) y = -3x + 1

B) y = 3x - 5

C) 2y = 6x + 6

D) 2x + y = 8

Slopes of Parallel Lines and Perpendicular Lines Test

The graph of line A passes through the point (2, 5) and has a slope of 3. The graph of line B passes through the point (-1, 4) and is parallel to line A. What is the equation of line B?

A) $y = 3x + 7$

B) $y = 4x - 7$

C) $y = 3x + 1$

D) $y = 4x + 1$

Which of the following pairs of lines is parallel?

A) $y = 2x + 3$ and $y = 2x - 5$

B) $y = 3x + 1$ and $y = -3x + 2$

C) $y = 4x - 2$ and $y = -4x + 2$

D) $y = 5x + 4$ and $y = -5x - 2$

The graph of line A passes through the point (2, 5) and has a slope of 3. The graph of line B is perpendicular to line A and passes through the point (4, -1). What is the equation of line B?

A) $y = -\frac{1}{3}x + 3$

B) $y = -3x - 13$

C) $y = \frac{-1}{3}x + \frac{1}{3}$

D) $y = 3x - 13$

$$x + 3ky = 12$$

$$5x - 12y = 18$$

In the system of equations above, k is a constant. For what value of k will the system of equations have no solutions?

A) $-\frac{4}{5}$

B) $\frac{4}{5}$

C) $\frac{5}{4}$

D) $-\frac{5}{4}$

1.	B	2.	C	3.	A	4.	B	5.	C	6.	D	7.	C	8.	B	9.	A	10.	C	11.	A	12.	A

1. Solution:

To determine the value of k, we need to find the slope of line q and then use the perpendicular property to find the slope of line p. The equation of line q is x - 2y = 6. We can rewrite this equation in slope-intercept form (y = mx + b) by isolating y:

$-2y = -x + 6$

$y = x - 3$

The slope of line q is $\frac{1}{2}$. Since line p is perpendicular to line q, the slopes of the two lines will be negative reciprocals of each other. Therefore, the slope of line p is $-\frac{2}{1} = -2$.

Now, let's use the slope and one of the given points on line p (5, -2)

Use the two-point slope formula to find k:

(5, -2) and (-4, k).

$$m_p = \frac{(y_2 - y_1)}{(x_2 - x_1)},$$

$$-2 = \frac{(k - (-2))}{(-4 - 5)}$$

$$-2 = \frac{(k + 2)}{(-9)} \quad \text{cross multiply}$$

$18 = k + 2$, Therefore, the value of k is 16.

Correct Answer is B

2. Solution:

The equation of line q is x - 2y = 10. We can rewrite this equation in slope-intercept form (y = mx + b) by isolating y: $-2y = -x + 10$ $y = \frac{1}{2}x - 5$

The slope of line q is $\frac{1}{2}$.

Since line p is parallel to line q, the slopes of the two lines will be equal.

Therefore, the slope of line p is also $\frac{1}{2}$.

Use the two-point slope formula to find k:

(5, -2) and (4, k).

$$m_p = \frac{(y_2 - y_1)}{(x_2 - x_1)},$$

$$\frac{1}{2} = \frac{(k - (-2))}{(4 - 5)}$$

$$\frac{1}{2} = \frac{(k + 2)}{(-1)} \quad \text{cross multiply}$$

$-1 = 2k + 4$, then $2k = -5$

$$k = \frac{-5}{2}$$

Correct Answer is C

3. Solution:

To determine which line is parallel to y = 2x + 3, we need to compare the slopes of the given lines with the slope of the original line, which is 2.

A) The slope of y = 2x + 5 is also 2. This line is parallel to the original line.

B) The slope of y = 3x - 2 is 3, which is not equal to 2. This line is not parallel to the original line.

C) The slope of $y = \frac{1}{2}x - 1$ is $\frac{1}{2}$, which is not equal to 2.

This line is not parallel to the original line.

D) The slope of y = -2x + 3 is -2, which is not equal to 2. This line is not parallel to the original line.

Correct Answer is A

4. Solution:

To determine which point lies on the line, we can use the

Using the given point (2, 5) and slope $\frac{1}{4}$, we can write the equation of the line as follows:

$y - 5 = \frac{1}{4}(x - 2)$

Now, let's check which of the given points satisfy this equation.

For point B) (6, 6):

$6 - 5 = \frac{1}{4}(6 - 2)$

$1 = 1$

Correct Answer is B

5. Solution:

Line m passes through the points (-3, 0) and (0, 1). We can find the slope of line m using the formula:

$m = \frac{(y_2 - y_1)}{(x_2 - x_1)}$, $1 = \frac{(1 - 0)}{(0 - (-3))}$, then $m = \frac{1}{3}$

Since line n is parallel to line m, it will have the same slope.

So, the slope of line n is also $\frac{1}{3}$.

Line n passes through the points (0, -5) and (p, 0).

$m = \frac{(y_2 - y_1)}{(x_2 - x_1)}$,

$\frac{1}{3} = \frac{(0 - (-5))}{(p - 0)}$

$\frac{1}{3} = \frac{5}{p}$, then p = 15

Correct Answer is C

6. Solution:

To find the value of a + b, we need to determine the coordinates of the point of intersection (a, b) between the two lines.

The equation of the first line can be found using the point-slope form $y - y_1 = m(x - x_1)$ Plugging in the values (4, 3) and a slope of $\frac{1}{2}$, we have:

$y - 3 = \frac{1}{2}(x - 4)$

$y - 3 = \frac{1x}{2} - 2$

$y = \frac{1x}{2} + 1$

Similarly, the equation of the second line can be found using the point-slope form and the values (2, -5) and a slope of $-\frac{2}{3}$:

$y - (-5) = -\frac{2}{3}(x - 2)$

$y + 5 = \frac{-2}{3}x + \frac{4}{3}$

$y = -\frac{2x}{3} - \frac{11}{3}$

To find the point of intersection, we set the two equations equal to each other:

$\frac{1}{2}x + 1 = \frac{-2}{3}x - \frac{11}{3}$

Multiplying both sides of the equation by 6 to eliminate the fractions, we get:

$3x + 6 = -4x - 22$

Combining like terms, we have:

$7x = -28$, then x = -4

Substituting this value of x back into either equation, we can find the value of y:

$y = \frac{1}{2}x + 1$

$y = \frac{1}{2}(-4) + 1$

$y = -2 + 1$, then y = -1

Therefore, the point of intersection is (-4, -1).

The value of a + b is:

$a + b = -4 + (-1) = -5$

Correct Answer is D

7. Solution:

To determine which line is perpendicular to $y = 2x + 3$,

The slope of $y = 2x + 3$ is 2. The negative reciprocal of 2 is $-\frac{1}{2}$.

Now let's check the slopes of the given answer choices:

Only Choice C has the slope is $-\frac{1}{2}$.

Correct Answer is C

8. Solution:

To determine which line is parallel to $y = 3x - 5$, we need to find the line with the same slope of 3. and difrent y - intercept

The slope-intercept form of $y = 3x - 5$ already gives us the slope, which is 3.

Now let's check the slopes of the given answer choices:

From all choices only B has slope of 3 and different y - intercept.

Correct Answer is B

9. Solution:

To determine the equation of line B, we can use the point-slope form of a linear equation:

$y - y_1 = m(x - x_1)$,

where (x_1, y_1) is a point on the line and m is the slope.

Given that line B is parallel to line A, it will have the same slope of 3.

We can use the point (-1, 4) to find the equation of line B.

Using the point-slope form, we have:

$y - 4 = 3(x - (-1))$,

$y - 4 = 3(x + 1)$,

$y - 4 = 3x + 3$,

$y = 3x + 7$.

Correct Answer is A

10. Solution:

To determine the equation of line B, we first need to find its slope.

Since line B is perpendicular to line A, its slope will be the negative reciprocal of the slope of line A.

The slope of line A is 3, so the slope of line B will be $-\frac{1}{3}$.

Write equation of line B using the point (4, -1) and the slope $-\frac{1}{3}$:

$y - (-1) = -\frac{1}{3}(x - 4)$,

$y + 1 = -\frac{1}{3}x + \frac{4}{3}$

$y = -\frac{1}{3}x + \frac{4}{3} - 1$

$y = -\frac{1}{3}x + \frac{4}{3} - \frac{3}{3}$

$y = -\frac{1}{3}x + \frac{1}{3}$

Correct Answer is C

11. Solution:

Two lines are parallel if and only if their slopes are equal.

Looking at the slopes of the given equations,

we find that the slopes of Option A,

$y = 2x + 3$ and $y = 2x - 5$, are both equal to 2.

Correct Answer is A

12. Solution:

$x + 3ky = 12$

$5x - 12y = 18$

$m_1 = \frac{-1}{3k}, \ m_2 = \frac{+5}{12}$

if a system has no solution then, $m_1 = m_2$

$\frac{-1}{3k} = \frac{+5}{12}, \ k = \frac{-4}{5}$

Correct Answer is A

CHAPTER 2
Problem-Solving and Data Analysis
(15%. 5–7 Questions)

➡️ Ratios & Proportions

➡️ Unit Rates & Percentages

➡️ Reading Charts & Graphs

➡️ Measures Of Center and Spread

➡️ Probability and Conditional Probability

➡️ Sample Statistics and Margin of Error

Ratio:

A ratio is a comparison of two quantities or numbers. It shows how one quantity relates to another.

Ratios are typically expressed in the form "a: b" or "$\frac{a}{b}$," where "a" and "b" represent the quantities being compared.

Proportions: A proportion is an equation that is equivalent to two ratios. $\frac{a}{b} = \frac{c}{d}$, then use cross multiplication ad = bc.

Digital SAT Sample Question:

The ratio of Sarah's salary to the number of hours she worked at is 25:1. If she earned $500, how many hours did she work in total?

A) 20 hours

B) 25 hours

C) 30 hours

D) 35 hours

Solution:

The ratio of Sarah's salary to the number of hours worked is 25:1. This means that for every $25 she earns, she works for 1 hour.

Let's represent the number of hours Sarah worked as "x".

We can set up the proportion as follows:

$$\frac{25 \text{ dollars}}{1 \text{ hour}} = \frac{500 \text{ dollars}}{x \text{ hours}}$$

To solve the proportion, we can cross-multiply:

25x = 1 x 500

25x = 500

x = 20

Correct answer is A

Digital SAT Sample Question:

The ratio between the number of apples and oranges in a basket is 4:7. If there are 120 apples, how many oranges are there in the basket?

A) 70

B) 140

C) 210

D) 280

Solution:

The ratio between the number of apples and oranges in the basket is 4:7, which means for every 4 apples, there are 7 oranges.

We know that there are 120 apples in the basket.

We can set up a proportion to find the number of oranges:

$$\frac{4 \text{ apples}}{7 \text{ oranges}} = \frac{120 \text{ apples}}{x \text{ oranges}}$$

To solve the proportion, we can cross-multiply:

4x = 7 x 120

4x = 840

x = 210

Correct answer is C

A recipe for a cake requires 2 cups of flour for every 3 cups of sugar. If Jane wants to make a cake and has 6 cups of sugar, how many cups of flour does she need?

A) 2 cups

B) 3 cups

C) 4 cups

D) 6 cups

A recipe for a fruit salad requires 2 cups of apples, 3 cups of grapes, and 1.5 cups of pineapples. If you want to make a larger batch of the fruit salad and maintain the same ratio of ingredients, how many cups of each ingredient do you need if you use 6 cups of grapes?

A) 2 cups of apples, 3 cups of grapes, and 1.5 cups of pineapples

B) 4 cups of apples, 6 cups of grapes, and 3 cups of pineapples

C) 8 cups of apples, 12 cups of grapes, and 6 cups of pineapples

D) 12 cups of apples, 18 cups of grapes, and 9 cups of pineapples

A car travels 180 miles in 3 hours. If the car continues to travel at the same speed, how far will it travel in 6 hours?

A) 180 miles

B) 360 miles

C) 540 miles

D) 720 miles

$$\frac{3x + 5}{2x - 1} = \frac{7}{4}$$

Which of the following represents all the possible values of x that satisfy the equation above?

A) $x = -\frac{27}{2}$

B) $x = 2$

C) $x = 27$

D) $\frac{27}{2}$

Ratios & Proportions Test

If $3(x+2) = 2(2x-1)$, which of the following represents all the possible values of x that satisfy the equation?

A) x = -8

B) x = 6

C) x = 8

D) x = -6

If the ratio of X to Y is 4: 9 and the ratio of Y to Z is 3: 7, what is the ratio of X to Z, provided that Y represents the same number in both ratios?

A) 4: 7

B) 3: 9

C) 4: 21

D) 7: 4

The ratio of the lengths of two sides of a rectangle is 2:7. If the perimeter of the rectangle is 36 units, what is the length of the longer side?

A) 14 units

B) 12 units

C) 18 units

D) 21 units

In a bag, there are red, blue, and green marbles in a ratio of 2:3:5, respectively. If there are a total of 100 marbles in the bag, how many blue marbles are there?

A) 15

B) 30

C) 45

D) 60

Medium

9

Of the 30 students in a class, 18 of them are girls and the rest are boys. If the ratio of the number of girls to the number of boys is 3:2, how many boys are in the class?

A) 9

B) 12

C) 15

D) 18

Medium

11

The ratio of the ages of two siblings, Alex and Ben, is 3:7. The sum of their ages is 40 years. What is Alex's age?

A) 9 years

B) 12 years

C) 15 years

D) 18 years

Hard

10

If the ratio of A to B is 5:2 and the ratio of B to C is 3:1, what is the ratio of A to C?

A) 5:1

B) 5:3

C) 15:2

D) 15:6

Medium

12

There are 28 students in Mr. Tong's math class, and they are completing their classwork and then turn to their group to discuss their work.

The ratio of complete work to incomplete work was 3 to 4. How many students did not complete their classwork?

A) 3

B) 7

C) 8

D) 16

Ratios & Proportions Test Solution

| 1. | C | 2. | B | 3. | B | 4. | D | 5. | C | 6. | A | 7. | C | 8. | B | 9. | B | 10. | C | 11. | B | 12. | D |

1. Solution:

To solve this problem, we can set up a ratio of cups of flour to cups of sugar using the given information:

2 cups of flour: 3 cups of sugar.

Since Jane has 6 cups of sugar, we can set up a proportion:

$$\frac{2 \text{ cups of flour}}{3 \text{ cups of sugar}} = \frac{x \text{ cups of flour}}{6 \text{ cups of sugar}}$$

Cross-multiplying, we get:

2 cups of flour · 6 cups of sugar = 3 cups of sugar · x cups of flour

12 cups of flour = 3 cups of sugar · x cups of flour

4 cups of flour = x cups of flour

Correct answer is C

2. Solution:

To maintain the same ratio of ingredients, we need to scale each ingredient proportionally.

Since we are using 6 cups of grapes instead of the original 3 cups, we need to double the quantities of the other ingredients.

2 x (2 cups of apples, 3 cups of grapes, and 1.5 cups of pineapples).

4 cups of apples, 6 cups of grapes, and 3 cups of pineapples

Correct answer is B

3. Solution:

To solve this proportion problem, we can set up a ratio

of distance to time for the given situation:

$$\frac{180 \text{ miles}}{3 \text{ hours}} = \frac{x \text{ miles}}{6 \text{ hours}}$$

To find the value of x, we can cross-multiply:

180 miles · 6 hours = 3 hours · x miles

1080 miles = 3x miles

x = 360 miles

Correct answer is B

4. Solution:

To solve this proportion equation, we can cross-multiply and simplify:

$$\frac{3x + 5}{2x - 1} = \frac{7}{4}$$

12x + 20 = 14x − 7

12x - 14x = -7 – 20

-2x = -27

$$x = \frac{27}{2}$$

Correct answer is D

5. Solution:

To solve this equation, we will simplify and solve for x:

3(x + 2) = 2(2x - 1)

3x + 6 = 4x - 2

Subtracting 3x from both sides:

6 = x - 2

Adding 2 to both sides:

8 = x

Correct answer is C.

6. Solution:

To solve this problem, let's assume the shorter side of the rectangle is 2x units and the longer side is 7x units, where x represents the common ratio.

The perimeter of a rectangle is given by the formula: 2(length + width)

Since the ratio of the lengths is 2:7, the perimeter can be expressed as:

2(2x + 7x) = 36

Simplifying the equation, we have:

2(9x) = 36

18x = 36

x = 2

Therefore, the longer side of the rectangle is 7x = 7(2) = 14 units.

Correct answer is A

7. Solution:

To find the ratio of X to Z, we can combine the given ratios of X to Y and Y to Z. Since Y represents the same number in both ratios, we can multiply the numerators and denominators:

$$\frac{X}{Y} \cdot \frac{Y}{Z} = \frac{X}{Z}$$

Substituting the given ratios:

$$\frac{4}{9} \cdot \frac{3}{7} = \frac{12}{63}$$

Simplifying the ratio:

$$\frac{4}{21}$$

Therefore, the ratio of X to Z is 4: 21.

Correct answer is C

8. Solution:

The ratio of blue marbles to the total number of marbles is $\frac{3}{10}$

Since the ratio of blue marbles is 3 and the total ratio is $2 + 3 + 5 = 10$.

$10x = 100$, then $x = 10$

Blue marbles = $3(10) = 30$

Therefore, there are 30 blue marbles in the bag.

Correct answer is B

9. Solution:

Number of girls = 18,   Ratio of girls to boys = 3:2

Let's set up a proportion to find the number of boys:

$$\frac{18 \text{ girls}}{x \text{ boys}} = \frac{3 \text{ girls}}{2 \text{ boys}}$$ Cross-multiplying,
we have: $18 \cdot 2 = 3 \cdot x$

$36 = 3x$

Dividing both sides by 3,

$x = 12$

Therefore, there are 12 boys in the class.

Correct answer is B

10. Solution:

To find the ratio of A to C, we can combine the given ratios of A to B and B to C by multiplying them together:

$(A: B) \cdot (B: C) = A : C$

$(5: 2) \cdot (3: 1) = (5 \cdot 3) : (2 \cdot 1) = 15 : 2$

Correct answer is C

11. Solution:

To solve this problem, let's assume Alex's age is 3x years and Ben's age is 7x years, where x represents the common ratio.

The sum of their ages is given as 40 years, so we can set up the equation:

$3x + 7x = 40$

Combining like terms, we have:

$10x = 40$

Dividing both sides by 10, we find:

$x = 4$

Now, substituting the value of x back into Alex's age, we get:

$3x = 3(4) = 12$ years

Therefore, Alex is 12 years old.

Correct answer is B

12. Solution:

Ratio of complete to incomplete is 3 to 4.

$3x + 4x = 28$

$7x = 28$

$x = 4$

Complete = $3x = 12$

Incomplete = $4x = 16$

Correct answer is D

Unit Rates:

A unit rate tells us how much of something is happening per one unit of something else. It helps us compare quantities in a standardized way, making it easier to make comparisons and understand the relationship between different quantities.

Example:

If we have 120 miles traveled in 3 hours, we can calculate the unit rate as follows:

$$\frac{\text{Unit rate}}{120 \text{ miles}} = \frac{3 \text{ hours}}{40 \text{ miles per hour}}$$

Digital SAT Sample Question:

A car is traveling at 60 mph and a motorcycle is traveling at 80 mph in the same direction.

If they start from the same place, in how many hours will the motorcycle be 120 miles ahead of the car?

A) 1 hour

B) 1.5 hours

C) 2 hours

D) 2.5 hours

Solution:

To find the time it takes for the motorcycle to be 120 miles ahead of the car, we need to consider their relative speed. Since they are traveling in the same direction, we can subtract the car's speed from the motorcycle's speed to get their relative speed.

Relative speed = Motorcycle speed - Car speed
Relative speed = 80 mph - 60 mph

Relative speed = 20 mph

Now we can use the formula:

$$\text{Time} = \frac{\text{Dis}\tan\text{ce}}{\text{Speed}}$$

Plugging in the values:

$$\text{Time} = \frac{120 \text{ miles}}{20 \text{ mph}} = 6 \text{ hours}$$

Correct answer is C

Percentages:

Percentages are a way to express a portion or fraction of a whole quantity in terms of 100.

Percentages are integrated by the symbol %.

For example, 25% represents 25 out of 100 parts, or

$\frac{25}{100}$, which can also be simplified to $\frac{1}{4}$.

Digital SAT Sample Question:

The price of a laptop has been discounted by 15%.

The sale price is $850. What was the original price of the laptop?

A) $765

B) $900

C) $935

D) $1,000

Solution:

To find the original price of the laptop, we need to reverse the discount calculation.

The discounted price is $850, which is 15% less than the original price.

This means that the discounted price is equal to 85% of the original price.

Discounted price = Original price - (15% of original price) $850 = 0.85P

To solve for P (the original price), we can divide both sides by 0.85:

$$\frac{\$850}{0.85} = P, \quad \$1,000 = P$$

Therefore, the original price of the laptop was $1,000.

Correct answer is D

Easy
1

A car travels 360 kilometers in 6 hours.

What is the unit rate of the car's speed in kilometers per hour?

A) 30 km/h

B) 60 km/h

C) 90 km/h

D) 120 km/h

Medium
3

A shirt originally priced at $40 is on sale for 25% off. What is the sale price of the shirt?

A) $10

B) $25

C) $30

D) $35

Medium
2

A construction crew can complete a building project in 12 days by working 8 hours per day. How many days will it take to complete the project if they work 6 hours per day.

A) 9 days

B) 16 days

C) 17 days

D) 18 days

Medium
4

A store initially marks up the price of a product by 25%. If the final selling price of the product is $80, what was the original price of the product?

A) $60

B) $64

C) $75

D) $100

Medium

5

A company has experienced a 15% decrease in revenue. If the current revenue is $1,275,000, what was the original revenue before the decrease?

A) $1,500,000

B) $1,500,800

C) $1,500,900

D) $1,504,500

Hard

6

A car starts traveling from City A to City B at 9:00 AM at a speed of 60 km/h. At 10:00 AM, another car starts traveling from City B to City A at a speed of 70 km/h. The distance between the two cities is 320 kilometers. At what time will the two cars meet?

A) 11:00 AM

B) 12:00 PM

C) 12:30 PM

D) 1:00 PM

Hard

7

Two trains, Train A and Train B, are traveling towards each other on parallel tracks.

Train A is traveling at a speed of 80 kilometers per hour, and

Train B is traveling at a speed of 100 kilometers per hour.

If they are initially 720 kilometers apart, how long will it take for the trains to meet?

A) 2 hours

B) 3 hours

C) 4 hours

D) 5 hours

Medium

8

A delivery truck and a motorcycle start from the same location at the same time, traveling toward each other. The delivery truck travels at an average rate of 40 miles per hour, while the motorcycle travels at an average rate of 60 miles per hour. If they are initially 300 miles apart, how long will it take for them to meet?

A) 2 hours

B) 3 hours

C) 4 hours

D) 5 hours

In a school election, there are 500 eligible voters. Candidate A receives 30% of the votes, Candidate B receives 20% of the votes, and Candidate C receives the remaining votes. If Candidate C receives 100 votes more than Candidate A, how many votes did Candidate B receive?

A) 100

B) 150

C) 200

D) 250

There are 8 students on Mr. Robert's math team. If 75% of the team members are girls, how many students on the math team are boys?

A) 1

B) 2

C) 3

D) 4

A store initially marks up the price of a product by 50%. During a clearance sale, the store offers a discount of 30% off the marked price. If the final selling price after the discount is $84, what was the original price of the product?

A) $80

B) $85

C) $90

D) $95

At dealership, a car sale price is $18,000 plus 7.5% sales tax. If the dealer applies a discount of 25% off from the sales price, find the price after including the discount and sales tax

A) $14,512.5

B) $14,450

C) $14,520

D) $14,530

Unit Rates & Percentages Test Solution

1. Solution:

To find the unit rate, divide the total distance by the total time. In this case, the unit rate is 360 km ÷ 6 hours = 60 km/h.

Correct answer is B

2. Solution:

To find the unit rate, we need to determine how much work is completed per hour.

$$\frac{12 \text{ days}}{8 \text{ hours}} = \frac{x \text{ days}}{6 \text{ hours}},$$
$$x = 16 \text{ days}$$

Correct answer is B

3. Solution:

To find the sale price, we need to subtract the discount from the original price.

The discount amount is 25% of $40,

which is $\left(\frac{25}{100}\right)$ x $40 = $10.

Subtracting $10 from the original price gives us the sale price: $40 - $10 = $30.

Correct answer is C

4. Solution:

To find the original price, we need to calculate the price before the 25% markup.

Let's assume the original price is x.

Since the price was marked up by 25%, the selling price becomes (100% + 25%) = 125% of the original price.

So, we can set up the equation: 125% of x = $80

To solve for x, we need to convert 125% to decimal form (1.25): 1.25x = $80

Dividing both sides by 1.25: x = $\frac{\$80}{1.25}$ = $64

Correct answer is B

5. Solution:

To find the original revenue before the decrease, we need to calculate the revenue before the 15% decrease. Let's assume the original revenue is x.

Since the revenue decreased by 15%, the current revenue represents 100% - 15% = 85% of the original revenue.

We can set up the equation: 85% of x = $1,275,000

0.85x = $1,275,000

x = $1,500,000

Correct answer is A

6. Solution:

Let's calculate the time it takes for the cars to meet:

Distance covered by the first car from 9:00 AM to the meeting time = 60 km/h × t hours (where t is the time in hours from 9:00 AM)

Distance covered by the second car from 10:00 AM to the meeting time = 70 km/h × (t - 1) hours (since the second car started one hour later)

The sum of these distances should be equal to 320 kilometers: 60t + 70(t - 1) = 320

Simplifying the equation: 60t + 70t - 70 = 320

130t = 390

t = 3

Therefore, it takes 3 hours from 9:00 AM for the cars to meet.

Adding 3 hours to 9:00 AM, we get 12:00 PM.

Correct answer is B

7. Solution:

Speed of Train A + Speed of Train B

Relative speed = 80 km/h + 100 km/h Relative speed = 180 km/h

Now, we can calculate the time it takes for the trains to meet by dividing the initial distance between them by their relative speed.

$$\text{Time} = \frac{\text{Dis} \tan ce}{\text{Relative Speed}}$$

$$\text{Time} = \frac{720 \text{ km}}{180 \text{ km/h}}$$

Time = 4 hours

Correct answer is C

8. Solution:

$$\text{Time} = \frac{\text{Dis}\tan\text{ce}}{\text{Relative Speed}}$$

The relative speed is the sum of the speeds of the two vehicles, which is 40 mph + 60 mph = 100 mph.

Given that they are initially 300 miles apart,

we can calculate the time it takes for them to meet:

$$\text{Time} = \frac{300 \text{ miles}}{100 \text{ mph}} = 3 \text{ hours}$$

Therefore, it will take 3 hours for the delivery truck and the motorcycle to meet.

Correct answer is B

9. Solution:

Let's start by finding the number of votes Candidate A received.

We know that Candidate A received 30% of the votes, so we can calculate it as follows:

Votes for Candidate $A = \frac{30}{100} \cdot 500 = 0.3 \cdot 500 = 150$ votes.

Now, let's find the number of votes Candidate C received.

We are given that Candidate C received 100 votes more than Candidate A, so, we can calculate it as:

Votes for Candidate C = Votes for Candidate A + 100

Votes for Candidate C = 150 + 100 = 250 votes

Since the total number of votes is 500 and we know the votes for

Candidate A and Candidate C, we can find the votes for Candidate B:

Votes for Candidate B = Total votes - Votes for Candidate A - Votes for Candidate C

V_B= 500 - 150 - 250 = 100 votes

Therefore, Candidate B received 100 votes.

Correct answer is A

10. Solution:

Step 1: Let the original price of the product be P.

After a 50% markup, the price becomes P + 50% of P = P + 0.5P = 1.5P.

Step 2: Calculate the selling price after the discount.

The selling price after a 30% discount is 70% of the marked price.

70% of 1.5P = 0.7 x 1.5P = 1.05P.

Step 3: Set up an equation based on the given information.

According to the problem, the final selling price after the discount is $84:

1.05P = $84.

P = $80

Therefore, the original price of the product was $80.

Correct answer is A

11. Solution:

From 8 students, if 75° are girls

$\neq$ of girls = $\frac{75 \times 8}{100}$

$\neq$ girls = 6

$\neq$ boys = 2

Correct answer is B

12. Solution:

Discount 25%

$$\frac{25}{100} \times \$18,000 = \$4,500$$

New price = $18,000 - $4,500

$$= \$13,500$$

Sale Tax 7.5% = $\frac{7.5}{100}$ x $13,500

Sale Tax = $1,012.5

Final Price = $13,500 + $1,012.5

$$= \$14,512.5$$

Correct answer is A

Bar Graphs:

Bar Graphs is a topic that involves interpreting and extracting information from graphical representations called bar graphs or bar charts. Bar graphs are used to display categorical data and show the relationship between different categories and their corresponding values.

Scatter Plot:

A scatter plot is a graphical representation that displays the relationship between two numerical variables. It is useful for identifying patterns, trends, and potential correlations between the variables. The plot consists of individual data points, each representing a combination of values from both variables.

Digital SAT Sample Question:

The bar graph below represents the number of students participating in various sports activities in a school.

What is the total number of students who participate in sports?

```
Sports          Number of Students
-------------------------------------------
Football:       | | | | | |
Basketball:     | | | | | | |
Tennis:         | | |
Swimming:       | | | | | |
Volleyball:     | | | | | | | |
```

A) 20 students

B) 30 students

C) 40 students

D) 50 students

Solution:

To find the total number of students who participate in sports, we need to sum up the heights of all the bars in the graph.

Counting the number of bars in each sport category:

- Football: 6 bars

- Basketball: 7 bars

- Tennis: 3 bars

- Swimming: 6 bars

- Volleyball: 8 bars

To calculate the total number of students, we add up the number of bars for each sport category:

$6 + 7 + 3 + 6 + 8 = 30$

Correct answer is B

Solve the next two questions related to the graph below.

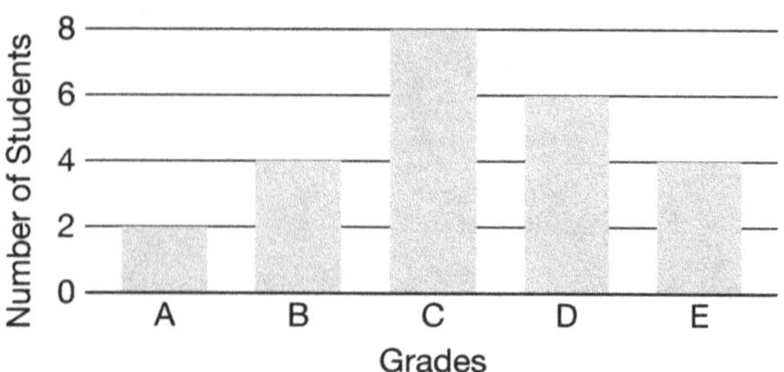

Students' math grades are given in the table. According to the table, how many students get grade C than get grade A?

A) 8

B) 6

C) 4

D) 2

What percentage of students did get grade D in the class?

A) 12%

B) 18%

C) 25%

D) 28 %

Solve the next three questions related to the line graph below.

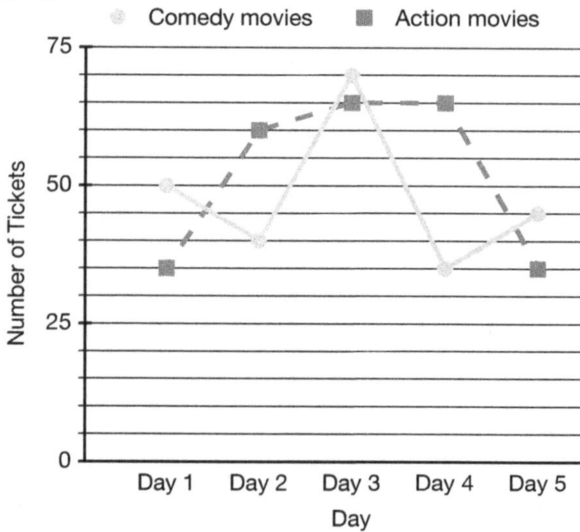

The number of tickets sold for comedy and action movies in a cinema is given. What is the difference between the number of tickets sold for comedy movies and action movies for five days?

A) 10

B) 18

C) 20

D) 26

What is the percent increase in the number of tickets sold on day 3 compared to the number of tickets sold on day 2?

A) 4%

B) 15%

C) 24%

D) 35%

Reading Charts & Graphs Test

Which day has the fewest comedy movie tickets sold?

A) Day 1

B) Day 2

C) Day 3

D) Day 4

Solve the next three questions according to the table in the below.

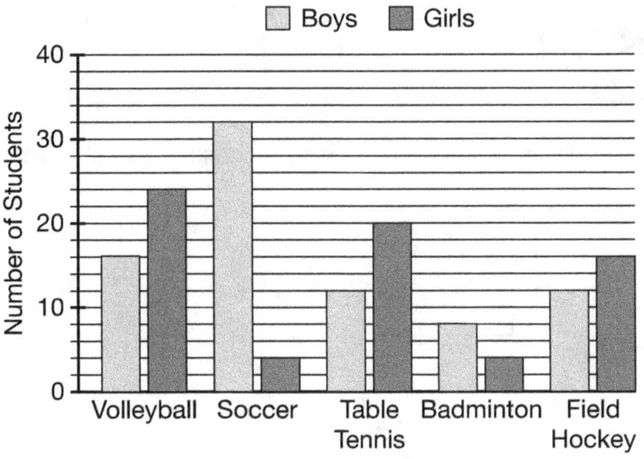

Which sport has the biggest difference between the number of male and female students?

A) Volleyball

B) Soccer

C) Table Tennis

D) Badminton

What is the percentage of boys playing volleyball among boy students in the school?

A) 4%

B) 8%

C) 20%

D) 36%

Which of the following information <u>cannot</u> be answered by looking at the graph?

A) The number of boys playing soccer is 9 times the number of girls.

B) The difference between the number of male students who play soccer and table tennis is 20.

C) 60% of the students who play volleyball are girls.

D) The number of students playing badminton is 12.

Solve the next two questions according to the table in the below.

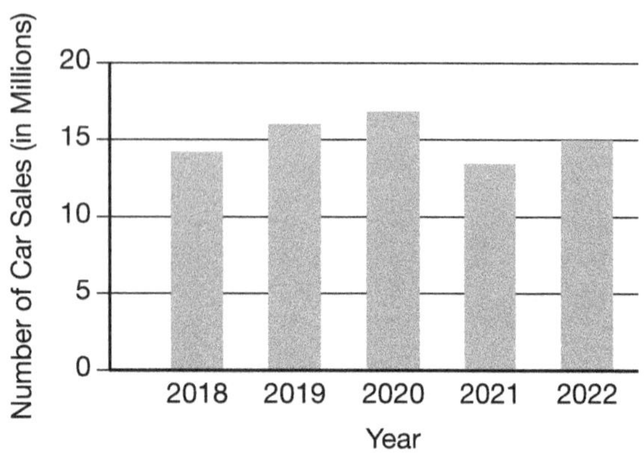

Easy
9

In the graph, how many cars were sold during five years are given. Which year had the most car sales?

A) 2018

B) 2019

C) 2020

D) 2021

Medium

10

In how many years more than 15 million cars were sold?

A) 1

B) 2

C) 3

D) 4

Easy

11

How many cars could be sold in 2018?

A) 8 million

B) 10 million

C) 14 million

D) 16 million

Easy

12

Which of following graphs has no correlation?

A) 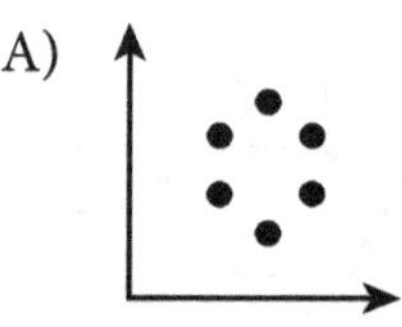

B) 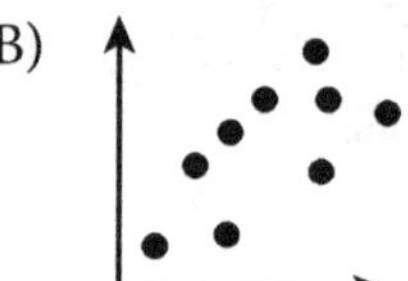

C) 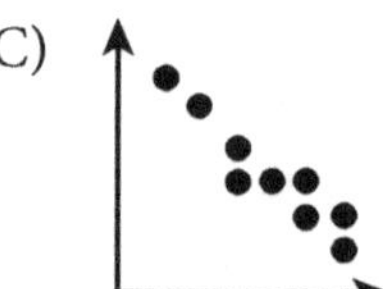

D) 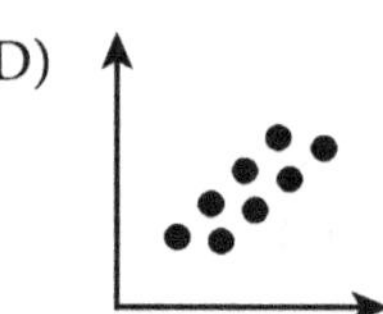

| 1. | B | 2. | C | 3. | C | 4. | D | 5. | D | 6. | B | 7. | C | 8. | A | 9. | C | 10. | B | 11. | C | 12. | A |

1. Solution:

There are 8 students who got grade C. There are 2 students who got grade A.

$8 - 2 = 6$

Correct answer is B

2. Solution:

Total number of students is 24. The number of students who got grade D is 6.

To find percentage $\frac{6}{24} = \frac{1}{4} = 25\%$

Correct answer is C

3. Solution:

The number of tickets sold for comedy movies is 240.

The number of tickets sold for action movies for five days is 260.

$260 - 240 = 20$

Correct answer is C

4. Solution:

The number of tickets sold on day 3 is 135.

The number of tickets sold on day 2 is 100.

so the increase from day 2 to day 3 is

$135 - 100 = 35$

Correct answer is D

5. Solution:

The day with the least comedy tickets sold is day 4.

Correct answer is D

6. Solution:

The biggest difference between the number of male and female students is in Soccer.

Correct answer is B

7. Solution:

The number of the boys playing volleyball is 16. The total number of boys in the class is 80.

$$\frac{16 \times 100}{80} = 20\%$$

Correct answer is C

8. Solution:

The number of boys playing soccer is 32. The number of girls playing soccer is 4.

$32 : 4 = 8$

Correct answer is A

9. Solution:

2020 had the most car sales.

Correct answer is C

10. Solution:

In 2018 and 2021, less than 15 million cars were sold.

In 2022, 15 million cars were sold. In 2019 and 2020, more than 15 million cars were sold.

Correct answer is B

11. Solution:

In 2018, the amount of cars sold will be between 10 million and 15 million. Also, it is close to 15 million. So, 14 million can be the answer.

Correct Answer is C

12. Solution:

No Correlation

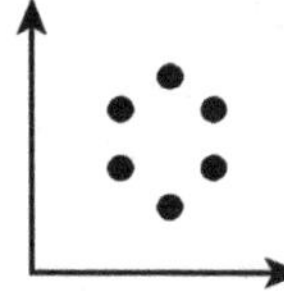

Correct Answer is A

Mean:

The mean is the average value of a dataset and is calculated by summing all the data points and dividing by the number of data points.

Median:

The median is the middle value in a dataset when it is arranged in ascending or descending order.

Range:

The range is the difference between the maximum and minimum values in a dataset. It gives an idea of the spread of the data.

Interquartile Range (IQR):

The IQR is the range of the middle 50% of the data, specifically the difference between the third quartile (Q3) and the first quartile (Q1). It provides a measure of the spread of the central portion of the data.

Standard Deviation:

The standard deviation is the square root of the variance and provides a measure of the average deviation of the data points from the mean. It is widely used as a measure of the spread.

Digital SAT Sample Question:

Consider the following dataset: 12, 15, 17, 20, 22, 25, 28.

Which of the following statements is true about this dataset?

A) The mean is 25

B) The median is 18

C) The range is 16

D) The mode is 12

Solution:

To find the answer, let's calculate the measures for the given dataset:

Mean =

$$\frac{\left(12 + 15 + 17 + 20 + 22 + 25 + 28 \right)}{7} = \frac{139}{7} = 19.857$$

Median = The middle value in the ordered dataset is 20.

Range = The difference between the maximum and minimum values is 28 - 12 = 16.

Mode: The most of repeating number. (No repainting number no mode)

Based on the calculations the correct answer is C

Digital SAT Sample Question:

The average height of 5 students in a class is 160 cm. Four of the students have heights of 150 cm, 155 cm, 165 cm, and 170 cm.

What is the height of the fifth student?

A) 155 cm

B) 160 cm

C) 165 cm

D) 170 cm

Solution:

Total height of the 5 students = (4 known heights) + (height of the fifth student)

Total height = 150 cm + 155 cm + 165 cm + 170 cm + (height of the fifth student)

$$\text{Average height} = \frac{\text{Total height}}{\text{Number of students}}$$

$$160 \text{ cm} = \frac{\text{Total height}}{5}$$

Total height = 160 cm x 5 = 800 cm

Now we can find the height of the fifth student:

800 cm = 150 cm + 155 cm + 165 cm + 170 cm + (height of the fifth student)

800 cm = 640 cm + (height of the fifth student)

Height of the fifth student = 160 cm

Correct answer is B

Measures Of Center and Spread Test

Medium
1

The average weight of 6 students in a class is 60 kg.

Five of the students have weights of 55 kg, 62 kg, 58 kg, 61 kg, and 64 kg.

What is the weight of the sixth student?

A) 55 kg

B) 58 kg

C) 60 kg

D) 64 kg

Medium
2

The ages of a group of 8 friends are as follows:

22, 25, 28, 22, 30, 28, 22, 23.

What are the mean, median, and mode of the ages?

A) Mean: 25, Median: 26, Mode: 22

B) Mean: 25, Median: 24, Mode: 25

C) Mean: 25, Median: 24, Mode: 22

D) Mean: 27, Median: 24, Mode: 22

Hard
3

John received grades of 80, 85, 90, and 75 on his four math exams.

What is the lowest score he can receive on his next math exam and still have an average of at least 80 on the five exams?

A) 65

B) 70

C) 75

D) 85

Easy
4

In a survey conducted among a group of students, the following data represents their favorite colors:

Red, Blue, Green, Blue, Red, Yellow, Blue, Green, Green, Red, Blue, Yellow, Green, Green

What is the mode of the favorite colors chosen by the students?

A) Red

B) Blue

C) Green

D) Yellow

In a survey conducted among a group of students, the following data represents their ages:

15, 16, 14, 17, 13, 15, 16, 18, 13, 15

What is the median age of the students?

A) 14

B) 15

C) 16

D) 17

If a is the average of 4k and 6, b is the average of 2k and 12 and c is the average 6k and 18, then what is the average of a, b, c in terms of k?

A) $k + 6$

B) $2k + 6$

C) $k + 12$

D) $2k + 12$

In a statistics class, the scores of 20 students on a test are as follows:

75, 81, 68, 72, 90, 86, 78, 82, 79, 88, 91, 70, 85, 83, 76, 84, 77, 73, 80, 87

What is the value of the interquartile range (IQR) for the test scores?

A) 9

B) 10

C) 11

D) 12

The average of five consecutive positive integers is 28.

What is the greatest possible value of one of these integers?

A) 24

B) 26

C) 30

D) 32

Medium

9

If the average of k + 2 and 3k + 6 is m and if the average of 5k and 7k - 12 is n, what is the average of m and n?

A) 2k + 1

B) 4k - 1

C) 3k - 1

D) 5k - 1

Hard

10

In a dataset of 8 numbers, the mean is 20 and the standard deviation is 5.

If a new number, 25, is added to the dataset, which of the following statements about the standard deviation of the updated dataset is true?

A) The standard deviation will remain the same.

B) The standard deviation will increase.

C) The standard deviation will decrease.

D) The standard deviation cannot be determined.

Medium

11

Sarah has taken four assessments, and her grades are 85, 90, 92, and 80.

She wants to maintain an average grade of 88 or above.

What minimum grade should she aim to score in her next assessment to achieve this target?

A) 58

B) 64

C) 75

D) 93

Medium

12

John has an average of 88 after three tests.

He dropped his average to 80 on his fourth test.

What score did he get on the fourth test?

A) 56

B) 65

C) 72

D) 82

| 1. | B | 2. | C | 3. | B | 4. | C | 5. | B | 6. | B | 7. | B | 8. | C | 9. | B | 10. | B | 11. | D | 12. | A |

1. Solution:

Step 1: Calculate the sum of the weights of all 6 students.

Sum of weights = Average weight × Number of students
Sum of weights

$= 60 \text{ kg} \times 6 = 360 \text{ kg}$

$= 360 \text{ kg} - (55 \text{ kg} + 62 \text{ kg} + 58 \text{ kg} + 61 \text{ kg} + 64 \text{ kg})$

Weight of the sixth student = 360 kg - 300 kg

Weight of the sixth student = 60 kg

Therefore, the weight of the sixth student is 60 kg.

Correct answer is B

Solution:

Mean: To find the mean, we sum up all the ages and divide by the number of friends.

Mean =

$$\frac{(22 + 25 + 28 + 22 + 30 + 28 + 22 + 23)}{8} = \frac{200}{8} = 25.$$

Median: To find the median, we arrange the ages in ascending order:

22, 22, 22, 23, 25, 28, 28, 30

$$\text{Median} = \frac{(23 + 25)}{2} = \frac{48}{2} = 24$$

Mode: The mode is the age that appears most frequently.

Mode = 22.

Therefore, the mean is 25, the median is 24, and the mode is 22.

Correct answer is C

3. Solution:

To find the lowest score John can receive on his next math exam and still have an average of at least 80 on the five exams, we can set up an equation:

$(80 + 85 + 90 + 75 + x)/5 \geq 80$

Multiplying both sides of the inequality by 5 to eliminate the denominator:

$330 + x \geq 400$

$x \geq 400 - 330$

$x \geq 70$

Therefore, the lowest score John can receive on his next math exam a and still have an average of at least 80 on the five exams is 70.

Correct answer is B

4. Solution:

By counting the occurrences of each color:

Red: 3 Blue: 4 Green: 5 Yellow: 2

The color that appears most frequently is Green with a frequency of 5.

Correct answer is C

5. Solution:

To find the median, we need to arrange the ages in ascending order and determine the middle value. If there is an even number of values, the median is the average of the two middle values. Arranging the ages in ascending order:
13, 13, 14, 15, 15, 15, 16, 16, 17, 18

The middle two values are 15 and 15.

Since there are two middle values, we take their average:

$$\text{Median} = \frac{15 + 15}{2}, \qquad \text{Median} = \frac{30}{2}$$

Median = 15

Correct answer is B

6. Solution:

To find the interquartile range (IQR), we need to calculate the first quartile (Q1) and the third quartile (Q3) of the data set and then subtract Q1 from Q3.

First, we need to sort the scores in ascending order:

68, 70, 72, 73, 75, 76, 77, 78, 79, 80, 81, 82, 83, 84, 85, 86, 87, 88, 90, 91

Next, we find the positions of Q1 and Q3 in the sorted data set.

Q1 is the median of the lower half of the data set, which consists of the scores from the 1st to the 10th position. Since there are an even number of values, we take the average of the two middle values:

$$Q1 = \frac{85 + 86}{2}$$
$$Q1 = 85 \cdot 5$$

Q3 is the median of the upper half of the data set, which consists of the scores from the 11th to the 20th position. Again, since there are an even number of values, we take the average of the two middle values:

$$Q3 = \frac{85 + 86}{2}$$
$$Q3 = 85 \cdot 5$$

We can calculate the interquartile range (IQR) by subtracting Q1 from Q3:

IQR = Q3 - Q1

$$IQR = 85 \cdot 5 - 75 \cdot 5$$

IQR = 10

Therefore, the value of the interquartile range (IQR) for the test scores is B

Correct answer is B

7. Solution:

To find the average, we add the values and divide by the total number of values.

Let's calculate the values of a, b, and c:

$$a = \frac{4k + 6}{2}$$
$$b = \frac{2k + 12}{2}$$
$$c = \frac{6k + 18}{2}$$

Now, to find the average of a, b, and c, we add them up and divide by 3:

$$\text{Average} = \frac{a + b + c}{3}$$

Substituting the values of a, b, and c:

$$\text{Average} = \frac{\left[\left(\frac{4k + 6}{2}\right) + \frac{2k + 12}{2} + \frac{6k + 18}{2}\right]}{3}$$

Simplifying the expression:

$$\text{Average} = \frac{4k + 6 + 2k + 12 + 6k + 18}{6}$$

Combining like terms:

$$\text{Average} = \frac{12k + 36}{6}$$
$$\text{Average} = 2k + 6$$

Correct answer is B

8. Solution:

Let's assume that the first positive integer is x.

Since we are dealing with five consecutive positive integers, the other four consecutive integers would be

(x + 1), (x + 2), (x + 3), and (x + 4).

$$\text{Average} = \left(\frac{x + (x + 1) + (x + 2) + (x + 3) + (x + 4)}{5} \right)$$

Simplifying the expression:

$$28 = \frac{5x + 10}{5}$$

Multiplying both sides of the equation by 5

$$140 = 5x + 10$$

Subtracting 10 from both sides:

$$130 = 5x$$

$$x = 26$$

Therefore, the first positive integer is 26,

and the consecutive integers are 26, 27, 28, 29, and 30.

greatest possible value of one of these integers is 30.

Correct answer is C

9. Solution:

To find the average of m and n:

$$m = \frac{k + 2 + 3k + 6}{2}$$

$$n = \frac{5k + 7k - 12}{2}$$

Now, let's simplify these expressions:

$$m = \frac{4k + 8}{2}$$

$$n = \frac{12k - 12}{2}$$

Simplifying further:

$$m = 2k + 4$$

$$n = 6k - 6$$

To find the average of m and n, we add them up and divide by 2:

$$\text{Average} = \frac{m + n}{2}$$

Substituting the values of m and n:

$$\text{Average} = \frac{[(2k + 4) + (6k - 6)]}{2}$$

Simplifying the expression:

$$\text{Average} = \frac{8k - 2}{2}$$

$$\text{Average} = 4k - 1$$

Correct answer is B

10. Solution:

Adding a new number to the dataset can change the standard deviation. In this case, the new number, 25, is larger than the mean of the dataset, which means it introduces additional variability.

As a result, the standard deviation will increase

Correct answer is B

11. Solution:

Sarah's assessments grade are 85, 90, 92, and 80.

She wants to make her average is 88 and she will take last one assessment.

So, she takes 5 assessments.

We need to find what sum is needed to make mean 88 with five exams.

Sum = 88 x 5 = 440

Sum of the four assessments;

85 + 90 + 92 + 80 = 347

To get fifth assessment grade to make average 88;

440 - 347 = 93

Correct answer is D

12. Solution:

$$\text{Average} = \frac{\text{the sum of all test scores}}{\text{number of tests}}$$

We know that John took three tests, and his average is 88.

We can find sum of his three test scores.

Sum of three test score= 88 x 3 =264

Then, he got one more exam and his average was dropped to 80.

So, we can find sum of four test score,

Sum of four test score= 80x4 = 320

To find how much he got from fourth test subtract sum of test scores, 320 - 264 = 56

Correct answer is A

Probability is expressed as a number between 0 and 1, where 0 represents an impossible event and 1 represents a certain event. The probability of an event A is denoted by P(A).

Conditional probability is the probability of an event occurring given that another event has already occurred. It is denoted by P(A|B), which represents the probability of event A given that event B has occurred.

Conditional probability allows us to adjust the probability based on additional information or conditions.

The formula for conditional probability is:

$$P(A \mid B) = \frac{P(A \text{ and } B)}{P(B)}$$ where P(A and B) represents

the probability of both events A and B occurring, and P(B) represents the probability of event B occurring.

Digital SAT Sample Question:

A bag contains 5 red balls and 7 blue balls.

If one ball is randomly selected from the bag, what is the probability of selecting a red ball?

A) $\frac{1}{6}$

B) $\frac{5}{12}$

C) $\frac{5}{7}$

D) $\frac{7}{12}$

Solution:

The total number of balls in the bag is

5 (red) + 7 (blue) = 12.

The probability of selecting a red ball can be calculated as the number of favorable outcomes (red balls) divided by the total number of possible outcomes (all balls).

Therefore, the probability of selecting a red ball is
$$\frac{5 (\text{number of red balls})}{12 (\text{total number of balls})} = \frac{5}{12}$$

Correct answer is B

Digital SAT Sample Question:

Use the following chart to answer questions.

The chart is about the students in the class and their situation with glasses.

	With glasses	No glasses
Girl	10	6
Boy	6	12

What is the probability of the selected student having no glasses?

A) 3

B) 9

C) $\frac{10}{17}$

D) $\frac{9}{17}$

Solution:

The total number of students are 34.

The probability of selecting number of students with no

$$\text{glasses} = \frac{(\text{number of students with no glasses})}{(\text{total number of possible outcomes})}$$

Therefore, the probability of selecting number of students with no glasses is

$$= \frac{18}{34} = \frac{9}{17}$$

Correct answer is D

Probability and Conditional Probability Test

A bag contains 5 red and 3 blue toy cars. If two toy cars are chosen randomly and without replacement, what is the probability that both are red?

A) $\frac{3}{32}$

B) $\frac{5}{14}$

C) $\frac{3}{8}$

D) $\frac{5}{8}$

A coin is flipped three times. What is the probability that it lands heads exactly on three flips?

A) $\frac{1}{64}$

B) $\frac{1}{16}$

C) $\frac{1}{8}$

D) $\frac{1}{4}$

In a basketball game, a player has a 70% chance of making a free throw. The player will make two throws. What is the probability the player will <u>NOT</u> make two free throws?

A) 0.7

B) 0.49

C) 0.3

D) 0.51

Jack will play chess match in which there are 3 outcomes: win, loss, and tie. For each game, let P(win) = 0.7 and P(loss) = 0.1 and P(tie) = 0.2 . If Jack plays the chess two times, what is the probability that he will win the first game, and not loss the second game?

A) 0.63

B) 0.09

C) 0.16

D) 0.14

Easy

5

Emma conducted a survey for students to ask which kind of ice cream and chocolate they like. The results are given in the table:

	Strawberry ice-cream	Vanilla ice-cream
White chocolate	10	12
Dark chocolate	8	6

What is the probability that randomly selected one student who likes vanilla ice cream with <u>NOT</u> like dark chocolate?

A) $\frac{1}{2}$

B) $\frac{1}{3}$

C) $\frac{5}{6}$

D) $\frac{3}{5}$

Hard

6

In a pencil case, there are crayons and pens. The probability that randomly selected acrayon is 3a+1, the probability that a randomly selected pen is 2a+1. What is the percentage of crayons?

A) 40

B) 50

C) 60

D) 80

Medium

7

Amy finds common positive factors of 24 and 36 to choose a number. What is the probability that a randomly selected number is the greatest common factor of 24 and 36?

A) $\frac{1}{5}$

B) $\frac{1}{6}$

C) $\frac{1}{7}$

D) $\frac{1}{8}$

Medium

8

Six numbers and six letters are written on the cards one by one, and the numbers are put in the green box. Letters put in then yellow box.

Green box: 13, 27, 37, 11,39, 18

Yellow box: A , B, C ,L , E, T

Amy will choose a card from each box. What is the sum of the probability of having a prime number written on the card drawn from the green box and the probability of having a vowel on the card drawn from the yellow box?

A) $\frac{1}{3}$

B) $\frac{1}{2}$

C) 1

D) $\frac{5}{6}$

What is the probability of the pointer landing on odd number when the given spinner is spun?

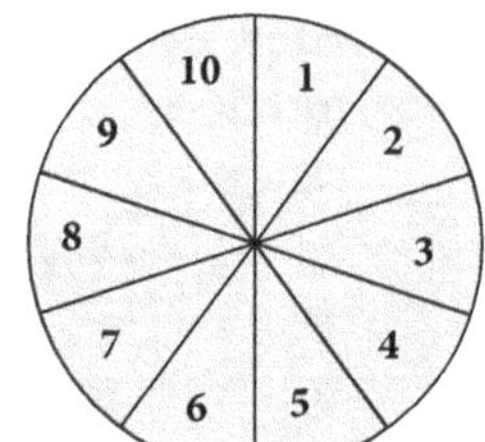

A) $\frac{1}{2}$

B) $\frac{2}{3}$

C) $\frac{1}{5}$

D) $\frac{2}{5}$

Emma asked their friends which sport activity they will register for the school year. The results are displayed in the table below.

	Choose hiking	Does Not Choose Hiking
Choose Canoe	57	63
Does Not Choose Canoe	32	48

What is the probability that randomly selected a student chooses neither canoe nor hiking?

A) 10 %

B) 14%

C) 24%

D) 35%

A box contains 8 green socks and 4 orange socks. If two socks are chosen randomly and without replacement, what is the probability that both are orange?

A) $\frac{1}{11}$

B) $\frac{1}{3}$

C) $\frac{3}{4}$

D) $\frac{1}{12}$

A die is rolled two times. What is the probability of getting 3 in the first roll and 5 in the second roll?

A) $\frac{1}{2}$

B) $\frac{1}{6}$

C) $\frac{2}{3}$

D) $\frac{1}{36}$

1.	B	2.	C	3.	D	4.	A	5.	B	6.	A	7.	B	8.	D	9.	A	10.	C	11.	A	12.	D

1. Solution:

The probability of choosing a red toy car on the first draw is $\frac{5}{8}$, since there are 5 red toy cars out of 8 total toy cars. Since we don't replace the first toy car before the second draw, there are now only 4 red toy cars left out of a total of 7 toy cars. Therefore, the probability of choosing another red toy car on the second draw is $\frac{4}{7}$.

To find the probability of both events happening, we need to multiply the probabilities of each event. So, the probability of choosing two red toy cars is: $\frac{5}{8} \cdot \frac{4}{7} = \frac{20}{56} = \frac{5}{14}$

Correct answer is B

2. Solution:

The probability of getting heads on a single flip is $\frac{1}{2}$. So, for three flips: $\frac{1}{2} \cdot \frac{1}{2} \cdot \frac{1}{2} = \frac{1}{8}$

Correct answer is C

3. Solution:

The probability of making a free throw is 0.70.

The probability that the player will make two free throws is

0.70 x 0.70 = 0.49

The probability will not make two free throws is

1 - 0.49 = 0.51

Correct answer is D

4. Solution:

The probability of Jack win is 0.7.

The probability of Jack loss is 0.1.

The probability of Jack tie is 0.2.

The probability he will win the first game is 0.7.

The probability he will <u>not</u> loss the second game is

1 - 0.1 = 0.9.

To find the probability of both events happening, we need to multiply the probabilities of each event.

0.7 x 0.9 = 0.63

Correct answer is A

5. Solution:

Number of students who like vanilla ice cream with white chocolate is 12.

The total number of students is 36.

The probability that randomly selected one student who likes vanilla ice cream with white chocolate is $\frac{12}{36} = \frac{1}{3}$

Correct answer is B

6. Solution:

In a pencil case , there are crayons and pens. So, sum of the probability of choosing a crayon and the probability of selecting a pen is 1.

$(3a + 1) + (2a + 1) = 1$

$5a + 2 = 1$

$5a = -1$

$a = -\frac{1}{5}$

$\text{crayons} = 3a + 1 = 3 \cdot \left(-\frac{1}{5}\right) + 1 = \frac{2}{5}$

$\text{pen} = 2a + 1 = 2 \cdot \left(-\frac{1}{5}\right) + 1 = \frac{3}{5}$

To find percentage of crayons:

$100 \cdot \frac{2}{5} = 40$

Correct answer is A

7. Solution:

Factors of 24 : 1, 2, 3, 4, 6, 8, 12, 24

Factors of 36 : 1, 2, 3, 4, 6, 9, 12, 18, 36

Common factors of 24 and 36: 1, 2, 3, 4, 6, 12

GCF(24, 26) = 12

The probability of choosing greatest common factor (24 ,36) among common factors: $\frac{1}{6}$

Correct answer is B

8. Solution:

Green box: 13, 27, 37, 11, 39, 18

Yellow box: A, B, C, L, E, T

The probability of having a prime number (it is selected from green box): $\frac{3}{6}$

The probability of having a vowel on the card drawn from the yellow box: $\frac{2}{6}$

Sum of these probabilities: $\frac{2}{6} + \frac{3}{6} = \frac{5}{6}$

Correct answer is D

9. Solution:

On the spinner 1, 2, 3, 4, 5, 6, 7, 8, 9, 10 are written. We have totally 10 numbers.

Odd numbers are 1, 3, 5, 7, 9

We have 5 odd numbers.

The probability to get odd number is : $\frac{5}{10} = \frac{1}{2}$

Correct answer is A

10. Solution:

The total number of student is 200.

The number of student chooses neither canoe nor hiking is 48.

The probability to chooses a student neither canoe nor hiking is $\frac{48}{200} = \frac{24}{100} = 24\%$

Correct answer is C

11. Solution:

The probability of choosing a orange sock on the first draw is $\frac{4}{12}$, since there are 4 orange socks out of 12 socks. Since we don't replace the first socks before the second draw, there are now only 3 orange socks left out of a total of 11 socks. Therefore, the probability of choosing other orange socks the second draw is $\frac{3}{11}$.

To find the probability of both events happening, we need to multiply the probabilities of each event. So, the probability of choosing orange socks is:

$$\frac{4}{12} \cdot \frac{3}{11} = \frac{1}{11}$$

Correct answer is A

12. Solution:

Numbers on a die: 1, 2, 3, 4, 5, 6

The probability of getting three is $\frac{1}{6}$.

The probability of getting five is $\frac{1}{6}$.

$$\frac{1}{6} \cdot \frac{1}{6} = \frac{1}{36}$$

Correct answer is D

Inference from sample statistics and margin of error is a topic that deals with making conclusions or inferences about a population based on information obtained from a sample. It involves using sample statistics, such as sample means or proportions, to estimate population parameters and quantify the uncertainty associated with those estimates.

Digital SAT Sample Question:

A survey was conducted to estimate the average height of students in a school. A random sample of 100 students was selected, and their heights were measured. The sample mean height was found to be 165 cm with a standard deviation of 10 cm.

What is the 95% confidence interval for the true average height of the students?

A) 160 cm to 170 cm

B) 162 cm to 168 cm

C) 163 cm to 167 cm

D) 164 cm to 166 cm

Solution:

Step 1: Identify the sample mean, sample size, and standard deviation.

Sample mean $(\bar{x})$ = 165 cm Sample size (n) = 100 Standard deviation (σ) = 10 cm

Step 2: Compute the margin of error. The margin of error

(E) can be calculated using the formula: $E = z \times \left(\dfrac{\sigma}{\sqrt{n}} \right)$

$E = 1.96 \times \left(\dfrac{10}{\sqrt{100}} \right) = 1.96 \times 1 = 1.96$ cm

Step 3: The confidence interval is given by the formula:

Confidence Interval = $\bar{x} \pm E$

Confidence Interval = 165 ± 1.96

Lower Bound = 165 - 1.96 = 163.04 cm

Upper Bound = 165 + 1.96 = 166.96 cm

Correct answer is C

Sample Statistics and Margin of Error Test

In a survey conducted to estimate the average salary of employees in a company, a random sample of 100 employees was taken. The sample mean was $50,000 with a margin of error of $2,000. Which of the following statements is correct regarding the inference from sample statistics and the margin of error?

A) The true average salary of all employees falls between $48,000 and $52,000.

B) The sample mean is exactly $50,000.

C) The margin of error represents the variability in the sample mean.

D) The sample size should have been larger to reduce the margin of error.

A company conducted a survey to gather data on the heights of its employees.

The following table shows the heights (in inches) of a sample of employees:

Employee	Height
1	62
2	65
3	68
4	63
5	66

Which of the following statements is true about the data in the table?

I.   The mode of the heights is 65 inches.

II. The median of the heights is 65 inches.

III. The range of the heights is 6 inches.

A) I only

B) II only

C) I and II only

D) II and III only

In a certain survey, a random sample of 100 participants was selected, and their average age was found to be 35 years.

The margin of error for the average age of the entire population was determined to be 3 years.

What is a reasonable range for the average age of the entire population?

A) 25 to 45 years

B) 30 to 40 years

C) 32 to 38 years

D) 33 to 37 years

A study was conducted to estimate the average time spent by students on homework per week.

A random sample of 150 students was surveyed, and their average weekly homework time was found to be 7 hours.

The margin of error for the average homework time of the entire student population was determined to be 1.5 hours.

What is a reasonable range for the average weekly homework time of the entire student population?

A) 5.5 to 8.5 hours

B) 6 to 8 hours

C) 6.5 to 7.5 hours

D) 7 to 9 hours

A statistics professor wants to determine the relationship between students' study hours and their test scores.

The following table shows the data collected from a sample of students:

Student	Study Hours (hours)	Test Score
1	4	85
2	6	92
3	3	78
4	5	88
5	7	95

Which of the following statements is true about the relationship between study hours and test scores?

I. There is a positive correlation between study hours and test scores.

II. Students who study more hours tend to have lower test scores.

III. There is a negative correlation between study hours and test scores.

A) I only

B) II only

C) III only

D) None of the above

A survey was conducted to estimate the percentage of people in a city who support a new environmental policy. The survey obtained responses from a random sample of 500 individuals, and it was found that 60% of the respondents supported the policy. The margin of error for this estimation is 3%.

What is the range within which the true percentage of people in the city who support the policy is likely to fall with 95% confidence?

A) 54% to 66%

B) 57% to 63%

C) 58% to 62%

D) 59% to 61%

A study is being conducted to estimate the average score of students on a math test.

Four different sampling scenarios are being considered.

In which case will the margin of error for the average test score be the least?

A) 50 students from the 7th grade

B) 50 students from the entire school

C) 100 students from the 7th grade

D) 100 students from the entire school

Sample Statistics and Margin of Error Test

Two different surveys were conducted to estimate the percentage of people in favor of a new policy.

The results of the surveys are shown below

Sample	Percentage in favor	Margin of error
A	48%	3.5%
B	52%	2.2%

Both samples were selected from the same population, and the margins of error were calculated using the same method.

Which of the following is the most appropriate reason why the margin of error for sample A is greater than the margin of error for sample B

A) Sample A had a smaller number of respondents.

B) Sample A had a higher percentage of respondents in favor.

C) Sample A had a larger sample size.

D) Sample A had a smaller sample size.

A bag contains 5,000 marbles of various colors.

To estimate the percentage of blue marbles in the bag, a random sample of marbles is selected. The estimated percentage of blue marbles is found to be 20% with a margin of error of 3%.

If b represents the actual number of blue marbles in the bag, which of the following ranges is the most plausible for b?

A) b > 900

B) 700 < b < 900

C) 500 < b < 800

D) b < 700

A poll is conducted to estimate the mean salary of a certain profession.

The sample size is 400, and the margin of error is calculated to be $2000.

What does the margin of error indicate?

A) The range of salaries within the sample.

B) The maximum difference between the sample mean and the true mean in the population.

C) The level of confidence associated with the sample estimate.

D) The maximum difference between the sample proportion and the true proportion in the population.

A survey is conducted to estimate the average number of hours high school students spend studying per week.

A random sample of 200 students is taken, and the sample mean is found to be 8 hours with a margin of error of 1.5 hours.

What can be inferred from this information?

A) Approximately 95% of high school students spend between 6.5 and 9.5 hours studying per week.

B) The average number of hours high school students spend studying per week is 8 hours.

C) The margin of error represents the range of values within which the sample mean falls.

D) The sample mean is the best estimate of the true population mean for all high school students

1.	A	2.	D	3.	C	4.	A	5.	A	6.	B	7.	C	8.	D	9.	B	10.	B	11.	B

1. Solution:

The margin of error represents the range within which the true population parameter is likely to fall. In this case, with a sample mean of $50,000 and a margin of error of $2,000, we can infer that the true average salary of all employees in the company is likely to be between $48,000 and $52,000.

Correct answer is A

2. Solution:

To determine the solution, let's analyze each statement:

The mode of the heights is 65 inches. The mode refers to the value that appears most frequently in a set of data. In this case, the mode is not 65 inches since no height value appears more than once.

II. The median of the heights is 65 inches. The median is the middle value in a sorted set of data. To find the median, we need to arrange the heights in ascending order: 62, 63, 65, 66, 68. The middle value is 65 inches, so this statement is true.

III. The range of the heights is 6 inches. The range is calculated by subtracting the smallest value from the largest value in a set of data. In this case, the range is 68 - 62 = 6 inches, so this statement is also true.

Correct answer is D

3. Solution:

To determine a reasonable range for the average age of the entire population, we need to consider the margin of error.

Given that the average age of the random sample of 100 participants is 35 years, and the margin of error is 3 years, we can calculate the range within which the true average age of the entire population is likely to fall.

Highest possible average age: 35 years + 3 years = 38 years

Lowest possible average age: 35 years - 3 years = 32 years

Therefore, a reasonable range for the average age of the entire population would be between 32 and 38 years.

Correct answer is C

4. Solution:

To determine a reasonable range for the average weekly homework time of the entire student population, we need to consider the margin of error.

Given that the average weekly homework time of the random sample of 150 students is 7 hours, and the margin of error is 1.5 hours, we can calculate the range within which the true average homework time of the entire student population is likely to fall.

Highest possible average homework time: 7 hours + 1.5 hours = 8.5 hours

Lowest possible average homework time: 7 hours - 1.5 hours = 5.5 hours

Therefore, a reasonable range for the average weekly homework time of the entire student population would be between 5.5 and 8.5 hours.

Based on the options provided, the correct answer is A

Correct answer is A

5. Solution:

By observing the data, we can see that as study hours increase, the corresponding test scores also increase. This indicates a positive correlation between study hours and test scores. Therefore, statement I is true.

Statement II is incorrect because it contradicts the positive correlation observed in the data.

Statement III is also incorrect as it suggests a negative correlation, which is not supported by the given data.

Correct answer is A

6. Solution:

The margin of error of 3% indicates that the estimated percentage of 60% has an uncertainty of ±3%.

To determine the range within which the true percentage is likely to fall with 95% confidence, we can subtract and add the margin of error to the estimated percentage.

Lower Bound = 60% - 3% = 57%

Upper Bound = 60% + 3% = 63%

Therefore, with 95% confidence, the true percentage of people in the city who support the policy is likely to fall within the range of 57% to 63%.

Correct answer is B

7. Solution:

To minimize the margin of error for estimating the average test score, we would want a larger sample size from the specific group of interest, which is the 7th grade in this case. This allows for a more accurate estimation of their average score.

Among the given options, the case that will likely have the least margin of error is:

C) 100 students from the 7th grade

By selecting a larger sample size (100 students) from the specific group of interest (the 7th grade), we increase the representation of that grade level in the sample, leading to a more reliable estimation of their average test score.

This larger sample size helps reduce the margin of error, resulting in a more precise estimation.

Correct answer is C

8. Solution:

The most appropriate reason why the margin of error for sample A is greater than the margin of error for sample B is:

D) Sample A had a smaller sample size.

As mentioned earlier, the margin of error is typically inversely related to the sample size.

Larger sample sizes tend to yield smaller margins of error, while smaller sample sizes result in larger margins of error.

Given that sample A has a greater margin of error than sample B, it indicates that sample A had a smaller sample size, leading to a wider range of possible outcomes and less precision in estimating the true percentage of people in favor of the new policy.

Correct answer is D

9. Solution:

To determine the most plausible range for the actual number of blue marbles (b) in the bag, we consider the estimated percentage and associated margin of error.

Given that the estimated percentage of blue marbles in the bag is 20% and the associated margin of error is 3%, we can calculate the plausible range for the actual number of blue marbles.

The highest possible percentage of blue marbles:

20% + 3% = 23%

The lowest possible percentage of blue marbles:

20% - 3% = 17%

To find the plausible range for the actual number of blue marbles, we consider the highest and lowest possible percentages and multiply them by the total number of marbles (5,000):

Highest plausible range: 23% of $5{,}000 = 0.23 \cdot 5{,}000 = 1{,}150$ marbles

Lowest plausible range: 17% of $5{,}000 = 0.17 \cdot 5{,}000 = 850$ marbles

Therefore, the most plausible option is:

B) 700 < b < 900

This range suggests that the actual number of blue marbles in the bag is likely to be between 850 and 1150.

Correct answer is B

10. Solution:

The margin of error indicates the maximum difference between the sample mean and the true mean in the population.

Correct answer is B

11. Solution:

The margin of error provides a range within which the true population parameter is likely to fall. In this case, the sample mean is 8 hours, and the margin of error is 1.5 hours.

To construct a confidence interval, we can say that with approximately 95% confidence, the true average number of hours high school students spend studying per week falls within the range of 8 - 1.5 to 8 + 1.5, which is 6.5 to 9.5 hours.

Correct answer is B

- Radical Equations in One Variable
- Rational Exponents
- Simplifying Rational Expressions
- Quadratic Equations
- Function Notation
- Zeros of Polynomial Functions
- Nonlinear Functions
- Isolating Quantities
- Complex Numbers
- Problem Solving

To solve simple radical equations:

- Check for extraneous solutions by substituting each derived solution into the equation.

Digital SAT Sample Question:

Which of the following values of x satisfy the equation $\sqrt{x-3} = x-5$?

A) 2

B) 3

C) 4

D) 7

Solution:

We need to substitute each value of x into the equation and see which one satisfies it.

Let's evaluate each option:

A) x = 2: $\sqrt{2-3}$ = 2-5 then $\sqrt{-1}$ = -3 This is not a valid solution since the square root of a negative number is not a real number.

B) x = 3: $\sqrt{3-3}$ = 3-5 then $\sqrt{-1}$ = -2 This is not a valid solution

C) x = 4: $\sqrt{4-3}$ = 4-5 then 1 = -1 This is not a valid solution

D) x = 7: $\sqrt{7-3}$ = 7-5 then 2 = 2 This is valid

Correct answer is D

Digital SAT Sample Question:

Solve the equation for x: $\sqrt{2x+3} = x+2$?

A) x = -7

B) x = -3

C) x = -1

D) x = 7

Solution:

To solve the equation $\sqrt{2x+3} = x+2$, we need to isolate the variable x.

Let's follow the steps:

Square both sides of the equation to eliminate the square root:

$$\left(\sqrt{2x+3}\right)^2 = (x+2)^2$$

$$2x + 3 = (x+2)(x+2)$$

$$2x + 3 = x^2 + 4x + 4$$

Rearrange the equation and combine like terms:

$$x^2 + 2x + 1 = 0$$

Factor the quadratic equation: $(x+1)(x+1) = 0$

Setting each factor equal to zero and solving for 'x':

$$x + 1 = 0$$

$$x = -1$$

Therefore, the solution to the equation is x = -1.

Correct answer is C

Radical Equations in One Variable Test

Simplify the following equation and find the value of x: $\sqrt{2x+5} = 9$

A) 4

B) 16

C) 20

D) 38

Which of the following values of x satisfies the equation $\sqrt{x+5} - 3 = 2$?

A) -10

B) 15

C) 20

D) 25

Which of the following values of x satisfies the equation $\sqrt{2x-1} = x-1$?

A) $1 \pm \sqrt{2}$

B) $2 \mp \sqrt{2}$

C) $\pm \sqrt{2}$

D) $2 \pm \sqrt{3}$

$$2\sqrt{x-p} = x-4$$

If p = 1 what is the solution of the equation above?

A) {2, 5}

B) {2}

C) {2, 10}

D) {10}

Radical Equations in One Variable Test

Medium
5

$$f(x) = a\sqrt{1-x}$$

Function f is defined by the equation above.

If f (-4) = 100, what is the value of a?

A) $10\sqrt{5}$

B) $20\sqrt{5}$

C) $25\sqrt{5}$

D) $30\sqrt{5}$

Medium
7

$$g(x) = \sqrt{2x+5}$$

Function f is defined by the equation above.

If g (x) = 7, what is the value of x?

A) 22

B) 25

C) 27

D) 30

Medium
6

$$g(x) = b\sqrt{x-3}$$

Function f is defined by the equation above.

If g (7) = 45, what is the value of b?

A) 18

B) 21

C) 22

D) 22.5

Medium
8

Which of the following values of 'x' satisfies the equation $\sqrt{2x-1} = x-2$?

A) 1

B) 3

C) 5

D) 7

Which of the following values of x satisfies the equation $\sqrt{x+4} = 3$?

A) 9

B) 7

C) 5

D) 1

Which of the following values of 'x' satisfies the equation $\sqrt{2x+3} - 2 = 0$?

A) 2

B) 1

C) -1

D) $\frac{1}{2}$

Which of the following values of 'x' satisfies the equation $\sqrt{3x-8} - 1 = \sqrt{x+1}$?

A) 3

B) 5

C) 6

D) 8

Which of the following values of 'x' satisfies the equation $\sqrt{5x+2} = 3$?

A) 1

B) 2

C) 3

D) $\frac{7}{5}$

| 1. | D | 2. | B | 3. | C | 4. | D | 5. | B | 6. | D | 7. | A | 8. | C | 9. | C | 10. | D | 11. | D | 12. | D |

1. Solution:

To solve the equation $\sqrt{2x+5}=9$, we need to isolate the radical term and square both sides of the equation. Here's the step-by-step solution:

$\sqrt{2x+5}=9$ Square both sides:

$(\sqrt{2x+5})^2=9^2$

$2x+5=81$

Now, isolate x by subtracting 5 from both sides:

$2x = 81 - 5$

$2x = 76$

$x = 38$

Correct answer is D

2. Solution:

To find the value of x that satisfies the equation, we need to isolate the square root term and solve for x.

$\sqrt{2x-1}=x-1$

Squaring both sides of the equation, we have:

$2x - 1 = (x - 1)^2$

$2x - 1 = x^2 - 2x + 1$

Rearranging the equation, we get: $x^2 - 4x + 2 = 0$

In this case, a = 1, b = -4, and c = 2.

Substituting these values into the quadratic formula:

$$\frac{-b \pm \sqrt{b^2 - 4ac}}{2a}$$

$$= \frac{-(-4) \pm \sqrt{(-4)^2 - 4(1)(2)}}{2(1)}$$

$$= \frac{4 \pm \sqrt{16 - 8}}{2}$$

$$= 2 \pm \sqrt{2}$$

Correct answer is B

3. Solution:

To solve this equation, we can isolate the square root term and solve for x.

$\sqrt{x+5} - 3 = 2$

Adding 3 to both sides of the equation:

$\sqrt{x+5} = 5$

Squaring both sides of the equation:

$(x + 5) = 25$

Subtracting 5 from both sides of the equation:

$x = 20$

Correct answer is C

4. Solution:

To solve the equation $2\sqrt{x-p}=x-4$, where p = 1,

Square both sides of the equation to eliminate the square root:

$(2\sqrt{x-1})^2 = (x-4)^2$

$4(x - 1) = (x - 4)^2$

Expand the equation on the right-hand side:

$4x - 4 = x^2 - 8x + 16$

Rearrange the equation and combine like terms:

$x^2 - 12x + 20 = 0$

can factor the quadratic:

$(x - 10)(x - 2) = 0$

Set each factor equal to zero and solve for x:

$x - 10 = 0 \to x = 10$

$x - 2 = 0 \to x = 2$

Therefore, the solutions to the equation are x = 10 and x = 2

but x cannot be 2.

Correct answer is D

5. Solution:

To find the value of 'a', we need to substitute the given values into the equation and solve for 'a'.

Given: $f(x) = a\sqrt{1-x}$

$f(-4) = 100$

Substituting x = -4 into the equation:

$f(-4) = a\sqrt{1-(-4)}$

$f(-4) = a\sqrt{1+4}$

$f(-4) = a\sqrt{5}$

$100 = a\sqrt{5}$

divide both sides of the equation by $\sqrt{5}$:

$a = \dfrac{100}{\sqrt{5}}$

rationalize the denominator:

$a = \left(\dfrac{100}{\sqrt{5}}\right) \cdot \left(\dfrac{\sqrt{5}}{\sqrt{5}}\right)$

$a = \dfrac{(100\sqrt{5})}{5}$

$a = 20\sqrt{5}$

Correct answer is B

6. Solution:

To find the value of b, we can substitute the given values into the equation:

$g(x) = b\sqrt{(x-3)}$

$g(7) = 45$

Substituting x = 7 and g (7) = 45:

$45 = b\sqrt{(7-3)}$

$45 = b\sqrt{4}$

$45 = 2b$

$22.5 = b$

Correct answer is D

7. Solution:

To find the value of x, we can substitute

$g(x) = 7$ into the given equation:

$g(x) = \sqrt{(2x+5)}$

$7 = \sqrt{(2x+5)}$

Squaring both sides of the equation, we get:

$2x + 5 = 7^2$

$2x + 5 = 49$

$2x = 44$

$x = 22$

Correct answer is A

8. Solution:

To find the value of 'x' that satisfies the equation,

we can square both sides of the equation and solve for 'x'.

Given equation: $\sqrt{(2x-1)}x - 2?$

Squaring both sides:

$(\sqrt{2x-1})^2 = (x-2)^2$

$2x - 1 = x^2 - 4x + 4$

Rearranging the equation: $x^2 - 6x + 5 = 0$

Factoring gives us:

$(x-5)(x-1) = 0$

Setting each factor equal to zero:

$x - 5 = 0$ or $x - 1 = 0$, $x = 5$ $x = 1$ but $x \neq 1$

Correct answer is C

9. Solution:

Square both sides of the equation and solve for 'x'.

Given equation: $\sqrt{(x+4)} = 3$

Squaring both sides:

$$\left(\sqrt{x+4}\right)^2 = (3)^2$$

$$x + 4 = 9$$

$$x = 5$$

Correct answer is C

10. Solution:

To determine which value of 'x' satisfies the equation

$$\sqrt{3x-8} - 1 = \sqrt{x+1}$$

Let's go through each option:

A) x = 3: Substituting x = 3 into the equation:

$$\sqrt{3(3)-8} - 1 = \sqrt{3+1}$$

$0 \neq 2$ (Not satisfied)

B) x = 5: Substituting x = 5 into the equation:

$$\sqrt{3(5)-8} - 1 = \sqrt{5+1}$$

$\sqrt{7} \neq \sqrt{6}$ (Not satisfied)

C) x = 6: Substituting x = 6 into the equation:

$$\sqrt{3(6)-8} - 1 = \sqrt{6+1}$$

$\sqrt{10} - 1 \neq \sqrt{7}$ (Not satisfied)

D) x = 8: Substituting x = 8 into the equation:

$$\sqrt{3(8)-8} - 1 = \sqrt{8+1}$$

$3 = 3$ (Satisfied)

Among the given options, only x = 8 satisfies the equation .

Correct answer is D

11. Solution:

To solve the equation $\sqrt{2x+3} - 2 = 0$?

we can isolate the square root term:

$$\sqrt{2x+3} = 2$$

Square both sides of the equation to eliminate the square root:

$$\left(\sqrt{2x+3}\right)^2 = (2)^2$$

$$2x + 3 = 4$$

$$x = \frac{1}{2}$$

Correct answer is D

12. Solution:

To solve the equation $\sqrt{(5x+2)} = 3$?

Square both sides of the equation to eliminate the square root:

$$(5x + 2)^2 = (3)^2$$

$$5x + 2 = 9$$

$$x = \frac{7}{5}$$

Correct answer is D

For any real number b and positive integer n, $b^{\frac{1}{n}} = \sqrt[n]{b}$, except when b < 0 and n is even. When b < 0 and n is even, a complex root may exist.

Digital SAT Sample Question:

If $x = 3\sqrt{2}$, and $5x = 3\sqrt{2y}$, what is the value of y?

A) 5

B) 10

C) 15

D) 25

Solution:

Since $x = 3\sqrt{2}$, one can substitute $3\sqrt{2}$ for x in 5x.

$5(3\sqrt{2}) = 3\sqrt{2y}$, then

$15\sqrt{2} = 3\sqrt{2y}$, divide by 3 both sides.

$5\sqrt{2} = \sqrt{2y}$, square each side.

$50 = 2y$, then $y = 25$.

Correct Answer is D

Digital SAT Sample Question:

$$\left(\sqrt[6]{3x}\right)^4$$

Which of following equations is equivalent to the expression above?

A) 3x

B) $9x^2$

C) $3^{\frac{2}{3}} x^{\frac{2}{3}}$

D) $3x^{\frac{1}{3}}$

Solution:

$$\left(\sqrt[6]{3x}\right)^4 = \left(3^{\frac{1}{6}} \cdot x^{\frac{1}{6}}\right)^4$$
$$= 3^{\frac{4}{6}} \cdot x^{\frac{4}{6}} = 3^{\frac{2}{3}} \cdot x^{\frac{2}{3}}$$

Correct Answer is C

Rational Exponents Test

$$\left(\left(64x^{12}\right)^{\frac{1}{6}}\right)$$

Which of following equations is equivalent to the expression above?

A) $2x^2$

B) $4x^2$

C) $8x^3$

D) $16x^4$

Simplify the expression

$$\left(\frac{8x^3}{27y^6}\right)^{\frac{2}{3}}$$

A) $\dfrac{2x}{3y^2}$

B) $\dfrac{4x^2}{9y^4}$

C) $\dfrac{16x^2}{27y^4}$

D) $\dfrac{64x^2}{81y^4}$

Simplify the expression

$$\left(\frac{1}{27x^6}\right)^{\frac{1}{3}}$$

A) $\dfrac{1}{3x^2}$

B) $\dfrac{1}{9x^2}$

C) $\dfrac{1}{27x^2}$

D) $\dfrac{1}{81x^2}$

Evaluate the expression

$$\frac{16^2}{4^3}$$

A) 1

B) 2

C) 4

D) 8

Rational Exponents Test

A rectangular box has a volume of 64 cm^3 and a length of 8cm.

If the width of the box is $\sqrt[3]{2}$ times the height, what is the height of the box?

A) $2^{\frac{4}{3}}$ cm

B) $2^{\frac{1}{3}}$ cm

C) 2cm

D) 4cm

If $81^{2x+1} = 27^{4x-1}$, what is the value of x?

A) $\dfrac{1}{4}$

B) $\dfrac{3}{4}$

C) $\dfrac{5}{4}$

D) $\dfrac{7}{4}$

Simplify the following expression using rational exponents:

$$\left(\frac{4}{9}\right)^{\frac{3}{2}} \cdot \left(\frac{9}{16}\right)^{\frac{1}{2}}$$

A) $\dfrac{1}{9}$

B) $\dfrac{2}{3}$

C) $\dfrac{2}{9}$

D) $\dfrac{4}{9}$

If, $125^{3x-2} = 25^{2x+1}$, what is the value of x?

A) 8

B) $\dfrac{8}{5}$

C) 5

D) $\dfrac{5}{8}$

Rational Exponents Test

Hard

9

$(5\sqrt{5})^n = 125^m$, what is the value of $\frac{n}{m}$?

A) 1

B) 2

C) 3

D) 4

Easy

11

If $7 = b^x$, then find $\frac{7}{b} = ?$

A) 1

B) b

C) b^{x+1}

D) b^{x-1}

Hard

10

If $2^{x+1} - 2^x = p$, what is 2^{x+3} in terms of p?

A) p

B) 5p

C) 8p

D) 10p

Medium

12

If $\dfrac{a^{22}}{a^p} = a^{18}$ and $(a^5)^k = a^{30}$, then find pk =

A) 15

B) 20

C) 24

D) 30

Rational Exponents Test Solution

| 1. | A | 2. | A | 3. | B | 4. | C | 5. | A | 6. | C | 7. | D | 8. | B | 9. | B | 10. | C | 11. | D | 12. | C |

1. Solution:

$$\left(\left(64x^{12}\right)^{\frac{1}{6}}\right)$$

Simplify the base by taking the sixth root:

$$\sqrt[6]{\left(64x^{12}\right)}$$

Simplify the expression under the root:

$$\left(\sqrt[6]{64}\right)\left(\sqrt[6]{x^{12}}\right)$$

$$\left(\sqrt[6]{2^6}\right)\cdot\left(\sqrt[6]{x^{12}}\right)$$

Simplify the exponent:

$$2x^2$$

Correct Answer is A

2. Solution:

To simplify the expression

$$\left(\frac{1}{27x^6}\right)^{\frac{1}{3}}$$

we can apply the rule of exponents which states that

$$\left(a^m\right)^n = a^{mn}$$

Using this rule, we can rewrite the expression as

$$\left(\frac{1}{27x^6}\right)^{\frac{1}{3}}$$

Now, let's simplify the expression within the parentheses.

Taking the cube root of 27

gives us 3, and taking the cube root of

x^6 gives us x^2.

Therefore, the simplified expression is

$$\frac{1}{3x^2}$$

Correct Answer is A

3. Solution:

To simplify the expression $\left(\dfrac{8x^3}{27y^6}\right)^{\frac{2}{3}}$, we apply the exponent

to both the numerator and the denominator:

$$\left(\frac{\left(8x^3\right)^{\frac{2}{3}}}{\left(27y^6\right)^{\frac{2}{3}}}\right)$$

Now, let's simplify the numerator and the denominator separately:

Numerator: $\left(8x^3\right)^{\frac{2}{3}} = \left(8\right)^{\frac{2}{3}}\left(x^3\right)^{\frac{2}{3}} = 4x^2$

To simplify this, we apply the power to both the coefficient and the variable:

$$\left(27y^6\right)^{\frac{2}{3}} = \left(27\right)^{\frac{2}{3}}\left(y^6\right)^{\frac{2}{3}} = 9y^4$$

Denominator: $9y^4$

Now, we substitute the simplified numerator and denominator back into the original expression:

$$\frac{4x^2}{9y^4}$$

Correct Answer is B

4. Solution:

$$\frac{16^2}{4^3} = \frac{\left(4^2\right)^2}{4^3} = \frac{4^4}{4^3} = 4$$

Correct answer is C

5. Solution:

To solve the problem, we can use the formula for the volume of a rectangular box:

$$V = l \cdot w \cdot h$$

where V is the volume, l is the length, w is the width, and h is the height.

Given that the volume of the box is

64 cm^3 and the length is 8 cm 8cm, we have:

$$64 = 8 \cdot w \cdot h$$

$$64 = 8 \cdot w \cdot h$$

We also know that the width (w) is $\sqrt[3]{2}$ times the height (h).

Substituting this relation into the equation above, we get:

$$64 = 8\sqrt[3]{2h} \cdot h$$

$$8 = \sqrt[3]{2} \cdot h^2$$

$$8 = 2^{\frac{1}{3}} \cdot h^2$$

$$\frac{2^3}{2^{\frac{1}{3}}} = h^2$$

$$2^{3-\frac{1}{3}} = h^2$$

$$2^{\frac{4}{3}} = h$$

Correct answer is A

6. Solution:

Simplify the following expression using rational exponents:

$$\left(\frac{4}{9}\right)^{\frac{3}{2}}\left(\frac{9}{16}\right)^{\frac{1}{2}}$$

To simplify the expression, we can evaluate each part separately and then multiply the results together.

Let's start with

$$\left(\frac{4}{9}\right)^{\frac{3}{2}} = \left(\frac{2^2}{3^2}\right)^{\frac{3}{2}} = \frac{2^3}{3^3} = \frac{8}{27}$$

$$\left(\frac{9}{16}\right)^{\frac{1}{2}} = \left(\frac{3^2}{4^2}\right)^{\frac{1}{2}} = \left(\frac{3}{4}\right)^1 = \frac{3}{4}$$

The simplified expression is:

$$\frac{8}{27} \cdot \frac{3}{4} = \frac{2}{9}$$

Correct answer is C

7. Solution:

To find the value of x, we can equate the exponents on both sides of the equation:

$$3^{4(2x+1)} = 3^{3(4x-1)}$$

Now we can equate the exponents:

$$4(2x + 1) = 3(4x - 1)$$

$$8x + 4 = 12x - 3$$

$$7 = 4x$$

$$\frac{7}{4} = x$$

Correct answer is D

8. Solution:

To find the value of x, we can equate the exponents on both sides of the equation:

$$125^{3x-2} = 25^{2x+1}$$

$$5^{3(3x-2)} = 5^{2(2x+1)}$$

$$5^{9x-6} = 5^{4x+2}$$

Now we can equate the exponents:

$$9x - 6 = 4x + 2$$

$$5x = 8$$

$$x = \frac{8}{5}$$

Correct answer is B

9. Solution:

To solve this, let's simplify the expression on both sides of the equation.

Starting with the left side:

$$\left(5\sqrt{5}\right)^n = 5^n\left(\sqrt{5}\right)^n = 5^n \cdot 5^{\frac{n}{2}} = 5^{\frac{3n}{2}}$$

right side of the equation:

$$5^{\frac{3n}{2}} = 5^{3m}$$

Equating the exponents, we have:

$$5^{\frac{3n}{2}} = 5^{3m}$$

$$\frac{3n}{2} = 3m$$

$$\frac{1n}{2} = m$$

$$\frac{n}{m} = 2$$

Correct answer is B

10. Solution:

Rewrite the left side in terms of 2^x:

$$2^{(x+1)} - 2^x = p$$

$$2^x \left(2 - 1\right) = p$$

$$2^x = p$$

$$2^{(x+3)} = 2^x \cdot 2^3 = 8p$$

Correct answer is C

11. Solution:

Starting with $7 = b^x$,

Now, we can substitute this value of $7 = b^x$

$$\frac{7}{b} = \frac{b^x}{b^1} = b^{x-1}$$

Correct answer is D

12. Solution:

Let's start with the first equation:

$$\frac{a^{22}}{a^P} = a^{18}$$

Using the properties of exponents, we can simplify the left side:

$$a^{22-P} = a^{18},$$

Since the bases are the same, we can equate the exponents:

$$22 - p = 18$$

$$4 = p$$

Now, let's move on to the second equation:

$$(a^5)^k = a^{30},$$

Using the properties of exponents, we can simplify the left side:

$$a^{5k} = a^{30},$$

$$5k = 30$$

$$k = 6$$

Therefore, the value of pk is $p \cdot k = 4 \cdot 6 = 24$

Correct answer is C

- A rational expression is the quotient of two polynomials.

- To get a rational expression in simplest form:

- Factor the numerator completely.

- Factor the denominator completely.

- Cancel out any common factors.

Digital SAT Sample Question:

Simplify : $\dfrac{5x - 10}{5x}$

Solution:

$$\dfrac{5x - 10}{5x} = \dfrac{\overset{\text{Factor}}{\cancel{5}}\,(x - 2)}{\cancel{5}\,x}$$
$$= \dfrac{x - 2}{x} = 1 - \dfrac{2}{x}$$

Digital SAT Sample Question: Simplify:

Simplify : $\dfrac{7x + 42}{x^2 + 3x - 18}$.

A) $6x$

B) $x - 3$

C) $\dfrac{7}{x + 3}$

D) $\dfrac{7}{x - 3}$

Solution:

$\dfrac{7x + 42}{x^2 + 3x - 18}$ Factor the numerator and denominator completely.

$\dfrac{7(x + 6)}{(x - 3)(x + 6)}$ Cancel out any common factors.

$= \dfrac{7}{x - 3}$

Correct Answer is D

Simplifying Rational Expressions Test

Simplify the following rational expression:

$$\frac{3x^2 - 12x}{6x^3 - 18x^2}$$

A) $\dfrac{x+4}{2x(x-3)}$

B) $\dfrac{x-4}{x-3}$

C) $\dfrac{x+4}{2x(x-3)}$

D) $\dfrac{x-4}{2x(x-3)}$

Simplify the rational expression:

$$\frac{3x^2 + 6x}{x^2 - 4} \div \frac{2x^2 + 5x}{x^2 + x - 6}$$

A) $\dfrac{3(3x+2)}{2x+5}$

B) $\dfrac{3(x+3)}{2x+5}$

C) $\dfrac{3(x-2)}{2x+5}$

D) $\dfrac{3(x-2)}{2x-5}$

Simplify the following rational expression:

$$\frac{4x^2 - 9}{2x + 3}$$

A) 1

B) 2x – 3

C) 2x + 3

D) x – 3

$$\frac{x^2 - 4}{x - 2} = -2$$

What are all values of x that satisfy the equation above?

A) 2

B) –1

C) –3

D) –4

Simplifying Rational Expressions Test

5

Which of the following is a value of x for which the expression $\dfrac{-2}{x^2 + 5x + 6}$ is undefined?

A) 2

B) 3

C) 5

D) –2

7

Which of the following is equivalent to $\dfrac{6x^2 + 2x}{3x + 2}$?

A) $\dfrac{2x}{3x + 2}$

B) $2x + \dfrac{2x}{3x + 2}$

C) $2x - \dfrac{2x}{3x + 2}$

D) $x - \dfrac{2x}{3x + 2}$

6

Which of the following is equivalent to $\dfrac{9x^2 + 6x}{3x + 2}$?

A) $3x$

B) $3x+1$

C) $3x+2$

D) $2x$

8

Which of the following is equivalent to $\left(x + \dfrac{y}{3} \right)^2$?

A) $x^2 + \dfrac{2xy}{3}$

B) $x^2 + \dfrac{2xy}{3} + \dfrac{y^2}{9}$

C) $\dfrac{2xy}{3} + \dfrac{y^2}{9}$

D) $x^2 - \dfrac{2xy}{3} + \dfrac{y^2}{9}$

Medium

9

If $x^2 + xy = 30$ and $y^2 + xy = 19$, then find $x + y$?

A) 2

B) 3

C) 7

D) 9

Medium

10

Simplif $\dfrac{x^2 y + xy^2 - xy}{x^2 + xy - x}$

A) x

B) y

C) 2xy

D) –x

Hard

11

Simplify $\dfrac{x^2 - 8x + 15}{x^2 - 9} \div \dfrac{x^2 - 4x - 5}{x^2 + 3x}$.

A) x – 1

B) $\dfrac{x}{x + 1}$

C) x + 1

D) $\dfrac{x + 1}{x - 1}$

Medium

12

Simplify $\dfrac{1}{x - 1} + \dfrac{1}{x + 1}$

A) x – 1

B) x + 1

C) 1

D) $\dfrac{2x}{x^2 - 1}$

Simplifying Rational Expressions Test Solution

1. D	2. B	3. B	4. D	5. D	6. A	7. C	8. B	9. C	10. B	11. B	12. D

1. Solution:

Start by factoring out the greatest common factor in both the numerator and denominator.

The numerator can be factored as

$3x^2 - 12x = 3x(x - 4)$ and the denominator can be factored as $6x^2(x - 3)$

Now, we can cancel out the common factors:

$$\frac{3x^2 - 12x}{6x^3 - 18x^2} = \frac{3x(x - 4)}{6x^2(x - 3)}$$

Cancelling the common factors 3x in the numerator and denominator, we get: $\dfrac{x - 4}{2x(x - 3)}$

Correct Answer is D

2. Solution:

Factor the numerator and denominator.

$$4x^2 - 9 = (2x - 3)(2x + 3)$$

Cancel out any common factors.

$$\frac{(2x - 3)(2x + 3)}{2x + 3} = 2x - 3$$

Correct Answer is B

3. Solution:

To solve this, we can start by multiplying the first fraction by the reciprocal of the second fraction:

$$\frac{3x^2 + 6x}{x^2 - 4} \cdot \frac{x^2 + x - 6}{2x^2 + 5x}$$

Next, we can factor the numerators and denominators:

$$\frac{3x(x + 2)}{(x + 1)(x - 2)} \cdot \frac{(x + 3)(x - 2)}{x(2x + 5)}$$

Now, we can cancel out the common factors:

$$\frac{3x(x + 2)}{(x + 2)(x - 2)} \cdot \frac{(x + 3)(x - 2)}{x(2x + 5)}$$

The simplified expression is:

$$\frac{3(x + 3)}{2x + 5}$$

Correct Answer is B

4. Solution:

$$\frac{x^2 - 4}{x - 2} = -2 \quad \text{factor the numerators}$$

$$\frac{(x - 2)(x + 2)}{X - 2} = -2$$

cancel out the common factors

$$x + 2 = -2$$

$$x = -4$$

Correct Answer is D

5. Solution:

Factor the quadratic equation

$$x^2 + 5x + 6 = 0$$

$$(x + 3)(x + 2) = 0$$

$$x = -3 \text{ and } x = -2$$

Correct Answer is D

6. Solution:

Let's simplify the given expression:

We can start by factoring out a common factor in both the numerator and the denominator, which is 3x:

$\dfrac{3x(3x + 2)}{3x + 2}$ cancel out the common factor of 3x + 2 in the numerator and the denominator:

$$3x$$

Correct Answer is A

7. Solution:

To simplify the expression $\dfrac{6x^2 + 2x}{3x + 2}$, let's factor out the common factors in the numerator:

$$\frac{2x(3x + 1)}{3x + 2}$$

Therefore, the simplified form of the expression

$$2x - \frac{2x}{3x + 2}$$

Correct Answer is C

8. Solution:

$$\left(x + \frac{y}{3}\right)^2 = \left(x + \frac{y}{3}\right) \cdot \left(x + \frac{y}{3}\right)$$

$$= x^2 + \frac{xy}{3} + \frac{xy}{3} + \frac{y^2}{9}$$

$$= x^2 + \frac{2xy}{3} + \frac{y^2}{9}$$

Correct Answer is B

9. Solution:

$$x^2 + xy = 30$$
$$+\ y^2 + xy = 19$$
$$\overline{}$$
$$x^2 + 2xy + y^2 = 49$$

$$(x + y)^2 = 49, \quad \sqrt{(x + y)^2} = \sqrt{49}$$

$$x + y = 7$$

Correct Answer is C

10. Solution:

$$\frac{x^2 y + xy^2 - xy}{x^2 xy - x}$$

$$= \frac{xy(x + y - 1)}{x(x + y - 1)}$$

$$= \frac{xy}{x} = y$$

Correct Answer is B

11. Solution:

$$\frac{x^2 - 8x + 15}{x^2 - 9} \div \frac{x^2 - 4x - 5}{x^2 + 3x}$$

$$\frac{(x - 5)(x - 3)}{(x - 3)(x + 3)} \cdot \frac{x(x + 3)}{(x - 5)(x + 1)}$$

$$= \frac{x}{x + 1}$$

Correct Answer is B

12. Solution:

$$\frac{1}{x - 1} + \frac{1}{x + 1} = \frac{x + 1 + x - 1}{(x - 1)(x + 1)}$$

$$= \frac{2x}{(x - 1)(x + 1)}$$

$$= \frac{2x}{x^2 - 1}$$

Correct Answer is D

Quadratic equations are equations of the form

$$ax^2 + bx + c = 0,$$

where a, b, and c are constants, and x is the variable.

- The highest power of x in a quadratic equation is 2, hence the term "quadratic.

- Quadratic equations can have one, two, or no real solutions.

- The quadratic formula:

$$x = \frac{-b \pm \sqrt{b^2 - 4ac}}{2a}$$

In the quadratic formula, the discriminant, denoted as

$\Delta = b^2 - 4ac$, plays a crucial role in determining the nature of the solutions.

If $\Delta > 0$, the equation has two distinct real solutions.

If $\Delta = 0$, the equation has one real solution (a repeated root).

If $\Delta < 0$, the equation has no real solutions (complex roots).

Digital SAT Sample Question

Which of the following quadratic equations will have exactly one solution?

A) $3x^2 + 4x + 2 = 0$

B) $2x^2 - 5x + 2 = 0$

C) $x^2 - 6x + 9 = 0$

D) $4x^2 + 7x + 3 = 0$

Solution:

To determine which quadratic equation will have exactly one solution, we need to calculate the discriminant.

For a quadratic equation $ax^2 + bx + c = 0$, the discriminant is calculated as follows:

Discriminant = $b^2 - 4ac$

If the discriminant is zero, the equation will have exactly one solution (a repeated root).

Let's calculate the discriminant for each option:

A) $3x^2 + 4x + 2 = 0$

Discriminant = $(4^2) - 4(3)(2) = -8$

Since the discriminant is negative, option A will have no real solutions.

B) $2x^2 - 5x + 2 = 0$

Discriminant = $(-5^2) - 4(2)(2) = 1$

Since the discriminant is positive, option B will have two distinct solutions.

C) $x^2 - 6x + 9 = 0$

Discriminant = $(-6^2) - 4(1)(9) = 0$

Since the discriminant is zero, option C will have exactly one solution.

D) $4x^2 + 7x + 3 = 0$

Discriminant = $(7^2) - 4(4)(3) = 1$ Since the discriminant is positive, option D will have two distinct solutions.

Based on the calculations, only option C, will have exactly one solution.

Quadratic Equations Test

If $(ax + 3)(bx + 4) = 18x^2 + cx + 12$ for all values of x, and $a + b = 9$, what are the two possible values for c?

A) 3 and 5

B) 7 and 9

C) 25 and 31

D) 30 and 33

If $(6x + 5)(6x + 4) = 36x^2 + cx + 20$ for all values of x, what is the value of c?

A) 12

B) 24

C) 30

D) 54

If $x < 0$ and $x^2 + 6x + 9 = 0$, what is the value of x?

A) 1

B) -1

C) -3

D) -5

If $2x^2 + 5x + 3 = 0$.

What is the value of the discriminant (D) for this equation?

A) 0

B) 1

C) -1

D) -2

Quadratic Equations Test

Hard

5

For constants a, b, and c, the equation

$$4x(2x+3)+5(2x+3)=ax^2+bx+c$$

In the equation above, a, b, and c are constants. If the equation is true for all values of x., what is the value of a + 2b + 3c ?

A) 67

B) 77

C) 97

D) 107

Hard

7

The equation $\dfrac{4x^2+7x+3}{ax-2}=-3x-5-\dfrac{7}{ax-2}$ is true for all values of x except $x=\dfrac{2}{a}$?

What is the value of a?

A) $a = 1$

B) $a = -2$

C) $a = \dfrac{1}{2}$

D) $a = -\dfrac{4}{3}$

Medium

6

Find a quadratic equation that has exactly one real solutions.

A) $x^2+5x+6=0$

B) $2x^2-8x+4=0$

C) $3x^2+4x+1=0$

D) $4x^2-12x+9=0$

Easy

8

What are the solutions to the quadratic equation $2x^2-5x+2=0$?

A) $x = 2, x = \dfrac{1}{2}$

B) $x = 1, x = 2,$

C) $x = \dfrac{1}{2}, x = 1$

D) $x = -1, x = -\dfrac{1}{2}$

Medium

9

If $2x(x^2 - 3) = 5x$, where $x > 0$, what is one possible solution to the equation?

A) 2

B) $\sqrt{\dfrac{2}{11}}$

C) $\sqrt{\dfrac{11}{2}}$

D) 11

Medium

10

If $(4x^2 - 3x + 2) - 3(2x^2 + x - 1)$ is rewritten in the form $ax^2 + bx + c = 0$, where a, b, and c are constants, what is the value of b?

A) 2

B) -6

C) 5

D) 6

Hard

11

$$x^2 - \frac{k}{3}x = m$$

In the quadratic equation above, k and p are constants.

What are the solutions for x?

A) $x = \dfrac{\dfrac{k}{3} \pm \sqrt{\dfrac{k^2}{9} + 4m}}{4}$

B) $x = \dfrac{\dfrac{k}{3} \pm \sqrt{\dfrac{k^2}{9} - 4m}}{2}$

C) $x = \dfrac{\dfrac{k}{3} \pm \sqrt{\dfrac{k^2}{9} + 4m}}{2}$

D) $x = \dfrac{-\dfrac{k}{3} \pm \sqrt{\dfrac{k^2}{3} + 4m}}{4}$

Hard

12

Which of the following values of x satisfies the equation $\dfrac{3x - 1}{x + 2} = \dfrac{2x + 5}{x + 4}$?

A) $-1 + \sqrt{15}$

B) $1 - \sqrt{15}$

C) $2 + \sqrt{15}$

D) $2 - \sqrt{15}$

1.	D	2.	C	3.	D	4.	B	5.	C	6.	D	7.	D	8.	A	9.	C	10.	B	11.	B	12.	A

1. Solution:

To find the two possible values for c, given that

$(ax + 3)(bx + 4) = 18x^2 + cx + 12$

Expanding the left side of the equation, we have:

$(ax + 3)(bx + 4) = abx^2 + (4a + 3b)x + 12 = 18x^2 + cx + 12$, we can equate the coefficients of corresponding terms:

Equating the coefficients of x^2: ab = 18

Equating the coefficients of x: 4a + 3b = c

Equating the constant terms: 12 = 12

We are given that a + b = 9. We can solve this system of equations to find the possible values of a, b, and c.

From a + b = 9, we can express aa in terms of b as a = 9 − b.

Substituting this into the equation ab = 18:

(9 − b) b = 18

Expanding and rearranging, we get:

$9b − b^2 = 18$

Rearranging further:

$b^2 − 9b + 18 = 0$

Now we can factor this quadratic equation:

(b − 3)(b − 6) = 0

Setting each factor to zero:

b − 3 = 0, b = 3

b − 6 = 0, b = 6

For each value of b, we can find the corresponding value of a using a = 9 − b.

For b = 3, a = 9 − 3 = 6

For b = 6, a = 9 − 6 = 3

Now, we can find the corresponding values of c using

4a + 3b = c

For a = 6 and b = 3:

c = 4(6) + 3(3) = 24 + 9 = 33

For a = 3 and b = 6:

c = 4(3) + 3(6) = 12 + 18 = 30

Therefore, the two possible values for c are 33 and 30.

Correct Answer is D

2. Solution:

To find the value of x, we can solve the quadratic equation $x^2 + 6x + 9 = 0$

This equation can be factored as $(x + 3)^2 = 0$.

Taking the square root of both sides, we have x + 3 = 0

Solving for x, we get x = -3

However, we are given that x < 0, which means the value of x can be -3.

Correct Answer is C

3. Solution:

Expanding the left side of the equation, we have:

$(6x + 5)(6x + 4) = 36x^2 + (24x + 30x) + 20 = 36x^2 + 54x + 20$

Comparing this with the given quadratic equation,

$36x^2 + cx + 20 = 36x^2 + 54x + 20$

cx = 54x

c = 54

Correct Answer is D

4. Solution:

The discriminant (D) of a quadratic equation

$ax^2 + bx + c = 0$ is given by the formula

$D = b^2 − 4ac$

For the quadratic equation

$2x^2 + 5x + 3 = 0$.

we have a = 2, b = 5, and c = 3.

Substituting these values into the formula for the discriminant, we get:

$D = (5)^2 − 4(2)(3) = 1$

Therefore, the value of the discriminant for the given quadratic equation is D = 1.

Correct Answer is B

5. Solution:

To find the value of a + 2b + 3c in the equation

$4x(2x + 3) + 5(2x + 3) = ax^2 + bx + c,$

we can simplify the equation and compare the coefficients.

Expanding the terms on the left side of the equation, we have:

$8x^2 + 12x + 10x + 15 = =ax^2 + bx + c$

Combining like terms, we get:

$8x^2 + 22x + 15= =ax^2 + bx + c$

Comparing the coefficients of the corresponding terms, we can equate them as follows:

Equating the coefficients of x^2: 8 = a

Equating the coefficients of x: 22 = b

Equating the constant terms: 15 = c

Now, we can find the value of a + 2b + 3c:

$a + 2b + 3c = 8 + 2(22) + 3(15)$

$a + 2b + 3c = 97$

Correct Answer is C

6. Solution:

The discriminant is given by the formula

$D = b^2 - 4ac$, where a, b, and c are the coefficients of the quadratic equation $ax^2 + bx + c$.

Now let's calculate the discriminant for each option:

A) $x^2 + 5x + 6 = 0$ In this equation,

a = 1, b = 5, and c = 6.

$D = ((5)^2 - 4(1)(6) = 25 - 24 = 1$

B) $2x^2 - 8x + 4 = 0$ In this equation,

a = 2, b = −8, and c = 4.

$D = (-8)^2 - 4(2)(4) = 64 - 32 = 32$

C) $3x^2 + 4x + 1 = 0$ In this equation,

a = 3, b = 4, and c = 1.

$D=(4)^2 - 4(3)(1) = 16 - 12 = 4$

D) $4x^2 - 12x + 9 = 0$ In this equation,

a = 4, b = −12, and c = 9.

$D = (-12)^2 - 4(4)(9) = 144 - 144 = 0$

Based on the values of the discriminants:

Options A, B, and C have positive discriminants, indicating two real solutions.

Option D has a discriminant of 0, indicating one real solution.

Correct Answer is D

7. Solution:

Given the equation:

$$\frac{4x^2 + 7x + 3}{ax - 2} = -3x - 5 - \frac{7}{ax - 2}$$

To find the value of a that satisfies the equation for all values of x except $x = \frac{2}{a}$, we need to simplify the equation and identify any restrictions on x. First, let's simplify the equation: $\frac{4x^2 + 7x + 3}{ax - 2} = -3x - 5 - \frac{7}{ax - 2}$

$4x^2 + 7x + 3 = (ax - 2)(-3x - 5) - 7$ Multiplying both sides by $(ax - 2)$ to eliminate the denominator, we get:

$4x^2 + 7x + 3 = (-3x - 5)(ax - 2) - 7$

Expanding and simplifying:

$4x^2 + 7x + 3 = -3ax^2 + -5ax + 6x + 10 - 7$

Combining like terms:

$4x^2 + 7x + 3 = -3ax^2 - 5ax + 6x + 3$

Comparing the coefficients of x^2 on both sides, we have:

$4 = -3a$

$a = -\frac{4}{3}$

Correct Answer is D

8. Solution:

The quadratic formula states that for an equation in the form $ax^2 + bx + c = 0$, the solutions for x are given by:

$$x = \frac{-b \pm \sqrt{b^2 - 4ac}}{2a}$$

In this case, we have a = 2, b = −5, and c = 2.

Plugging these values into the quadratic formula, we get:

$$x = \frac{-(-5) \pm \sqrt{(-5)^2 - 4(2)(2)}}{2(2)} = \frac{5 \mp \sqrt{25 - 16}}{4}$$

Simplifying further:

$$x = \frac{5 \pm 3}{4}$$

Simplify the expression:

$$x = \frac{5 + 3}{4} = 2 \text{ or } x = \frac{5 - 3}{4} = \frac{1}{2}$$

Correct Answer is A

9. Solution:

To find a possible solution to the equation

$2x(x^2 - 3) = 5x$, where x > 0

Simplify the equation and solve for x.

First, let's simplify the equation:

$2x(x^2 - 3) = 5x$,

Expanding the left side:

$2x^3 - 6x = 5x$,

Combining like terms:

$2x^3 - 11x = 0$,

Now, let's factor out xx from the equation:

$x(2x^2 - 11) = 0$,

We have two possible solutions: x = 0

$2x^2 - 11 = 0$.

Since the given condition is x > 0, we need to find the positive solution.

Solving $2x^2 - 11 = 0$

$$x^2 = \frac{11}{2}$$

$$x = \sqrt{\frac{11}{2}}$$

Correct Answer is C

10. Solution:

To rewrite the expression

$(4x^2 - 3x + 2) - 3(2x^2 + x - 1)$

In the form $ax^2 + bx + c$, we need to simplify it by combining like terms. Expanding the expression, we have:

$4x^2 - 3x + 2 - 6x^2 - 3x + 3$

Combining like terms, we get:

$(4x^2 - 6x^2) + (-3x - 3x) + (2 + 3)$

Simplifying further: $-2x + -6x + 5$,

$a = -2$, $b = -6$, $c = 5$

Therefore, the value of b is -6.

Correct Answer is B

11. Solution:

To find the solutions for the quadratic equation

$x^2 - \dfrac{k}{3} x - m = 0$, we can use the quadratic formula:

$$x = \frac{-b \pm \sqrt{b^2 - 4ac}}{2a}$$

Comparing the equation $x^2 - \dfrac{k}{3}x - m = 0$

with the standard quadratic equation $ax^2 + bx + c = 0$, we have: $a = 1$, $b = \dfrac{-k}{3}$ and $c = -m$

Substituting these values into the quadratic formula:

$$x = \frac{-\left(\frac{-k}{3}\right) \pm \sqrt{\left(\frac{-k}{3}\right)^2 - 4(1)(-m)}}{2(1)}$$

$$x = \frac{+\frac{k}{3} \pm \sqrt{\frac{k^2}{9} + 4m}}{2}$$

Correct Answer is C

12. Solution:

To solve the equation, we can cross-multiply and simplify:

$(3x - 1)(x + 4) = (2x + 5)(x + 2)$

Expanding both sides of the equation:

$3x^2 + 11x - 4 = 2x^2 + 9x + 10$

Combining like terms:

$x^2 + 2x - 14 = 0$

Factoring quadratic equation:

$a = 1$, $b = 2$, and $c = -14$

$$x = \frac{-2 \mp \sqrt{2^2 - 4(1)(-14)}}{2(1)}$$

$$x = \frac{-2 \mp \sqrt{4 + 56}}{2} = \frac{-2 \mp \sqrt{60}}{2}$$

$$x = \frac{-2 \mp 2\sqrt{15}}{2} = -1 \mp \sqrt{15}$$

Correct Answer is A

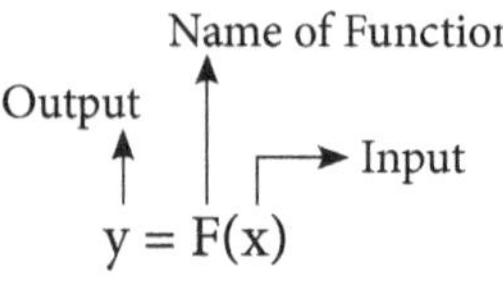

Not a Function: If the domain (x) is repeating, it's not a function. You do not need to check the range (y). It does not matter if range repeats.

Example: (a, 1), (b, 3), (c, 5) is a function because the domains do not repeat.

Example: (a, 1), (b, 3), (c, 5), (a, 10) is not a function because the domains repeat.

Digital SAT Sample Question:

If $f(x) = x + 9$ and $h(x) = 6x$, what is the value of $3f(5) - h(7)$?

A) -1

B) 0

C) 1

D) 2

Solution:

To find the value of 3f(5) - h(7), we need to substitute the given functions and compute the expression.

Given: $f(x) = x + 9$ and $h(x) = 6x$

First, let's evaluate f(5) using the function

$f(x) = x + 9: f(5) = 5 + 9 = 14$

Next, we'll evaluate h(7) using the function

$h(x) = 6x : h(7) = 6 \times 7 = 42$

Now, we can substitute these values into the expression 3f(5) - h(7) : $3f(5) - h(7) = 3 \times 14 - 42 = 42 - 42 = 0$

Correct Answer is B.

Digital SAT Sample Question:

If $f(x) = x + 11$ and $h(x) = 4x$, what is the value of $2f(3) + g(5)$?

A) 48

B) 52

C) 64

D) 72

Solution:

To find the value of 2f(3) + g(5), we need to substitute the given functions and compute the expression.

Given: $f(x) = x + 11$ and $g(x) = 4x$

First, let's evaluate f(3) using the function

$f(x) = x + 11 : f(3) = 3 + 11 = 14$

Next, we'll evaluate g(5) using the function

$g(x) = 4x : g(5) = 4 \times 5 = 20$

Now, we can substitute these values into the expression 2f(3) + g(5): $2f(3) + g(5) = 2 \times 14 + 20 = 28 + 20 = 48$

Correct Answer is A

Function Notation Test

$$g(x) = bx^2 + 10$$

For the function g defined above is a constant and g (2) = 18.

What is the value of g (−2)?

A) -18

B) 18

C) 22

D) 28

A function f satisfies f (1) = 4 and f (7) = 6.

A function g satisfies g (2) = 3 and g (4) = 7.

What is the value of f (g (4))?

A) 3

B) 4

C) 6

D) 7

In the xy-plane, the point (5, 3) lies on the graph of the function f(x) = 2x² + bx + 10. What is the value of b?

A) 11

B) -11.4

C) -12.4

D) -14

n	g(n)
1	5
2	9
3	13
4	17

The table below shows some values of the linear function g.

Which of the following options correctly defines the function g?

A) g(n) = 4n + 1

B) g(n) = 4n + 3

C) g(n) = 4n + 5

D) g(n) = 4n + 7

5

$h(x) = -2x^2 + 8x - 3$

What is the maximum value of the given function?

A) 5

B) 6

C) -3

D) 3

6

If $f(x) = 2x - 5$ and $g(x) = x^2 + 3$, what is the value of $3f(2) - g(4)$?

A) -4

B) -8

C) -22

 D) 22

7

Let $f(x) = 2x + 3$ and $g(x) = x^2 - 4x + 5$. Find the value of $f(g(2))$.

A) 1

B) 3

C) 4

D) 5

8

Let $f(x) = x^2 - 4$ and $g(x) = 3x + 2$.

Find the value of $f(g(1))$.

A) 21

B) 25

C) 30

D) 35

Hard

9

$$g(x) = \frac{2x - 3}{4} + k$$

In the function above, k is a constant. If g (3) = 5, what is the value of g (-1)?

A) 0

B) 1

C) 2

D) 3

Easy

11

If $f(x) = 5 - x^2$, what is the value of f(-2)?

A) -9

B) -1

C) 1

D) 9

Medium

10

If g(x) = 4x - 3, what is g(2x) equal to?

A) g(2x) = 8x - 3

B) g(2x) = 2x - 3

C) g(2x) = 16x - 3

D) g(2x) = 4x + 3

Easy

12

If $f(x) = 2^{(2x)}$, what is the value of f(0)?

A) 0

B) 1

C) 2

D) 4

Function Notation Test Solution

1. Solution:

Substitute 2 into the function g(x) and solve for the value. We are given that g (2) = 18,

which gives us: $g(2) = b(2)^2 + 10 = 18$

Simplifying this equation, we have:

$$\left.\begin{array}{l} 4b + 10 = 18 \\ 4b = 8, b = 2 \end{array}\right\} g(x) = 2x^2 + 10$$

substituting -2 into the function g(x):

$g(-2) = (2)(-2)^2 + 10 = 2(4) + 10 = 8 + 10 = 18$

Therefore, the value of g (-2) is 18.

Correct Answer is B

2. Solution:

To find the value of f (g (4)), we need to evaluate the functions step by step.

Given that g (4) = 7, we substitute this value into the function f(x): f (g (4)) = f (7)

From the given information, we know that f (7) = 6.

Correct Answer is C

3. Solution:

Substituting x = 5 and y = 3 into the function f(x), we have:

$3 = 2(5)^2 + b(5) + 10$

Simplifying the equation, we get:

3 = 2(25) + 5b + 10

Further simplifying, we have:

3 = 50 + 5b + 10

Combining like terms, we have:

3 = 60 + 5b

-57 = 5b, b = -11.4

Correct Answer is B

4. Solution:

Use the point-slope form of a linear equation:

$y - y_1 = m(x - x_1)$,

where (x_1, y_1) is a point on the line, and m is the slope.

Let's choose one point from the table, for example, (1, 5).

Plugging in the values into the equation, we have:

g(n) - 5 = 4(n - 1).

Simplifying the equation gives:

g(n) = 4n + 1.

Correct Answer is A

5. Solution:

Given function: $h(x) = -2x^2 + 8x - 3$

To find the maximum value of the function se axis of symmetry: $x = \dfrac{-b}{2a}$,

where a and b are the coefficients of x^2 and x, respectively.

In this case, a = -2 and b = 8.

Plugging these values into the formula,

$$x = \frac{-b}{2a} = \frac{-8}{2(-2)} = 2$$

Substitute the x-coordinate back into the function:

$h(2) = -2x^2 + 8x - 3$

$h(2) = -2(2)^2 + 8(2) - 3$

h (2) = 5

Correct Answer is A

6. Solution:

To find the value of $3f(2) - g(4)$,

Substitute the given values into the respective functions and perform the calculations.

First, let's find $f(2)$:

$f(2) = 2(2) - 5 = 4 - 5 = -1$

Next, let's find $g(4)$:

$g(4) = (4)^2 + 3 = 16 + 3 = 19$

Now, we can calculate the expression $3f(2) - g(4)$:

$= 3(-1) - 19 = -3 - 19 = -22$

Correct Answer is C

7. Solution:

To find the value of $f(g(2))$,

First, let's find $g(2)$:

$g(2) = (2)^2 - 4(2) + 5 = 4 - 8 + 5 = 1$

Next, substitute the value of $g(2)$, into the function $f(x)$:

$f(g(2)) = f(1) = 2(1) + 3 = 2 + 3 = 5$

Correct Answer is D

8. Solution:

To find the value of $f(g(1))$, we need to evaluate the expression step by step.

First, let's find $g(1)$: $g(1) = 3(1) + 2 = 3 + 2 = 5$

Next, substitute the value of $g(1)$ into the function

$f(x)$: $f(g(1)) = f(5) = 5^2 - 4 = 25 - 4 = 21$

Correct Answer is A

9. Solution:

Substitute -1 into the function and evaluate the expression.

Given that $g(3) = 5$, we can substitute $x = 3$ and $g(x) = 5$

into the function: $5 = \dfrac{2(3) - 3}{4} + k$

Simplifying the equation gives:

$5 = \dfrac{6 - 3}{4} + k$

$5 = \dfrac{3}{4} + k$

$\dfrac{17}{4} = k$

Substitute $x = -1$ into the function

$g(x) = \dfrac{2x - 3}{4} + \dfrac{17}{4}$

$g(-1) = \dfrac{2(-1) - 3}{4} + \dfrac{17}{4}$

$g(-1) = \dfrac{12}{4}$

$g(-1) = 3$

Correct Answer is D

10. Solution:

To find $g(2x)$, we substitute $2x$ into the function $g(x) = 4x - 3$ and evaluate the expression.

Given that $g(x) = 4x - 3$, we substitute $x = 2x$ into the function: $g(2x) = 4(2x) - 3$

Simplifying the expression gives: $g(2x) = 8x - 3$

Therefore, $g(2x)$ is equal to $8x - 3$.

Correct Answer is A

11. Solution:

Substitute $x = -2$ into the function:

$f(-2) = 5 - (-2)^2 = 5 - 4 = 1.$

Correct Answer is C.

12. Solution:

Substitute $x = 0$ into the function:

$f(0) = 2^{2 \times 0} = 2^0 = 1.$

Correct Answer is B

Zeros of Polynomial Functions

- The Zeros of a Polynomial Function are the solutions to the equation you get when you set the polynomial equal to zero.

- In other words, the Zeros are the x-values where y equals zero.

Digital SAT Sample Question:

If the polynomial function $f(x) = x^2 - 5x + 6$.

Which of the following is a zero of the function?

A) $x = 2$

B) $x = -1$

C) $x = 4$

D) $x = 6$

Solution:

To find the zeros of the function, we set $f(x) = 0$ and solve for x: $x^2 - 5x + 6 = 0$
We can factor the quadratic equation: $(x - 2)(x - 3) = 0$
Setting each factor equal to zero, we find the zeros:
$x - 2 = 0 \rightarrow x = 2$, $x - 3 = 0 \rightarrow x = 3$
Correct Answer is A.

Digital SAT Sample Question:

Which of the following options represents the number of distinct zeros for the function

$f(x) = 2x^3 - 6x^2 + 4x$?

A) 0

B) 1

C) 2

D) 3

Solution:
Set it equal to zero and solve for x:

$2x^3 - 6x^2 + 4x = 0$

We can factor out 2x from the equation:

$2x(x^2 - 3x + 2) = 0$

Now we have two parts to consider:

$2x = 0$: This gives us $x = 0$, which is one distinct zero.

$(x^2 - 3x + 2) = 0$: $(x - 2) \cdot (x - 1) = 0$

Setting each factor equal to zero, we find that $x = 1$ and $x = 2$ are the remaining distinct zeros.

Therefore, the function $f(x) = 2x^3 - 6x^2 + 4x$

has three distinct zeros: $x = 0$, $x = 1$, and $x = 2$.

Correct Answer is D.

Zeros of Polynomial Functions Test

Which of the following options represents the number of distinct zeros for the function $h(x) = 4x^2 - 12x + 9$?

A) Zero

B) One

C) Two

D) Three

Which of the following options represents a polynomial function with a single x-intercept at $x = 2$?

A) $f(x) = x^2 + 4x + 4$

B) $f(x) = x^3 - 8x^2 + 16x - 8$

C) $f(x) = x^2 - 2x + 1$

D) $f(x) = x^3 + x^2 + 4x - 8$

The graph of function g has x-intercepts at -2, 0, and 4.

Which of the following could define g?

A) $g(x) = x\,(x + 2)\,(x - 4)$

B) $g(x) = (x + 2)\,(x - 2)\,(x + 4)$

C) $g(x) = (x - 2)\,(x - 4)$

D) $g(x) = x\,(x + 2)\,(x + 4)$

Which of the following is a factor of the polynomial $x^3 - 7x^2 + 12x$?

A) $x - 2$

B) $x + 3$

C) $x - 3$

D) $x + 4$

Zeros of Polynomial Functions Test

Easy

5

$(x - 3) \cdot (x + 2) = 0$

How many distinct real solutions does the given equation have?

A) Exactly one

B) Exactly two

C) Infinitely many

D) Zero

Medium

7

If $(bx + 2)^2 = 16,$

b is a constant. If $x = 2$ is one solution to the equation, what is a possible value of b?

A) 0

B) 3

C) -1

D) -3

Hard

6

$ax^3 + bx^2 + cx + d = 0$

In the equation above, a, b, c, and d are constants. If the equation has roots -2, 3, and 4, which of the following is a factor of $ax^3 + bx^2 + cx + d$?

A) x - 2

B) x + 1

C) x - 3

D) x + 4

Medium

8

If $f(x)$ is a linear function and $f(3) = 12$ and $f(-2) = 2$, then find $f(-4)$?

A) 2

B) 4

C) -2

D) -4

Easy

9

$$x^2 + 6x - 16 = 0$$

Which of the following equations is the solution to the quadratic equation above?

A) $x = 2, x = -8$

B) $x = 3, x = -8$

C) $x = 8, x = -2$

D) $x = 0, x = -8$

Medium

11

For a polynomial q(x), the value of q (-1) is 3. Which of the following must be true about q(x)?

A) $x + 2$ is a factor of q(x).

B) $x - 3$ is a factor of q(x).

C) $q(1) = 3$.

D) The remainder when q(x) is divided by $x + 1$ is 3.

Easy

10

If 4 is one of the solutions of the equation

$x^2 - 4ax - 12 = 0$, what is the value of a?

A) 1

B) $\dfrac{1}{4}$

C) $\dfrac{1}{2}$

D) 2

Medium

12

If the polynomial function $f(x) = x^2 - 5x + 6$ has zeros a and b, what is the value of $a + b$?

A) 0

B) 1

C) 5

D) 6

| 1. | B | 2. | A | 3. | B | 4. | C | 5. | B | 6. | C | 7. | D | 8. | C | 9. | A | 10. | B | 11. | D | 12. | C |

1. Solution:

The discriminant is given by the formula $\Delta = b^2 - 4ac$, where a, b, and c are the coefficients of the quadratic equation ($ax^2 + bx + c = 0$).

In this case, the coefficients of $h(x) = 4x^2 - 12x + 9$ are

a = 4, b = -12, and c = 9.

Calculating the discriminant:

$$\Delta = (-12)^2 - 4(4)(9) = 144 - 144 = 0$$

Since the discriminant is equal to zero, the quadratic equation has exactly one real root.

Correct Answer is B

3. Solution:

The function to equal zero at x = 2 and have no other x-intercepts. Let's evaluate each option using this condition:

A) $f(2) = (2)^2 + 4(2) + 4 = 20$ **(does not satisfy the condition)**

B) $f(2) = 2^3 - 8(2)^2 + 16(2) - 8 = 0$ **(satisfies the condition)**

C) $f(2) = (2)^2 - 2(2) + 1 = 1$ **(does not satisfy the condition)**

D) $f(2) = 2^3 + (2)^2 + 4(2) - 8 = 12$ **(does not satisfy the condition)**

Correct Answer is B

2. Solution:

We know that the x-intercepts of a function are the values of x for which the function equals zero. In this case, the x-intercepts are -2, 0, and 4. Therefore, we can set up the following equations:

For x = -2: g (-2) = 0, x + 2 = 0

For x = 0: g (0) = 0, x = 0

For x = 4: g (4) = 0, x - 4 = 0

g(x) = x(x + 2) (x - 4)

Correct Answer is A

4. Solution:

First, we notice that each term has a common factor of

x: $x (x^2 - 7x + 12)$

Next, we factor the trinomial $x^2 + 7x + 12$.

We look for factors of -12 that add up to the coefficient of the middle term, which is 7. By trying different factor combinations, we find that: $x^2 - 7x + 12 = (x - 3)(x - 4)$

Therefore, the factored form of the polynomial is:

x(x - 3)(x - 4)

So, the polynomial $x^2 - 7x + 12$ can be factored as

x(x - 3)(x - 4).

Correct Answer is C

5. Solution:

Given equation: $(x - 3) \cdot (x + 2) = 0$

To satisfy the equation, either $(x - 3)$ must equal zero or $(x + 2)$ must equal zero. This can be written as: $x - 3 = 0$ or $x + 2 = 0$

Solving each equation separately, we find:

For $x - 3 = 0$: $x = 3$

For $x + 2 = 0$: $x = -2$

Thus, we have found two distinct real solutions:

$x = 3$ and $x = -2$.

Correct Answer is B

6. Solution:

If the equation has roots -2, 3, and 4, which of the following are factor:

for $x = -2$, $x + 2 = 0$,

for $x = 3$, $x - 3 = 0$,

for $x = 4$, $x - 4 = 0$, then from all options, option C is a factor of the given polynomials

Correct Answer is C

7. Solution:

Substitute $x = 2$ into the equation and solve for b:

$(2b + 2)^2 = 16$,

Taking the square root of both sides:

$|2b + 2| = 4$

Since the absolute value of a number can be positive or negative, we'll consider both cases:

Case 1: $2b + 2 = 4$ Solving for b: $2b = 4 - 2$,

$2b = 2$,

$b = 1$

Case 2: $-(2b + 2) = 4$, Solving for b:

$-2b - 2 = 4$,

$b = -3$

Correct Answer is D

8. Solution:

$3m + b = 12$

$+ \ \underline{-(-2m + b = 2)}$

$m = 2$, $b = 6$, $y = mx + b$

$f(x) = 2x + 6$

$f(-4) = 2(-4) + 6 = -8 + 6 = -2$

Correct Answer is C

9. Solution:

$x^2 + 6x - 16 = 0$ factoring form:

$(x - 2)(x + 8) = 0$, $x = 2$ or $x = -8$

Correct Answer is A

11. Solution:

Let's analyze statement D.

D) The remainder when q(x) is divided by x + 1 is 3:

Given that q (-1) = 3, it implies that the remainder when q(x) is divided by x + 1 is indeed 3.

Therefore, statement D is true.

Correct answer is D

10. Solution:

$x^2 - 4ax - 12 = 0$

If 4 is one of the solutions

$4^2 - 4a(4) - 12 = 0$

$16 - 16a - 12 = 0$

$\frac{1}{4} = a$

Correct Answer is B

12. Solution:

The polynomial function is given as $f(x) = x^2 - 5x + 6$.

To find the zeros, set f(x) equal to zero: $x^2 - 5x + 6 = 0$.

Factoring the equation gives $(x - 2)(x - 3) = 0$, which means the zeros are $x = 2$ and $x = 3$. Therefore, $a + b = 2 + 3 = 5$.

Correct answer is C

Quadratic Function $f(x) = ax^2 + bx + c$

a) When $a > 0$, parabola opens upward.

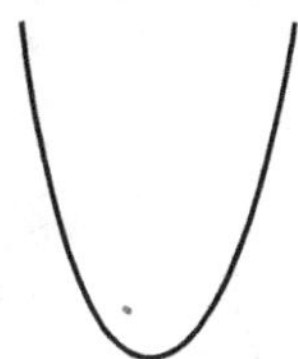

b) When $a < 0$, parabola opens downward.

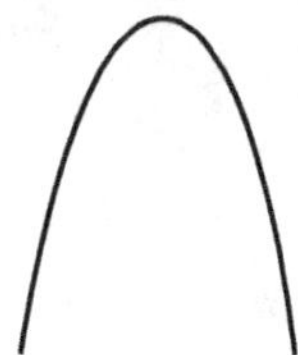

Vertex form:

$y = a(x - h)^2 + k$. The vertex of the parabola point is (h, k).

- The equation of the line of symmetry is $x = h = -\dfrac{b}{2a}$

Digital SAT Sample Question:

Which of the following is a root of the function

$f(x) = 3x^2 - 5x + 2$?

A) $x = \dfrac{1}{2}$

B) $x = \dfrac{2}{3}$

C) $x = 2$

D) $x = -1$

Solution:

Set $f(x)$ equal to zero:

$3x^2 - 5x + 2 = 0$

We can factor the quadratic equation:

$(3x - 2)(x - 1) = 0$

$3x - 2 = 0$: Solving for x, we get $x = \dfrac{2}{3}$

$x - 1 = 0$: Solving for x, we get $x = 1$.

Therefore, the function $f(x) = x^2 - 5x + 2$,

has two roots: $x = \dfrac{2}{3}$ and $x = 1$.

Correct answer is B.

Medium

1

If $f(x) = x^2 - 6x + 4$, what is the vertex point V(h,k)?

A) $(3, 5)$

B) $(3, -5)$

C) $(4, -3)$

D) $(-4, 3)$

Medium

2

$$g(x) = (x - 3)(x + 5)$$

where the maximum value appears as a constant or coefficient?

A) $g(x) = (x - 2)^2 - 19$

B) $g(x) = (x + 3)^2 - 10$

C) $g(x) = (x + 1)^2 - 16$

D) $g(x) = (x - 5)^2 - 10$

Medium

3

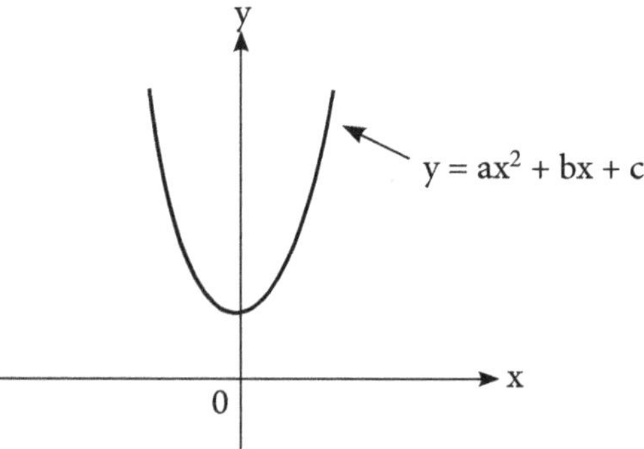

The vertex of the parabola in the xy-plane is (-2, 5).

Which of the following is true about the parabola with the equation $y = a(x + 2)^2 + 5$?

A) The vertex is (-2, 5) and the graph opens upward.

B) The vertex is (-2, 5) and the graph opens downward.

C) The vertex is (2, 5) and the graph opens upward.

D) The vertex is (2, 5) and the graph opens downward.

Medium

4

$$y = x^2 + 6x + 8$$

The equation above represents a parabola in the xy-plane.

Which of the following equivalent forms of the equation displays the x-intercepts as constants or coefficients?

A) $y = (x + 4)(x + 2)$

B) $y - 8 = x(x + 6)$

C) $y = (x + 3)^2 - 1$

D) $y = y = (x - 3)^2 + 1$

Nonlinear Functions Test

In the equation $y = x^2 - 8x + k$, where k is a constant, if the equation represents a parabola in the xy - plane that is tangent to the x-axis, what is the value of k?

A) $k = 4$

B) $k = 8$

C) $k = 16$

D) $k = 24$

If $f(x) = x^2 - 2mx + n$ and the vertex point V is (3,2) find m+n?

A) 6

B) 9

C) 11

D) 14

Which of the following parabola functions could represent the graph in the picture?

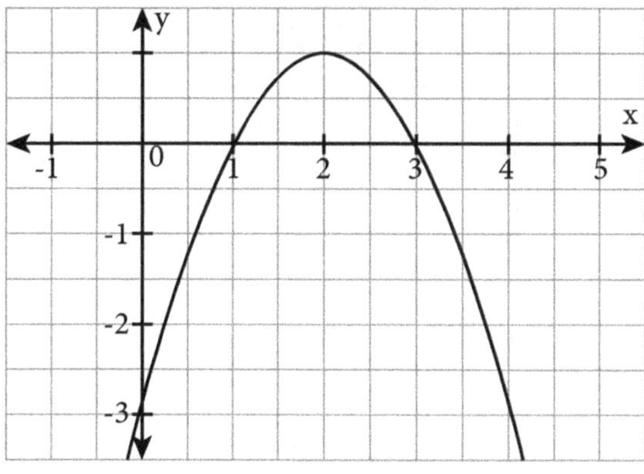

A) $f(x) = -x^2 + 4x + 3$

B) $f(x) = -x^2 - 4x + 3$

C) $f(x) = x^2 + 4x - 3$

D) $f(x) = -x^2 + 4x - 3$

$$f(x) = mx^2 + 18$$

For the function above, m is a constant and f (3) =48. What is the value of f (6)?

A) 38

B) 120

C) 138

D) 150

Medium
9

Which of the following is in vertex form for the quadratic equation $y = -2x^2 + 4x - 3$?

A) $y = -2(x + 1)^2 + 1$

B) $y = -2(x - 1)^2 - 1$

C) $y = -2(x + 1)^2 - 1$

D) $y = -2(x - 1)^2 + 1$

Medium
10

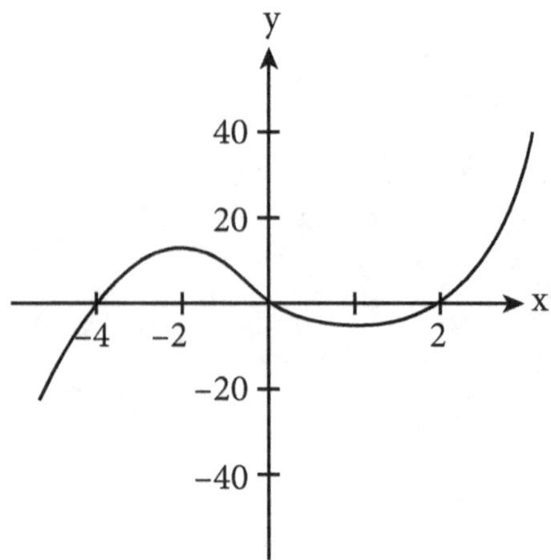

Which of the following could be the equation of the graph above?

A) $y = x(x + 4)(x - 2)$

B) $y = x^2(x + 4)(x - 2)$

C) $y = x(x - 4)(x + 2)$

D) $y = x^2(x - 4)(x + 2)$

Medium
11

The function $f(x) = -2x^2 + 4$ represents a quadratic function.

What is the vertex of the parabola?

A) $(0, 4)$

B) $(2, -4)$

C) $(2, 4)$

D) $(0, -4)$

Medium
12

The graph of a function passes through the points $(1, 2)$, $(2, 5)$, and $(3, 10)$.

Which of the following equations represents a nonlinear function that could produce this graph?

A) $y = x^2 - 1$

B) $y = x^2 + 1$

C) $y = x^2 + 2$

D) $y = x^2$

| 1. | B | 2. | C | 3. | A | 4. | C | 5. | C | 6. | D | 7. | D | 8. | C | 9. | B | 10. | A | 11. | A | 12. | B |

1. Solution:

$F(x) = x^2 - 6x + 4$ Vertex Form

$V(x) = a(x - h) + k$

$V(x) = (x - 3)^2 - 9 + 4$

$V(x) = (x - 3)^2 - 5$

$V(h, k) = (3, -5)$

Correct Answer is B

2. Solution:

To determine the correct option, we need to complete the square and compare it to the given choices. Expanding and simplifying the function

$g(x)$: $g(x) = (x - 3)(x + 5) = x^2 + 5x - 3x - 15 = x^2 + 2x - 15$

The maximum value appears as a constant or coefficient, we need to complete the square.

$g(x) = x^2 + 2x - 15 = (x^2 + 2x + 1) - 1 - 15 = (x + 1)^2 - 16$

Correct Answer is C

3. Solution:

To solve this, we can compare the given equation

$y = a(x + 2)^2 + 5$? with the standard vertex form

$y = a(x - h)^2 + k$, where (h, k) represents the vertex of the parabola. The vertex is given as (-2, 5), which corresponds to the values of (h, k). The graph opens upward if the coefficient 'a' is positive, and it opens downward if 'a' is negative. Let's analyze statement A: This statement is true because the vertex of the parabola is given as (-2, 5), and the graph opens upward when the coefficient 'a' is positive.

Correct Answer is A

4. Solution:

Starting with the equation $y = x^2 + 6x + 8$, we can rewrite it as: $y = (x^2 + 6x) + 8$. To complete the square, we need to add and subtract the square of half the coefficient of x. Half of 6 is 3, so we have:

$y = (x^2 + 6x + 9 - 9) + 8$.

Now, let's rearrange the terms:

$y = (x^2 + 6x + 9) - 9 + 8$.

Simplifying further:

$y = (x + 3)^2 - 1$

The equation $y = (x + 3)^2 - 1$ is in vertex form.

Correct Answer is C

5. Solution:

The discriminant is given by $\Delta = b^2 - 4ac$, where a, b, and c are the coefficients of the quadratic equation $ax^2 + bx + c$.

In this case, a = 1, b = -8, and c = k.

Setting the discriminant equal to zero:

$\Delta = (-8)^2 - 4(1)(k) = 0$.

Simplifying:

$64 - 4k = 0$.

Rearranging the equation:

$4k = 64$.

Dividing both sides by 4:

$k = 16$.

Correct Answer is C

6. Solution:

From the graph the Vertex Point is (2, 1).

$V(x) = a(x-h)^2 + k$

$V(x) = a(x-2)^2 + 1$

From the graph you can use (0, - 3)

$-3 = a(0 - 2)^2 + 1$

$-3 = 4a + 1$

$-4 = 4a, \quad a = -1$

$V(x) = -(x - 2)^2 + 1$

$V(x) = -(x^2 - 4x + 4) + 1$

$= -x^2 + 4x - 4 + 1$

$= -x^2 + 4x - 3$

Correct Answer is D

7. Solution:

$F(x) = x^2 - 2mx + n$

$V(3, 2)$

$2 = 3^2 - 2m(2) + n$

$2 = 9 - 4m + n$

$-7 = -6m + n$

From axis of symmetry $x = \dfrac{-b}{2a}$

$x = h = \dfrac{-(-2m)}{2(1)} = \dfrac{2m}{2}$

since h = 3 then

$\dfrac{2m}{2} = 3$, then

m = 3, from -7 = -6m + n

$-7 = -6(3) + n$

$11 = n$

$m + n = 11 + 3 = 14$

Correct Answer is D

8. Solution:

Since f (3) = 48

$f(3) = m(3)^2 + 18$

$48 = 9m + 18$

$m = \dfrac{10}{3}$ plug in to function:

$f(x) = \dfrac{10}{3}x^2 + 18$

$f(6) = \dfrac{10}{3}(6)^2 + 18$

$\qquad = 138$

Correct Answer is C

9. Solution:

The standard vertex form, $y = a(x - h)^2 + k$,

In the given equation, $y = -2x^2 + 4x - 3$,

the coefficient 'a' is -2, and to express it in vertex form,

we need to complete the square. Let's proceed:

$y = -2x^2 + 4x - 3$

$= -2(x^2 - 2x + 1) + 2 - 3$

$= -2(x - 1)^2 - 1$,

Vertex form: $y = -2(x - 1)^2 - 1$.

Correct Answer is B

10. Solution:

To determine which equation could represent the given graph, let's analyze the characteristics of the graph:

The x intercepts of graph are 0, 2, -4

This option represents a cubic function with three distinct linear factors.

Consider the option A: $y = x(x + 4)(x - 2)$:

It matches the form of the equation for the given graph.

Correct Answer is A

11. Solution:

The vertex of a parabola in the form $f(x) = ax^2 + bx + c$

is given by the coordinates $\left(-\dfrac{b}{2a}, f\left(-\dfrac{b}{2a}\right)\right)$.

In this case, a = -2 and b = 0.

$f(x) = -2x^2 + 4$

$f(0) = 4$

Therefore, the vertex is

$\left(-\dfrac{0}{2}(-2), f(0)\right) = (0, 4)$.

Correct Answer is A

12. Solution:

By substituting the given points into the equations, we can determine which equation represents a nonlinear function.

Option B) $y = x^2 + 1$ satisfies the given points and represents a quadratic function, which is nonlinear.

Correct Answer is B

Digital SAT Sample Question:

In the equation $x = 2y + 4z$, if we want to isolate y, which of the following expressions correctly represents y in terms of x and z?

A) $y = \dfrac{x - 4z}{2}$

B) $y = \dfrac{x + 4z}{2}$

C) $y = \dfrac{x - 4z}{4}$

D) $= \dfrac{x + 4z}{4}$

Solution:

To isolate y in the equation $x = 2y + 4z$, we need to rearrange the equation to have y alone on one side. Start with the given equation: $x = 2y + 4z$

To isolate y, we can begin by subtracting 4z from both sides of the equation: $x - 4z = 2y$

Now, divide both sides of the equation by 2 to isolate y: $\dfrac{x - 4z}{2} = y$

Correct answer is A.

Digital SAT Sample Question:

In the equation $V = u + at$, where V represents velocity, u represents initial velocity, a represents acceleration, and t represents time, which of the following expressions correctly represents time (t) in terms of V, u, and a?

A) $t = \dfrac{V - u}{a}$

B) $t = \dfrac{V + u}{a}$

C) $t = \dfrac{V - u}{u}$

D) $t = \dfrac{V + u}{u}$

Solution:

To isolate time (t) in the equation $V = u + at$, we need to rearrange the equation to have t alone on one side. Start with the given equation:
$V = u + at$
Subtract u from both sides of the equation:
$V - u = at$
Now, divide both sides of the equation by a to isolate t: $t = \dfrac{V - u}{a}$

Correct Answer is A.

Isolating Quantities Test

In the equation $S = ut + \frac{1}{2}at^2$ where S represents displacement, u represents initial velocity, a represents acceleration, and t represents time, which of the following expressions correctly represents time (t) in terms of S, u, and a?

A) $t = \dfrac{2S + u}{a}$

B) $t = \sqrt{\left(\dfrac{2(S - ut)}{a}\right)}$

C) $t = \sqrt{\left(\dfrac{2(S + ut)}{a}\right)}$

D) $t = \left(\dfrac{S + u}{a}\right)$

The formula $A = P(1 + r)^t$ represents the compound interest accrued on a principal amount P, with an annual interest rate of r, compounded annually for t years. Which of the following expresses the principal amount P in terms of the other variables?

A) $P = \dfrac{A}{(1 - r)^t}$

B) $P = \dfrac{A}{(1 + r)^t}$

C) $P = \dfrac{A}{(1 + r)^{\frac{1}{t}}}$

D) $P = \dfrac{A}{(1 - r)^{\frac{1}{t}}}$

$$2x + 3y = 9$$

which of the following equations represents y in terms of x?

A) $y = \dfrac{2 - 9x}{3}$

B) $y = \dfrac{9 + 2x}{3}$

C) $y = \dfrac{9 - 2x}{3}$

D) $y = \dfrac{2 + 9x}{3}$

The formula $A = \dfrac{B + C}{D}$ represents a calculation where A is determined by the sum of B and C divided by D. Which of the following expresses the value of B in terms of A, C, and D

A) B = AD - C

B) B = AC + D

C) B = AD + C

D) B = A - CD

Easy

5

The formula $C = \dfrac{A + 2B}{3}$ is used to calculate the average of three numbers, where A, B, and C represent the numbers.

Which of the following correctly expresses the value of B in terms of A, C, and the formula?

A) $B = 3C - A$

B) $B = \dfrac{3C - A}{2}$

C) $B = 2C - A$

D) $B = \dfrac{2C - A}{3}$

Medium

6

The area of a circle is given by the formula $A = \pi r^2$, where A is the area and r is the radius of the circle.

Which of the following gives the radius of the circle in terms of its area?

A) $r = \sqrt{\dfrac{A}{\pi}}$

B) $r = \dfrac{A}{\pi}$

C) $r = \sqrt{A \cdot \pi}$

D) $r = A \cdot \pi$

Medium

7

The formula for the area of a trapezoid is given by

$A = \left(\dfrac{b_1 + b_2}{2} \right)h$, where A is the area, b_1 and b_2 are the lengths of the parallel bases, and h is the height of the trapezoid.

Which of the following gives the height of the trapezoid in terms of its area and the lengths of the bases? $h = \dfrac{2A}{b_1 + b_2}$

A) $h = \dfrac{2A}{b_1 + b_2}$

B) $h = \dfrac{A}{2(b_1 + b_2)}$

C) $h = 2A(b_1 + b_2)$

D) $h = 2A(b_1 - b_2)$

Medium

8

If $2(a + b) = c$, solve for b in terms of a and c.

A) $b = \dfrac{c - 2a}{2}$

B) $b = \dfrac{2a - c}{2}$

C) $b = \dfrac{c - a}{2}$

D) $b = \dfrac{a - c}{2}$

$\frac{1}{a} = \frac{1}{b} + \frac{1}{c}$ Find b in terms of a and c.

A) $b = \dfrac{ac}{c-a}$

B) $b = \dfrac{ac}{a-c}$

C) $b = ac$

D) $b = \dfrac{1}{c-a}$

In the equation $A = x + at$, where A represents velocity, x represents initial velocity, a represents acceleration, and t represents time, which of the following expressions correctly represents time (t) in terms of A, x, and a?

A) $t = \dfrac{A-x}{a}$

B) $t = \dfrac{A+x}{a}$

C) $t = \dfrac{A-x}{x}$

D) $t = \dfrac{A+x}{x}$

Two-points slope formula is $m = \dfrac{y_2 - y_1}{x_2 - x_1}$.

What is x_2 in terms of the variables x_1, y_2, y_1 and m?

A) $x_2 = \dfrac{y_2 - y_1}{mx_1}$

B) $x_2 = \dfrac{y_2 - y_1 + mx_1}{m}$

C) $x_2 = y_2 - y_1 + mx_1$

D) $x_2 = y_2 + y_1 + mx_1$

Solve for y: $2(y - 3) = 4x$

A) $y = 2x + 3$

B) $y = 4x - 6$

C) $y = 2x - 3$

D) $y = 4x + 6$

| 1. | B | 2. | C | 3. | B | 4. | A | 5. | B | 6. | A | 7. | A | 8. | A | 9. | A | 10. | B | 11. | A | 12. | A |

1. Solution:

To find the expression that correctly represents time (t) in terms of S, u, and a, we need to rearrange the given equation.

Starting with the equation $S = ut + \frac{1}{2}at^2$ we can isolate the term with t^2 by subtracting ut from both sides:

$$S - ut = \frac{1}{2}at^2$$

To isolate t^2, we can divide both by $\frac{1}{2}a$:

$$\frac{2(S - ut)}{a} = t^2$$

$$\sqrt{\left(\frac{2(S - ut)}{a}\right)} = t$$

Correct Answer is B

2. Solution:

Solve for y by isolating it on one side of the equation.

Step 1: Start with the equation 2x + 3y = 9.

Step 2: Subtract 2x from both sides of the equation to move the term containing x to the other side:

3y = 9 - 2x.

Step 3: Divide both sides of the equation by 3 to solve for y:

$$y = \frac{9 - 2x}{3}$$

Correct Answer is C

3. Solution:

We'll rearrange the formula $A = P(1 + r)^t$ and solve for P.

Start with the given equation $A = P(1 + r)^t$

Divide both sides of the equation by $(1 + r)^t$

to eliminate the exponent: $\frac{A}{(1 + r)^t} = P$

Correct answer is B

4. Solution:

To express the value of B in terms of A, C, and D, we'll rearrange the formula $A = \frac{B + C}{D}$ and solve for B. Multiply both sides of the equation by D

to eliminate the denominator: AD = B + C

Now, let's isolate B by moving the constant term

to the other side: B = AD - C

So, the correct answer is A.

Correct answer is A

5. Solution:

To express the value of B in terms of A, C, and the formula, we'll rearrange the formula $C = \dfrac{A + 2B}{3}$ and solve for B.

Start with the given equation: $C = \dfrac{A + 2B}{3}$

Multiply both sides of the equation by 3 to eliminate the denominator: $3C = A + 2B$

Now, let's isolate B by moving the terms containing B to one side and the constant term to the other side: $2B = 3C - A$

Divide both sides by 2 to solve for B:

$$B = \dfrac{3C - A}{2}$$

Correct answer is B

6. Solution:

To express the radius of the circle in terms of its area, we'll rearrange the formula $A = \pi r^2$ and solve for r.

Start with the given equation: $A = \pi r^2$,

Divide both sides of the equation by π to eliminate

π: $\dfrac{A}{\pi} = r^2$,

To isolate r, we'll take the square root of both sides:

$$r = \sqrt{\dfrac{A}{\pi}}$$

Correct answer is A

7. Solution:

We'll rearrange the formula $A = \left(\dfrac{b_1 + b_2}{2}\right)h$ and solve for h.

Start with the given equation: $A = \left(\dfrac{b_1 + b_2}{2}\right)h$

Multiply both sides of the equation by $\dfrac{2}{b_1 + b_2}$ to isolate h:

$$h = \dfrac{2A}{b_1 + b_2}$$

Correct answer is A

8. Solution:

Starting with the equation: $2(a + b) = c$

Distribute the 2 on the left side: $2a + 2b = c$

Subtract 2a from both sides: $2b = c - 2a$

Divide both sides by 2: $b = \dfrac{c - 2a}{2}$

Correct answer is A

9. Solution:

$$\frac{1}{a} = \frac{1}{b} + \frac{1}{c}$$

$$\frac{1}{a} = \frac{c+b}{bc} \ (\text{cross multiply})$$

$$ac + ab = bc$$

$$ac = bc - ab$$

$$ac = b(c - a)$$

$$\frac{ac}{c-a} = b$$

Correct answer is A

10. Solution:

$$m = \frac{y_2 - y_1}{x_2 - x_1}$$

$$x_2 m - x_1 m = y_2 - y_1$$

$$x_2 = \frac{y_2 - y_1 + m x_1}{m}$$

Correct answer is B

11. Solution:

To isolate time (t) in the equation A = x + at, we need to rearrange the equation to have t alone on one side.

Start with the given equation: A = x + at

Subtract u from both sides of the equation: A - x = at

Now, divide both sides of the equation by a to isolate

$$t : t = \frac{A - x}{a}$$

Correct Answer is A

12. Solution:

To solve for y in the equation 2(y - 3) = 4x, follow these steps:

- Distribute the 2 on the left side of the equation: 2y - 6 = 4x.

- Add 6 to both sides to isolate the variable term: 2y = 4x + 6.

- Divide both sides by 2 to solve for $y : y = \frac{4x + 6}{2}$.

- Simplify the right side of the equation:

  y = 2x + 3.

The solution for y is y = 2x + 3.

Correct Answer is A

Complex Numbers

Imaginary Number:

An imaginary number is a number that can be expressed as a real number multiplied by the imaginary unit "i."

It is written in the form "bi," where "b" is a real number and "i" represents the square root of -1.

Imaginary Unit:

The imaginary unit "i" is defined as $\sqrt{-1}$, meaning that "i" squared equals -1: ($i^2 = -1$).

Complex Numbers:

Complex numbers are numbers that combine real numbers and imaginary numbers.

They are written in the form "a + bi," where "a" and "b" are real numbers.

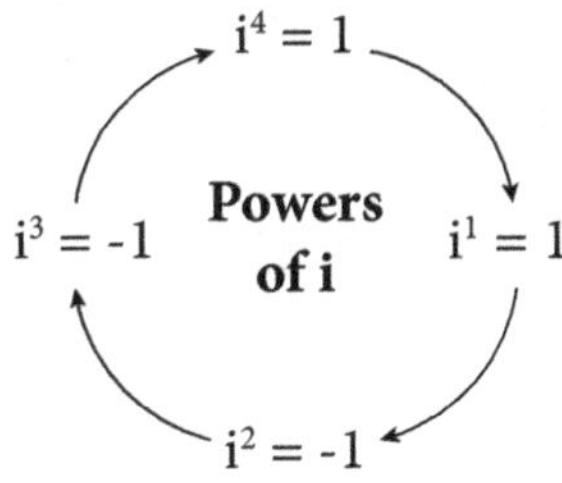

Complex Numbers

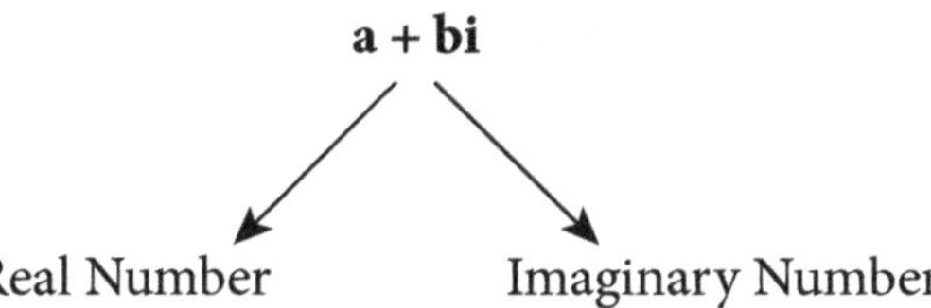

Complex number in standard form: a + bi

Example: (3 + 2i) + (4 + 3i) = 3 + 2i + 4 + 3i = 7 + 5i

Example: (6 + 4i) - (5 + 3i) = 6 + 4i - 5 - 3i = 1 + i

Example:

Simplify (2 + 3i)(-4 + 5i)

A) 23 - 2i

B) -2i – 23

C) -23 - 2i

D) -23 + 2i

Solution:

To multiply complex numbers, we use the distributive property and combine like terms.

Step 1: Multiply the real parts: (2 · -4) = -8

Step 2: Multiply the imaginary parts: (2 ·5i) = 10i

Step 3: Multiply the real part of the first number by the imaginary part of the second number:

(3i · -4) = -12i

Step 4: Multiply the imaginary part of the first number by the imaginary part of the second number:

(3i · 5i) = 15i².

Step 5: Combine the results: $-8 + 10i - 12i + 15i^2$

Simplify the terms: -8 - 2i + 15i²

Since i² is equal to -1: -8 - 2i + 15(-1)

Further simplification: -8 - 2i - 15

Combining like terms: -23 - 2i

Correct answer is C

Example:

Simplify $\dfrac{2 + 3i}{1 - i}$?

A) $\dfrac{1 + 5i}{2}$

B) $\dfrac{5i}{2}$

C) $\dfrac{2 + i}{5}$

D) $\dfrac{i}{5}$

Solution:

Step 1: Find the conjugate of the denominator:

The conjugate of $(1 - i)$ is $(1 + i)$.

Step 2: Multiply both the numerator and denominator by the conjugate of the denominator:

$$\left(\frac{2 + 3i}{1 - i} \right)\left(\frac{1 + i}{1 + i} \right)$$

Expanding the numerator and denominator:

$$\frac{3 + 2i + 3i + 3i^2}{1^2 - i^2}$$

Simplifying the terms:

$$\frac{3 + 2i + 3i - 3}{1 + 1}$$

Combining like terms:

$$\frac{5i}{2}$$

Correct answer is B

Medium

1

Simplify $(2 + 3i)(-1 + 5i)$

A) $17 + 7i$

B) $-17 + 7i$

C) $17 - 7i$

D) $7 - 17i$

Easy

3

Which of the following represents the difference of the complex numbers $(6 + 4i)$ and $(-3 - 2i)$?

A) $9 + 6i$

B) $9 - 6i$

C) $3 + 6i$

D) $3 - 6i$

Easy

2

Which of the following represents the sum of the complex numbers $(4 + 3i)$ and $(-2 - i)$?

A) $2 + 4i$

B) $2 - 4i$

C) $2 + 2i$

D) $2 - 2$

Medium

4

Which of the following represents the product of the complex numbers $(2 + 3i)$ and $(-1 + 4i)$?

A) $-11 + 5i$

B) $-5 + 14i$

C) $-14 + 5i$

D) $14 - 5i$

Complex Numbers Test

Hard
5

Simplify the expression $\dfrac{7+9i}{5-2i}$.

A) $\dfrac{17+59i}{29}$

B) $\dfrac{17-59i}{29}$

C) $\dfrac{17+59i}{13}$

D) $\dfrac{17-59i}{13}$

Hard
7

Which of the following is equal to $\dfrac{4}{1+i\sqrt{3}}$?

A) $1-i\sqrt{3}$

B) $1+i\sqrt{3}$

C) 1

D) $3i$

Medium
6

Simplify $\sqrt{-5}+\sqrt{-20}+\sqrt{-125}$?

A) $-8i\sqrt{5}$

B) $8i\sqrt{5}$

C) $8i$

D) $-8i$

Medium
8

Which of the following is a solution to the equation $x^2 = 6x - 11$?

A) $3 \pm i\sqrt{2}$

B) $-3 \pm i\sqrt{2}$

C) $2 \pm i\sqrt{3}$

D) $-2 \pm i\sqrt{3}$

Complex Numbers Test

Evaluate $7i^{20} + 10i^2 + 15i^{12}$?

A) 4

B) 6

C) 12i

D) 12

Simplify the expression $(2 + i\sqrt{3})(2 - i\sqrt{3})$?

A) 3i

B) 5i

C) 7

D) 7i

If $\dfrac{1 + 4i}{2 - 3i} = a + bi$, what is the value of $a + b$?

A) $\dfrac{1}{13}$

B) $\dfrac{-1}{13}$

C) $\dfrac{3}{13}$

D) $\dfrac{4}{13}$

What is the product of $(2 + 3i)(4 - 2i)$?

A) 8 - 14i

B) 2 + 6i

C) 14 + 8i

D) 10 + 4i

| 1. | B | 2. | C | 3. | A | 4. | C | 5. | A | 6. | B | 7. | A | 8. | A | 9. | D | 10. | A | 11. | C | 12. | C |

1. Solution:

To multiply complex numbers, we use the distributive property and combine like terms.

Step 1: Multiply the real parts: $(2 \cdot -1) = -2$

Step 2: Multiply the imaginary parts: $(2 \cdot 5i) = 10i$

Step 3: Multiply the real part of the first number by the imaginary part of the second number: $(3i \cdot -1) = -3i$

Step 4: Multiply the imaginary part of the first number by the imaginary part of the second number: $(3i \cdot 5i) = 15i^2$.

Step 5: Combine the results: $-2 + 10i - 3i + 15i^2$

Simplify the terms: $-2 + 7i + 15i^2$

Since i^2 is equal to -1: $-2 + 7i + 15(-1)$

Further simplification: $-2 + 7i - 15$

Combining like terms: $-17 + 7i$

Correct answer is B

2. Solution:

To solve this question, we can simply add the real parts and the imaginary parts separately.

Adding the real parts: $4 + (-2) = 2$

Adding the imaginary parts: $3i + (-1i) = 2i$

Combining the results, we have: $2 + 2i$

Correct answer is C

3. Solution:

To solve this question, we can simply subtract the real parts and the imaginary parts separately.

Subtracting the real parts: $6 - (-3) = 9$

Subtracting the imaginary parts: $4i - (-2i) = 6i$

Combining the results, we have: $9 + 6i$

Correct answer is A

4. Solution:

To solve this question, we can use the distributive property and combine like terms.

Multiplying the complex numbers: $(2 + 3i) \cdot (-1 + 4i)$

Expanding the expression: $= 2(-1) + 2(4i) + 3i(-1) + 3i(4i)$

Simplifying each term: $= -2 + 8i - 3i + 12i^2$

Since i^2 is defined as -1: $= -2 + 8i - 3i + 12(-1)$

Further simplifying: $= -2 + 8i - 3i - 12$

Combine like terms: $= (-2 - 12) + (8i - 3i) = -14 + 5i$

Correct answer is C

Complex Numbers Test Solution

5. Solution:

To simplify the division of complex numbers, multiplying both the numerator and denominator by the conjugate of the denominator.

The conjugate of 5 - 2i is 5 + 2i.

$$\frac{7+9i}{5-2i}\cdot\frac{5+2i}{5+2i}$$

Expanding the numerator and denominator:

$$\frac{(7+9i)(5+2i)}{(5-2i)(5+2i)}$$

Simplifying each term:

$$\frac{(7\cdot5)+(7\cdot2i)+(9i\cdot5)+(9i\cdot2i)}{(5\cdot5)+(5\cdot2i)+(-2i\cdot5)+(-2i\cdot2i)}$$

$$=\frac{35+14i+45i+18i^2}{25+10i-10i-4i^2}$$

Since i^2 is defined as -1:

$$=\frac{35+14i+45i+18(-1)}{25+10i-10i-4(-1)}$$

$$=\frac{35+14i+45i-18}{25+10i-10i+4}$$

$$=\frac{17+59i}{29}$$

Correct answer is A

6. Solution:

$$\sqrt{-5}+\sqrt{-20}+\sqrt{-125}$$

$$=i\sqrt{5}+2i\sqrt{5}+5i\sqrt{5}$$

$$=8i\sqrt{5}$$

Correct answer is B

7. Solution:

$$\frac{4}{1+i\sqrt{3}}=\frac{4}{1+i\sqrt{3}}\left(\frac{1-i\sqrt{3}}{1-i\sqrt{3}}\right)$$

$$=\frac{4-4i\sqrt{3}}{1-i^2\cdot(3)}=\frac{4-4i\sqrt{3}}{1+3}$$

$$=\frac{4-4i\sqrt{3}}{4}=1-i\sqrt{3}$$

Correct Answer is A

8. Solution:

$$x^2=6x-11$$

$$x^2-6x=-11$$

$$(x-3)^2-9=-11$$

$$(x-3)^2=-2 \qquad i^2=-1$$

$$\sqrt{(x-3)^2}=\sqrt{2i^2}$$

$$x-3=\mp i\sqrt{2}$$

$$x=3\mp i\sqrt{2}$$

Correct Answer is A

9. Solution:

$$7i^{20}+10i^2+15i^{12}$$

$$=7(i^2)^{10}+10i^2+15(i^2)^6$$

$$=7(-1)^{10}+10(-1)+15(-1)^6$$

$$=7-10+15$$

$$=12$$

Correct Answer is D

10 Solution:

multiplying both the numerator and denominator by the conjugate of the denominator.

The conjugate of 2 - 3i is 2 + 3i.

So, we have:

$$\frac{1+4i}{2-3i}\cdot\frac{2+3i}{2+3i}$$

Expanding the numerator and denominator:

$$\frac{(1+4i)(2+3i)}{(2-3i)(2+3i)}$$

Simplifying each term:

$$\frac{(1\cdot2)+(1\cdot3i)+(4i\cdot2)+(4i\cdot3i)}{(2\cdot2)+(2\cdot3i)+(-3i\cdot2)+(-3i\cdot3i)}$$

$$=\frac{2+3i+8i+12i^2}{4+6i-6i-9i^2}$$

Since i^2 is defined as -1:

$$=\frac{2+3i+8i-12}{4+6i-6i+9}$$

$$=\frac{-10+11i}{13}$$

Comparing this with a + bi, we can see that

$$a=\frac{-10}{13}$$

$$b=\frac{11}{13}$$

Therefore, $a+b=\dfrac{-10}{13}+\dfrac{11}{13}=\dfrac{1}{13}$

Correct Answer is A

11. Solution:

To simplify the expression $(2+i\sqrt{3})(2-i\sqrt{3})$

Use the difference of squares formula:

$(a+b)(a-b)=a^2-b^2$

Let's apply this formula to simplify the given expression:

$$(2+i\sqrt{3})(2-i\sqrt{3})=2^2-(i\sqrt{3})^2$$

Simplifying further:

$4-(-3)=7$

Correct answer is C

12. Solution:

To multiply complex numbers, use the distributive property.

$(2+3i)(4-2i)$

$=8-4i+12i-6i^2$

$=8+8i-6(-1)$

$=8+8i+6$

$=14+8i.$

Correct answer is C

Problem Solving

Problem solving tips and strategies:

- **Understand the problem:** Read the problem carefully and make sure you understand what is being asked. Identify the key information and any constraints or conditions given

- **Visualize the problem:** Create a mental or visual representation of the problem. Draw diagrams, charts, or graphs if necessary.

  Break it down: Break the problem into smaller, manageable parts.

  Identify the main steps or sub-problems that need to be solved.

- **Use logical reasoning:** Apply logical reasoning to analyze the problem and consider possible solutions.

- **Use prior knowledge and experience:** Draw upon your existing knowledge and past experiences to solve the problem

- **Try different approaches:** If one approach doesn't work, don't be afraid to try a different one. Be flexible and open to alternative solutions. Sometimes, thinking outside the box can lead to creative solution

Important Math Problem Solving formulas

Distance = rate · time

$D = r \cdot t$

Distance = $\dfrac{\text{mile}}{\text{miles}}$

Rate: mile per hour (mph)

Time: $\dfrac{\text{hour}}{\text{hours}}$

Work Problem Formula;

$$\frac{1}{x} + \frac{1}{y} = \frac{1}{t}$$

x = is the amount of time taken by first person to complete a job.

y = is the amount of time taken by second person to complete a job.

t = is the time taken if both do the together.

Increase/Decrease Problem Solving Formula:

Percent of change = $\dfrac{\text{Old Value} - \text{New Value}}{\text{Old Value}} \cdot 100$

If the result is positive, it is an increase.

If the result is negative, it is a decrease.

Problem Solving Test

Medium

1

Vera can clean a house in 12 hours. Working together, Vera and Nora take only 4 hours to clean a house.

How long would it take Nora to clean a house alone?

A) 4

B) 6

C) 8

D) 10

Easy

3

Jolie is 6 years younger than twice her sister's age.

If Jolie is 24 years old, then how old is Jolie's sister?

A) 7

B) 9

C) 15

D) 24

Hard

2

A new copy machine can print 120 pages per hour, and an older copy machine can print 80 pages per hour.

How many minutes will two copy machines working together, take to copy a total of 360 pages?

A) 72

B) 86

C) 96

D) 108

Medium

4

Nora is 10 years older than Vera. In 3 years, Nora will be twice as old as Vera.

Find Vera's age in 5 years' time.

A) 7

B) 9

C) 10

D) 12

Problem Solving Test

How many liters of 80% pure water must be added to 40 liters of 30% pure water to produce 60% pure water?

A) 30

B) 45

C) 60

D) 90

A train and a bus leave the same place and traveled in opposite directions. If the train is traveling at 35 mph and the bus is traveling at 45 mph, in how many hours will they be 600 miles apart?

A) 3

B) 5

C) 7.5

D) 10

How many grams of a 20% acid solution should be mixed with 30 grams of a 40% acid solution to get a mix that is a 30% acid.

A) 30

B) 35

C) 40

D) 45

In science study class had 32 students yesterday. Teacher miscounted the class of total and record it as 24 students. What is the percent error?

A) 5%

B) 15%

C) 25%

D) 35%

Problem Solving Test

Medium

9

A house in real estate market sold last year for $400,000.

The same property sold one year later for $560,000.

At what percent did the house price increase?

A) 25%

B) 30%

C) 35%

D) 40%

Medium

11

A restaurant bill comes to $50. If a 15% tip is added, what is the total amount to be paid, including the tip?

A) $52.50

B) $57.50

C) $60.00

D) $72.50

Hard

10

The radius of a cylinder is increased by 25% and its height is decreased by 20%.

What is the effect on the volume of a cylinder?

A) 25% increase

B) 25% decrease

C) 35% increase

D) 35% decrease

Easy

12

The sum of two consecutive even integers is 86.

What is the smallest integer?

A) 42

B) 44

C) 86

D) 88

Problem Solving Test Solution

1. Solution:

Vera can clean a house in x hours.

Nora cleans a house in y hours.

Nora and Vera together clean a house in t hours.

Job problem solving formula:

$$\frac{1}{x} + \frac{1}{y} = \frac{1}{t}$$

$$\frac{1}{y} = \frac{1}{4} - \frac{1}{12}$$

y = 6 hours.

Correct Answer is B

2. Solution:

$$\left(\frac{120}{60} + \frac{80}{60}\right)t = 360$$

$$\left(\frac{200}{60}\right)t = 360$$

$$\frac{10t}{3} = 360$$

$$\frac{t}{3} = 36, \ t = 108$$

Correct Answer is D

3. Solution:

Melisa age	Her sister
2x – 6	x

2x – 6 = 24,

2x = 30,

x = 15, her sister is 15 years old.

Correct Answer is C

4. Solution

	Current age	After 3 years
Vera	x	x+3
Nora	x + 10	x + 13

Since after 3 years,

Nora will be twice as old as Vera,

then x + 13 = 2(x + 3)

= x + 13 = 2x + 6

7 = x

After 5 years

Vera age will be x + 5 → 7 + 5 = 12 years old.

Correct Answer is D

5. Solution

	liters pure water	%water	total liters
80% water	x	.80	.80x
30% water	40	.30	.30(40) = 12
60% water	x + 40	.60	.60(x + 40)

From the last column, you get the equation:

0.80x + 12 = 0.6(x + 40)

Solve for x.

0.80x + 12 = 0.6x + 24

0.80x – 0.6x = 24 – 12

0.2x = 12

2x = 120

x = 60 liters.

Correct Answer is C

6. Solution

Let say x grams of %20 acid solution need to mix with 30 grams of acid solution then:

$20\% \cdot x + 40\% \cdot 30 = 30\% (x + 30)$

$20x + 1200 = 30x + 900$

$1200 - 900 = 30x - 20x$

$300 = 10x$

$30 = x$

Correct Answer is A

7. Solution:

$D = r \cdot t$

$D_{train} = 35 \text{ mph} \cdot t = 35t$

$D_{bus} = 45 \text{ mph} \cdot t = 45t$

Since the total distance is 600miles

$D_{train} + D_{bus} = 600 \text{ miles}$

$35t + 45t = 600$ miles, then $80t = 600$, $t = 7.5$ hours.

Correct Answer is C

8. Solution:

$$\text{Error percent} = \frac{\text{Old Value} - \text{New Value}}{\text{Old Value}}$$

$$\text{Error percent} = \frac{32 - 24}{32} = \frac{8}{32} = \frac{1}{4} = 25\% \text{ error percent.}$$

Correct Answer is C

9. Solution:

$560,000 - 400,000 = 160,000$

$$\text{Percent of change} = \frac{160,000}{400,000}$$

$$= \frac{4}{10} = \frac{40}{100}$$

$$= 40\% \text{ increase.}$$

Correct Answer is D

10. Solution:

Suppose $r = 4 \quad h = 5$

$V = \pi r^2 \quad V = r \cdot 16 \cdot 5 = 80\pi$

$r \longrightarrow 25\%$ increase $r = 5$

$h \longrightarrow 20\%$ decrease $h = 4$

$V = \pi r^2 = 25 \cdot 4 \cdot \pi = 100\pi$

$$\frac{100\pi - 80\pi}{80\pi} = \frac{1}{4} = 25\% \text{ increase}$$

Correct Answer is A

11. Solution:

To calculate the tip, multiply the bill amount by the tip percentage: $\$50 \cdot 0.15 = \$7.50$.

Add the tip to the bill amount to find the total amount to be paid:

$\$50 + \$7.50 = \$57.50$.

Correct Answer is B

12. Solution:

Let's denote the first even integer as "x".

Since the integers are consecutive, the second even integer can be represented as "x + 2".

We can set up the equation as follows:

$x + (x + 2) = 86$

Combining like terms, we have:

$2x + 2 = 86$

Next, we subtract 2 from both sides of the equation:

$2x = 84$

To find the value of x, we divide both sides of the equation by 2:

$$x = \frac{84}{2}$$

Simplifying, we find:

$x = 42$

Therefore, the smallest even integer is 42.

Correct Answer is A

CHAPTER 4
Geometry and Trigonometry
(15%. 5–7 Questions)

➡ Angles & Triangles

➡ Right Triangles

➡ Similarity Theorem

➡ Area and Perimeter of Quadrilaterals

➡ Circle and Circle Equations

➡ Volume

➡ Trigonometry

Angles:

An angle is formed by two rays with a common endpoint called the vertex.

Types of angles:

- Acute angle: An angle that measures less than 90 degrees.

- Right angle: An angle that measures exactly 90 degrees.

- Obtuse angle: An angle that measures between 90 and 180 degrees.

- Straight angle: An angle that measures exactly 180 degrees.

- Reflex angle: An angle that measures between 180 and 360 degrees.

Angle pairs:

- **Complementary angles:** Two angles whose measures sum up to 90 degrees.

- **Supplementary angles:** Two angles whose measures sum up to 180 degrees

Triangles:

A triangle is a polygon with three sides and three angles.

Types of triangles:

- **Equilateral triangle:** A triangle with three equal sides and three equal angles measuring 60 degrees each.

- **Isosceles triangle:** A triangle with two equal sides and two equal angles.

- **Scalene triangle:** A triangle with no equal sides or angles.

- **Right triangle:** A triangle with one right angle (90 degrees).

- **Obtuse triangle:** A triangle with one obtuse angle (greater than 90 degrees).

- **Acute triangle:** A triangle with three acute angles (less than 90 degrees)

Triangle properties:

- **Triangle inequality theorem:** The sum of the lengths of any two sides of a triangle is greater than the length of the third side.

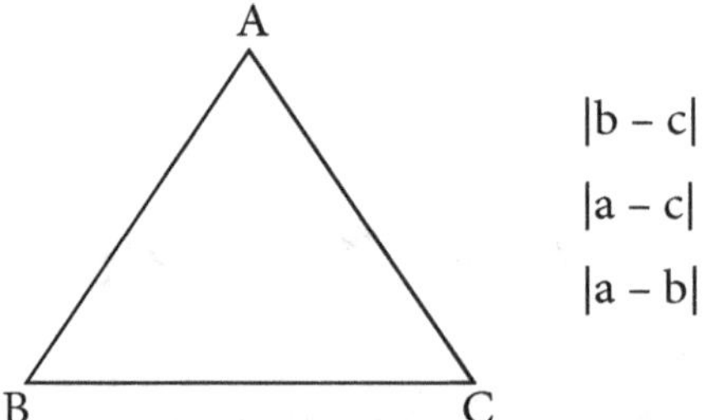

$$|b - c| < a < b + c$$
$$|a - c| < b < a + c$$
$$|a - b| < c < a + b$$

Angle sum property:

- The sum of the interior angles of a triangle is always 180 degrees.

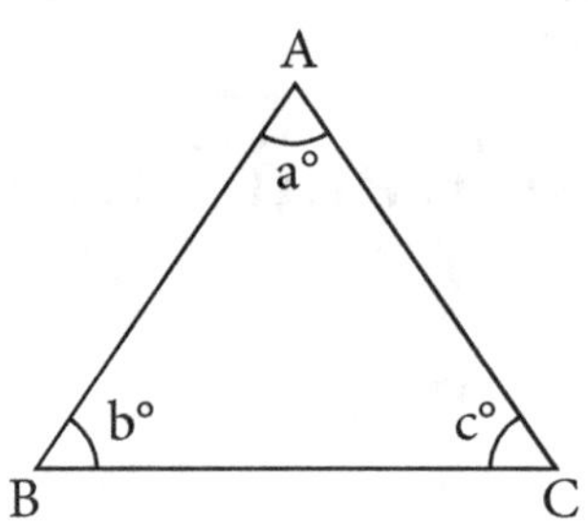

✓ Interior angles ; $\angle a°$, $\angle b°$, $\angle c°$,

✓ $m \angle a° + m \angle b° + m \angle c° = 180°$

Pythagorean theorem:

- In a right triangle, the square of the hypotenuse is equal to the sum of the squares of the other two sides.

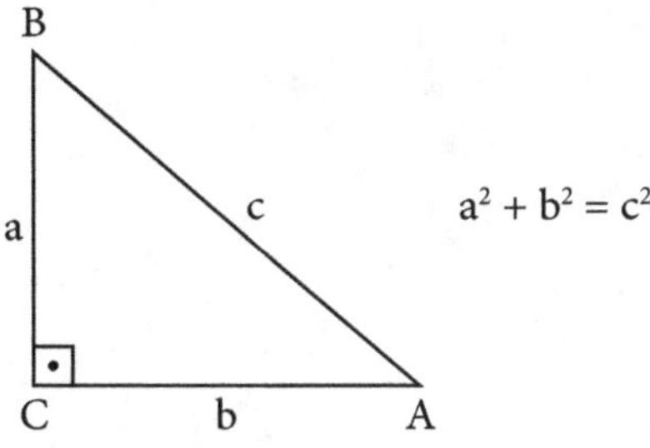

Digital SAT Sample Question:

In triangle ABC, angle A measures 50 degrees and angle B measures 70 degrees. What is the measure of angle C?

A) 30 degrees

B) 50 degrees

C) 60 degrees

D) 110 degrees

Solution:

In a triangle, the sum of the interior angles is always 180 degrees. To find the measure of angle C, we can subtract the measures of angles A and B from 180.

Given: Angle A = 50 degrees Angle B = 70 degrees

Calculating the measure of angle

C: 180 - (angle A + angle B)

= 180 - (50 + 70)

= 180 – 120

= 60 degrees

Correct answer is C

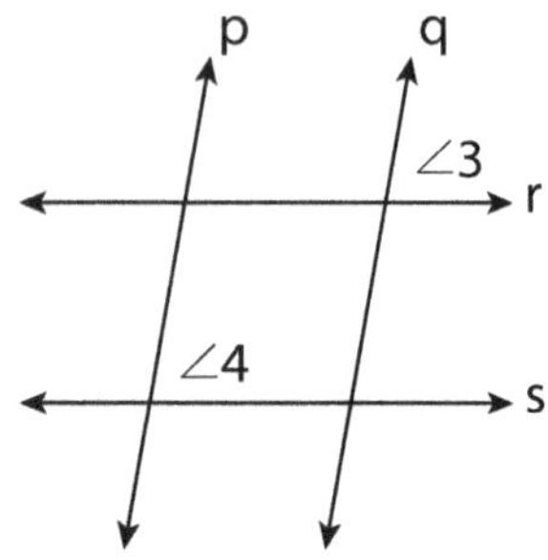

In the given figure, lines p and q are parallel, and lines r and s are parallel.

If the measure of ∠3 is 75°, what is the measure of ∠4?

A) 35°

B) 75°

C) 105°

D) 140°

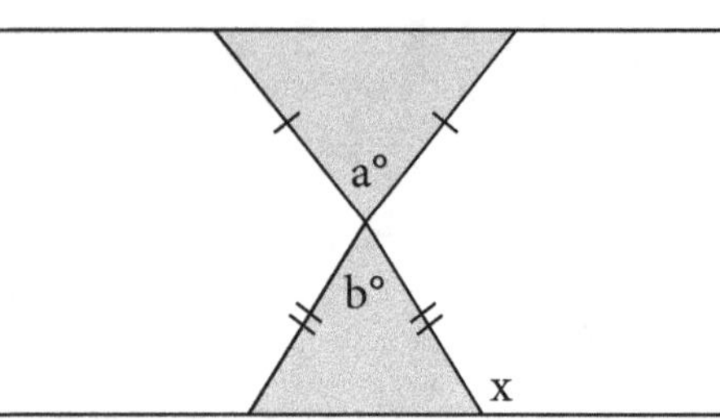

Two isosceles triangles are shown above. If $140 - b = 2a$ and $a = 55°$, what is the value of x?

A) 35°

B) 70°

C) 105°

D) 140°

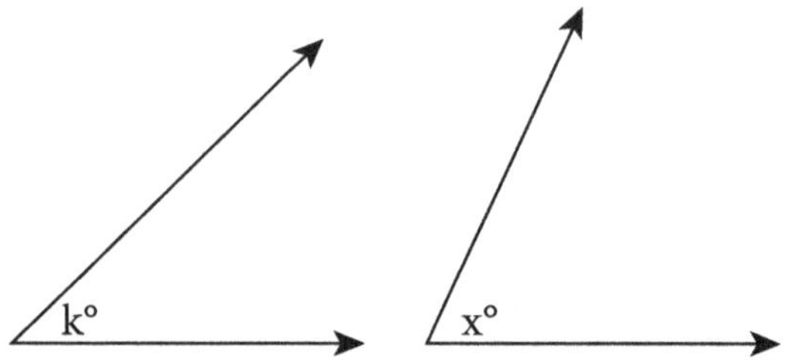

The angles shown above are acute.

If $x = 3k - 21$ and $x = 78°$, what is the value of k?

A) 23°

B) 33°

C) 43°

D) 53°

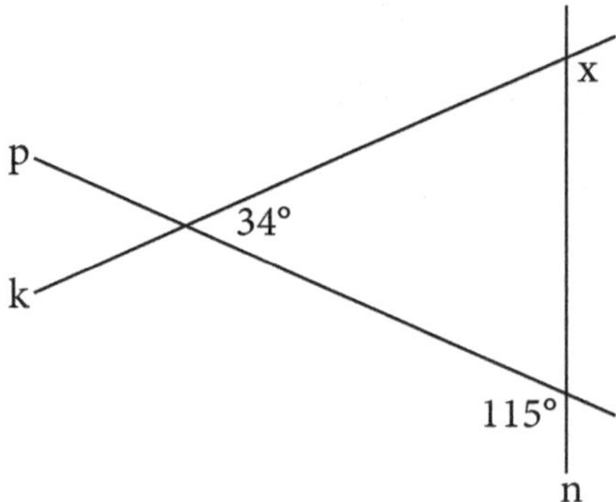

What is the value of x?

A) 99°

B) 105°

C) 106°

D) 108°

Medium

5

On AD above, AB = CD. What is the length of BC?

A) 18

B) 24

C) 36

D) 48

Medium

7

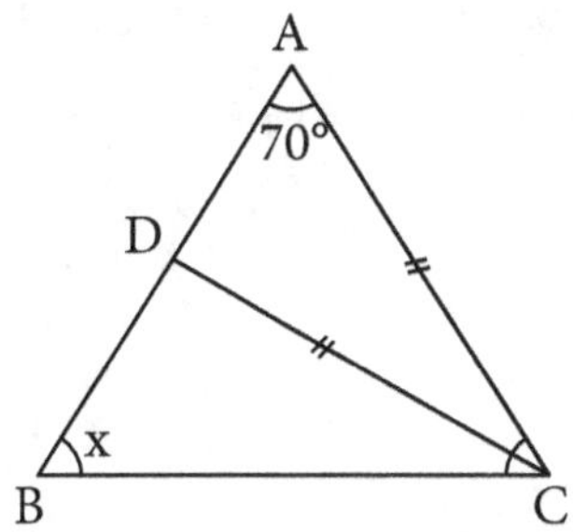

From above triangle $\angle(ACD) = \angle(DCB)$, and

$AC = CD$, If $\angle(BAC) = 70°$, find x =?

A) 30°

B) 40°

C) 50°

D 60°

Easy

6

Find the value of x in the diagram.

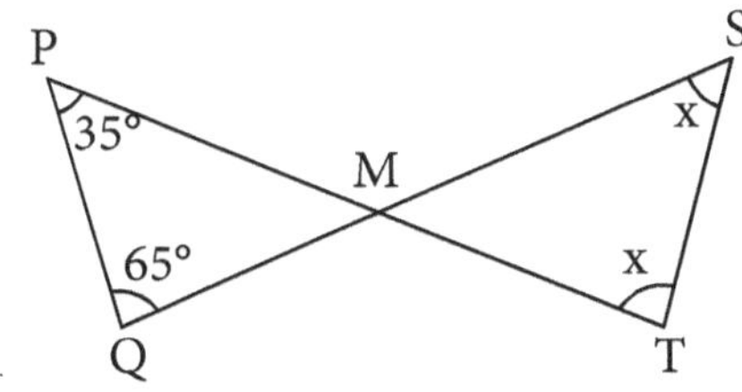

A) 25°

B) 35°

C) 45°

D) 50°

Hard

8

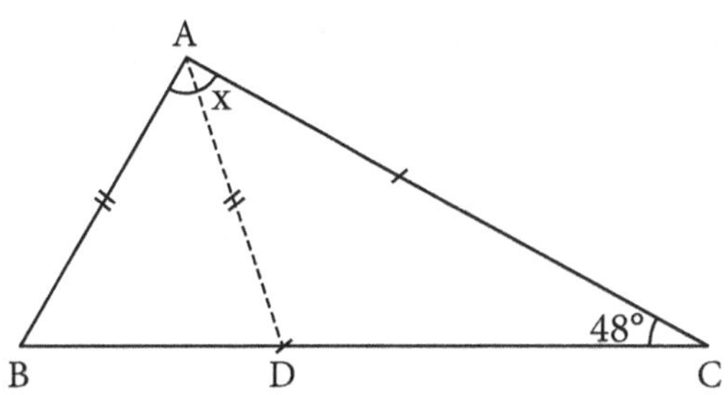

From the following triangle, if AB = AD and

BC = AC. What is the value of x?

A) 9°

B) 18°

C) 27°

D 36°

The angles of a triangle are in the ratio of 4:5:9.

What is the degree measure of the smallest angle?

A) 40°

B) 30°

C) 25°

D 20°

If C is between A and B and AB = 30,

AC = 3x + 5   CB = 2x + 10.

Find the value of x?

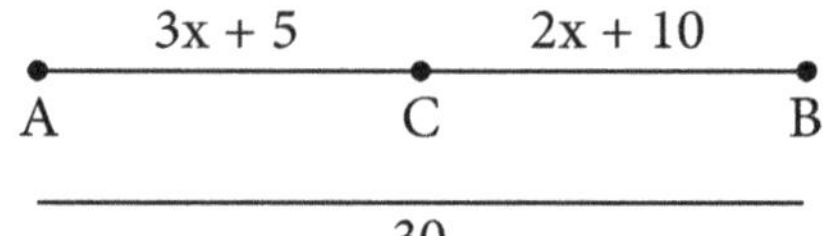

A) 1

B) 2

C) 3

D 4

EF is the angle bisector of m < DEG,

if m < DEF = 3x – 10°, and

m < FEG = 2x + 15°, then find x.

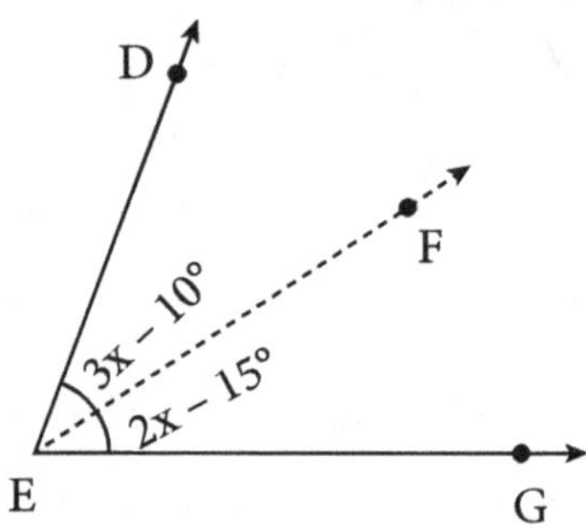

A) 10

B) 15

C) 20

D 25

Which of following is the sides of $\widehat{ABC}$ from shortest to longest.

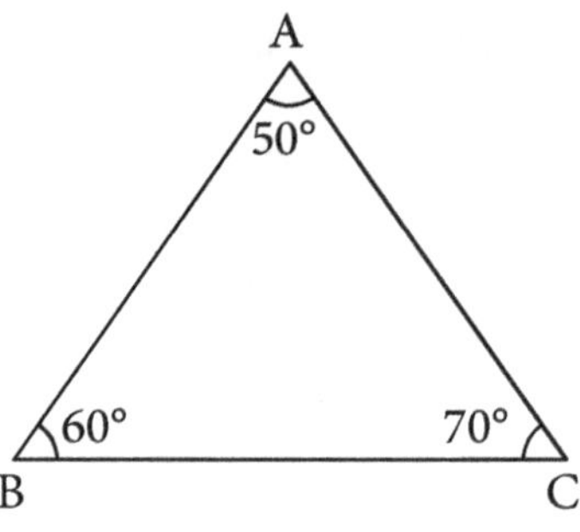

A) $\overline{AB} < \overline{BC} < \overline{AC}$

B) $\overline{BC} < \overline{AB} < \overline{AC}$

C) $\overline{AC} < \overline{BC} < \overline{AB}$

D $\overline{BC} < \overline{AC} < \overline{AB}$

| 1. | B | 2. | C | 3. | B | 4. | A | 5. | D | 6. | D | 7. | A | 8. | B | 9. | A | 10. | D | 11. | C | 12. | D |

1. Solution:

If lines p and q are parallel and lines r and s are parallel,

we can determine the measure of $\angle 4$ based on the given information that $\angle 3$ measures 75°.

$\angle 3$ and $\angle 4$ are corresponding angles since they are on the same side of the transversal line and parallel lines. Corresponding angles are congruent when the transversal intersects parallel lines.

Therefore, the measure of $\angle 4$ is also 75°

Correct answer is B

2. Solution:

The equation 140 - b = 2a and the information that a = 55, we can find the value of x.

Substituting a = 55 into the equation, we have:

140 - b = 2 x 55

Simplifying further:

140 - b = 110

To find the value of b, we subtract 110 from both sides:

-b = 110 - 140

b = 30

Now, to find the value of x, we can use the fact that the sum of the interior angles of a triangle is 180 degrees. Since the given triangles are isosceles, the base angles of each other is also 75° degrees. Since x is the vertex angle of the isosceles triangle, it is equal to the sum of the other two interior angles:

x = 30 + 75

x = 105

Correct Answer is C

3. Solution:

If x = 3k−21 and x = 78°, then

3k = 99°

k = 33°

Correct Answer is B

4. Solution:

Since x is the vertex angle of the triangle, it is equal to the sum of the other two interior angles:

x = 34° + 65°

x = 99°

Correct Answer is A

5. Solution:

Since AB = CD, then

3x + 4 = 5x - 12

12 + 4 = 5x - 3x

16 = 2x

8 = x

BC = 6x = 6(8) = 48,

Correct Answer is D

6. Solution:

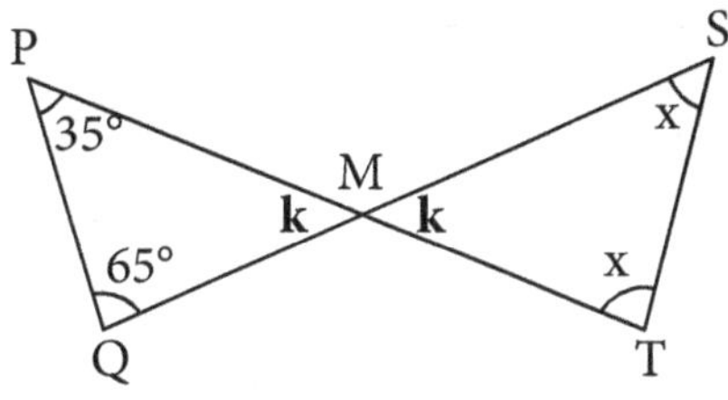

k + 65° + 35° = 180°

k + 100° = 180°

k = 80°

2x + k = 180°

2x + 80° = 180°

2x = 100°

x = 50°

Correct Answer is D

7. Solution:

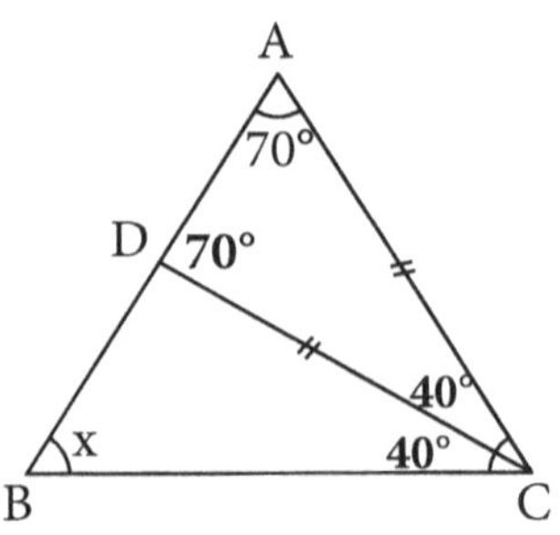

$x + 40° = 70°$

$x = 30°$

Correct Answer is A

8. Solution:

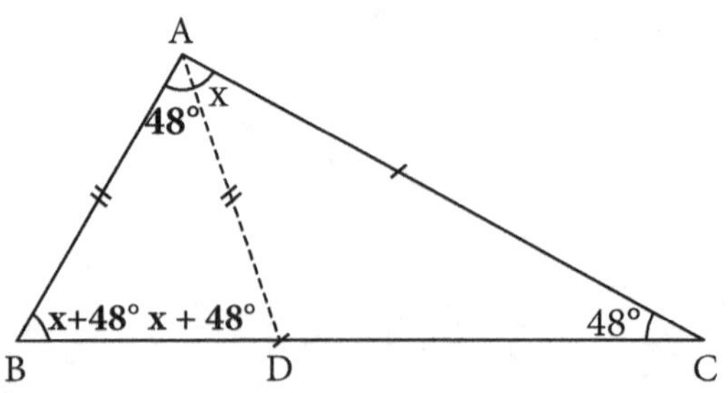

$2x + 144° = 180°$

$x = 18°$

Correct Answer is B

9. Solution:

$4k + 5k + 9k = 180°$

$18k = 180°$

$k = 10°$

smallest angle $= 4k = 40°$

Correct Answer is A

10. Solution:

$m \angle DEF = m \angle FEG,$

$3x - 10 = 2x + 15$

$\underline{+\quad -2x \qquad 2x}$

$x - 10 = 15, x = 25$

Correct Answer is D

11. Solution:

$3x + 5 + 2x + 10 = 30$

$5x + 15 = 30$

$\underline{+ \qquad -15 - 15}$

$5x = 15$

$x = 3$

Correct Answer is C

12. Solution:

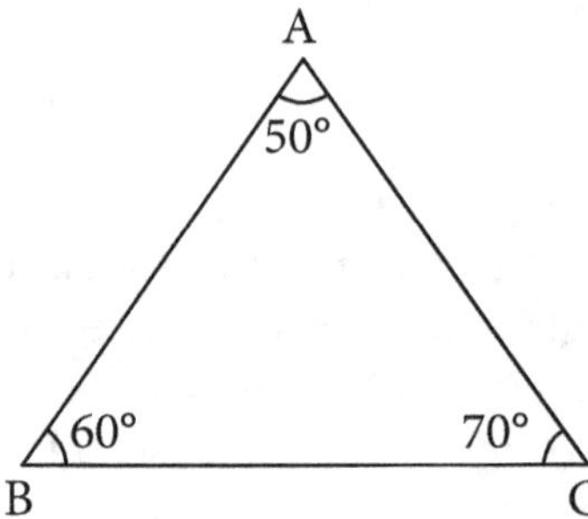

The shortest side is always opposite the smallest interior angle.

Sides of shortest to longest:

$\overline{AC} = 60°,$

$\overline{BC} = 50°,$ and

$\overline{AB} = 70°$

$\overline{BC} < \overline{AC} < \overline{AB}$

Correct Answer is D

30° – 60° – 90° Special right triangle:

In a triangel 30° – 60° – 90°, the hypotenuse is twice as long side as short side, and the longer side is $\sqrt{3}$ times as long as the shorter side.

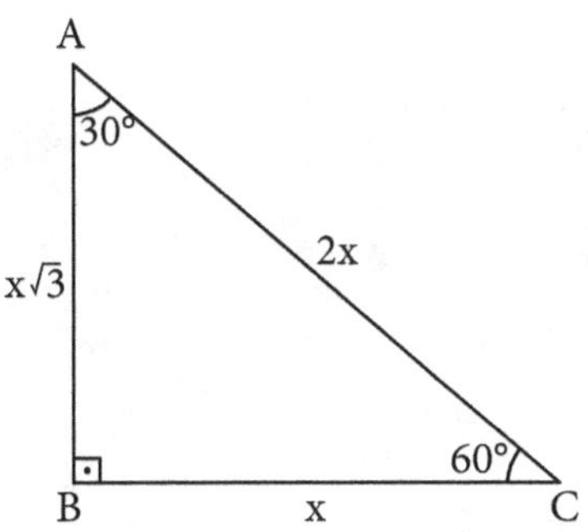

45° – 45° – 90° Special right triangle:

In a triangle 45°–45°–90°, the hypotenuse is $\sqrt{2}$ times the length of either of the other two sides, which are both equal.

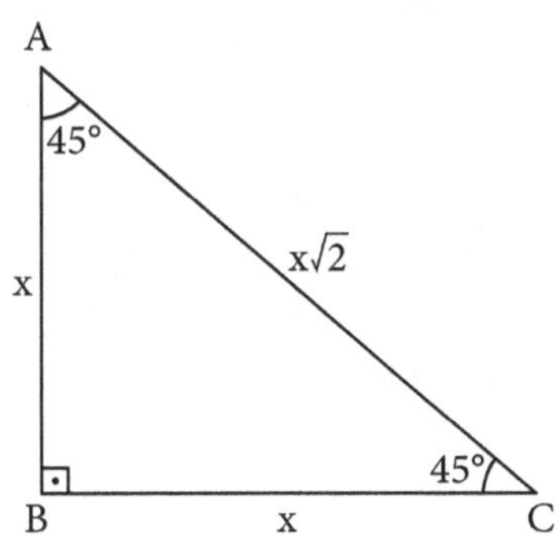

Digital SAT Sample Question:

Find the value of x.

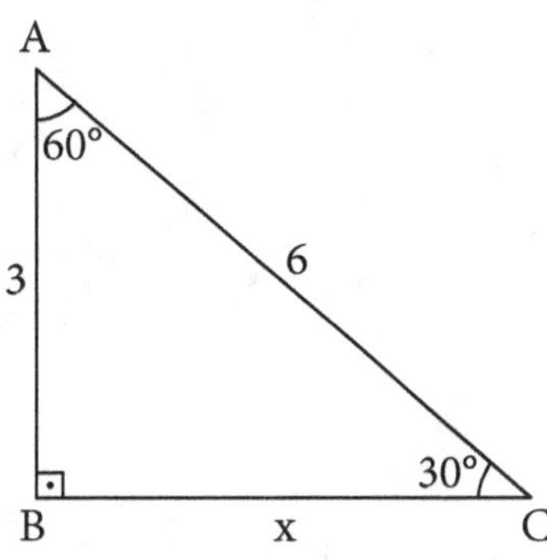

A) 3

B) $\sqrt{3}$

C) $3\sqrt{3}$

D) 6

Solution:

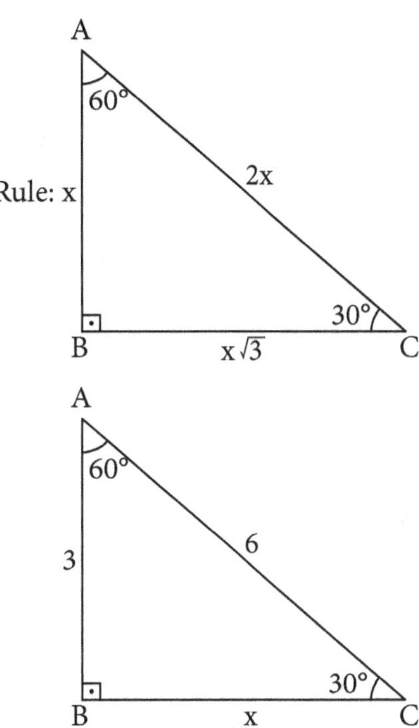

If 30° ise equal to 3, then 60° is $3\sqrt{3}$

x = $3\sqrt{3}$

Correct Answer is C

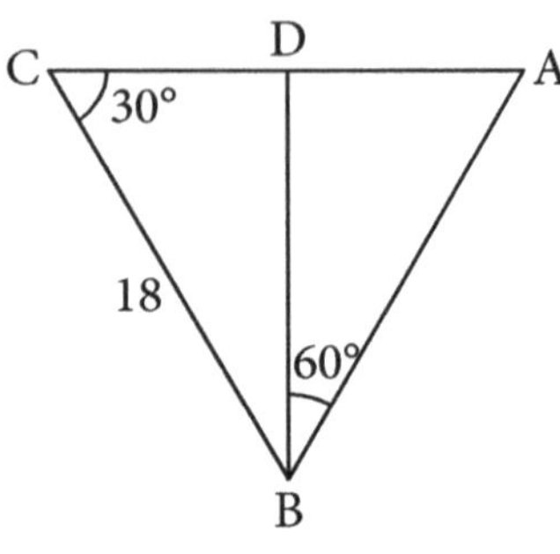

In $\left(\widehat{ABC}\right)$ above, what is the length of AB?

A) 9

B) 12

C) 18

D) 24

Find the value of x.

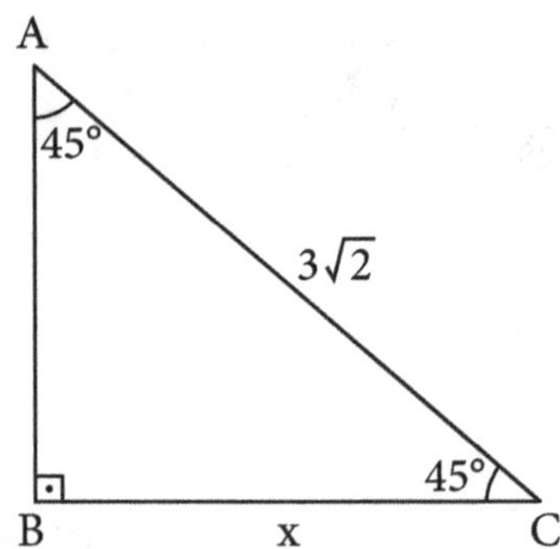

A) 1

B) 3

C) $\sqrt{3}$

D) 5

What is the area of an equilateral triangle with a side of 4?

A) $\sqrt{3}$

B) $2\sqrt{3}$

C) $4\sqrt{3}$

D) $6\sqrt{3}$

Find the value of x.

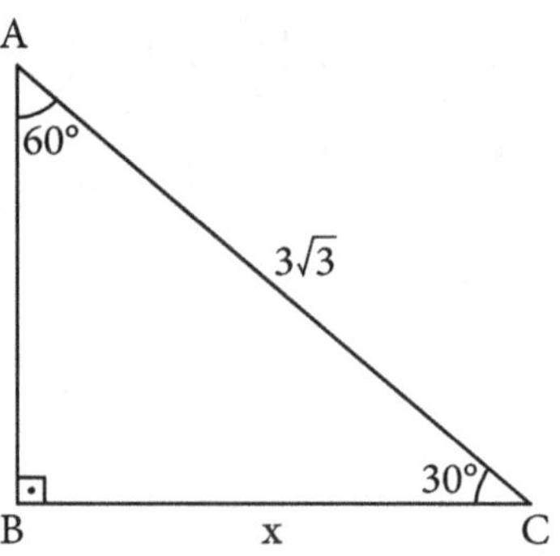

A) $\dfrac{1}{2}$

B) $\dfrac{3}{2}$

C) $\dfrac{9}{2}$

D) $6\sqrt{3}$

In a 30° -60° -90° degrees special triangle, if the shorter leg measures 6 units, what are the lengths of the other two sides?

A) Shorter leg: 6 units, longer leg: 12 units, hypotenuse: $6\sqrt{3}$ units

B) Shorter leg: 6 units, longer leg: $6\sqrt{3}$ units, hypotenuse: 12 units

C) Shorter leg: 6 units, longer leg: $3\sqrt{3}$ units, hypotenuse: 6 units

D) Shorter leg: 6 units, longer leg: 3 units, hypotenuse: $3\sqrt{3}$ units

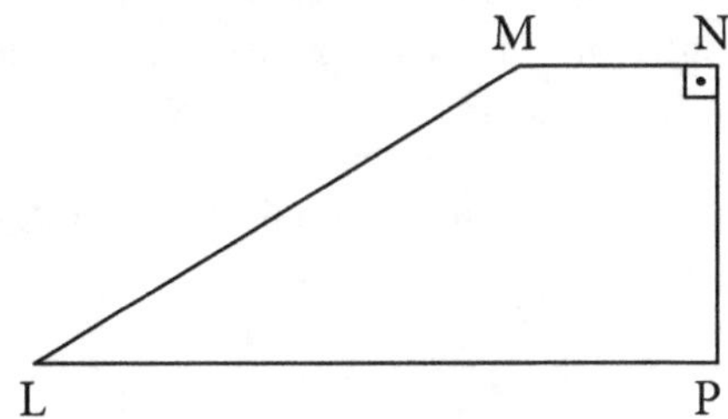

In quadrilateral LMNP above, LP || MN and

LM. =2NP. What is the measure of angle L?

A) 30°

B) 60°

C) 75°

D) 85°

In a 30° -60° -90° degrees special triangle, if the hypotenuse measures $12\sqrt{3}$ units, what is the length of the shorter leg?

A) $2\sqrt{3}$ units

B) $6\sqrt{3}$ units

C) 18 units

D) 24 units

In a 45°-45°-90° degrees triangle, the hypotenuse measures 10 units.

Determine the lengths of the other side (the legs) in the triangle.

A) 5 units

B) $5\sqrt{2}$ units

C) 10 units

D) $10\sqrt{2}$ units

In a 30-60-90 triangle, the longer leg is opposite the 60-degree angle, and it is equal to $\sqrt{3}$ times the length of the shorter leg.

If the longer leg is 9 units. What is the length of hypotenuse?

A) $\sqrt{3}$ units

B) $2\sqrt{3}$ units

C) $4\sqrt{3}$ units

D) $6\sqrt{3}$ units

In a 30-60-90 triangle, if the hypotenuse has a length of 24 units, what is the length of the longer leg?

A) 8 units

B) 12 units

C) $12\sqrt{3}$ units

D) 24 units

In a 45-45-90 triangle, the length of one leg is 10 units.

What is the length of the other leg?

A) 5 units

B) 10 units

C) $10\sqrt{2}$ units

D) 20 units

In a 45-45-90 triangle, if the hypotenuse has a length of $20\sqrt{2}$ units, what is the length of each leg?

A) 10 units

B) $10\sqrt{2}$ units

C) 20 units

D) 40 units

| 1. | C | 2. | B | 3. | C | 4. | C | 5. | B | 6. | B | 7. | A | 8. | B | 9. | D | 10. | B | 11. | C | 12. | C |

1. Solution:

From 30°, 60°, and 90° special triangle theorem if BC = 18, then BD = 9.

If BD = 9 then, AB = 18.

Correct Answer is C

2. Solution:

Rule:

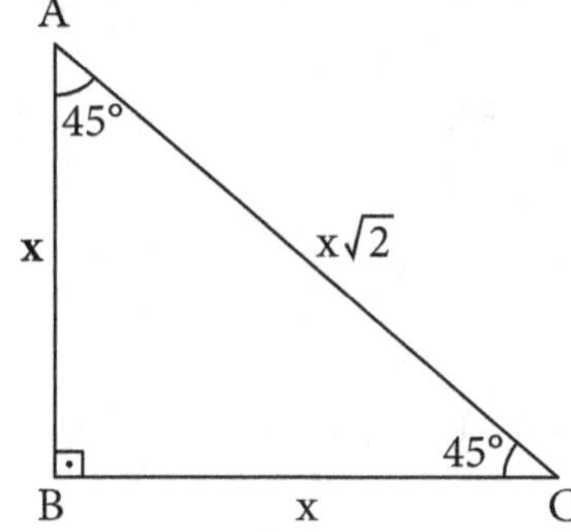

If $x\sqrt{2} = 3\sqrt{2}$

$\quad x = 3$

Correct Answer is B

3. Solution:

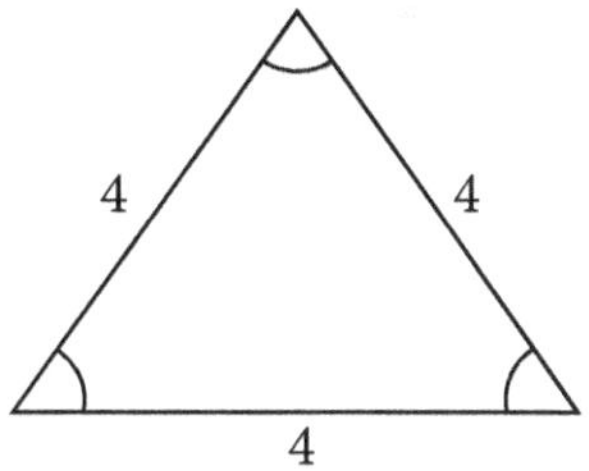

$Area = \dfrac{a^2\sqrt{3}}{4}$

$Area = \dfrac{(4)^2\sqrt{3}}{4}$

$\quad = \dfrac{16\sqrt{3}}{4}$

$\quad = 4\sqrt{3}$

Correct Answer is C

4. Solution:

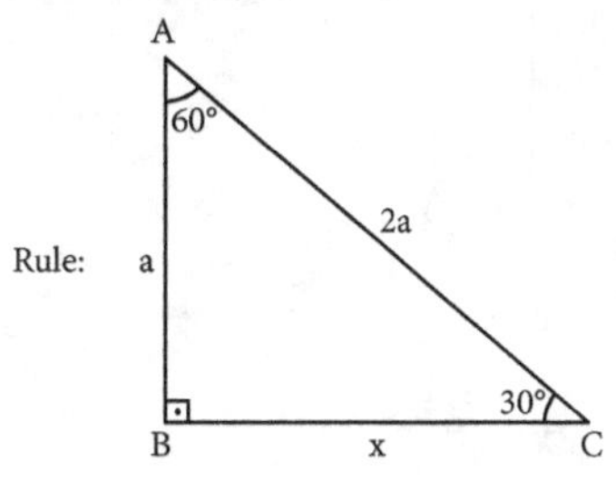 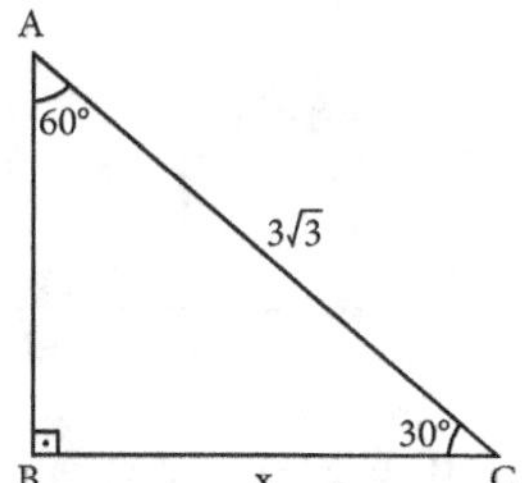

Rule:

If $2a = 3\sqrt{3}$, then $a = \dfrac{3\sqrt{3}}{2}$

since $x = a\sqrt{3}$ then $\dfrac{3\sqrt{3}}{2}\cdot(\sqrt{3}) = \dfrac{3\sqrt{9}}{2} = \dfrac{3\cdot 3}{2} = \dfrac{9}{2}$

Correct Answer is C

5. Solution:

In a 30° -60° -90° degrees special triangle, t he relationship between the sides is as follows:

Shorter leg: Longer leg: Hypotenuse = 1: $\sqrt{3}$: 2

Given that the shorter leg measures 6 units, we can determine the lengths of the other two sides:

Shorter leg = 6 units Longer leg = $6\sqrt{3}$ units

Hypotenuse = 2 • 6 = 12 units

Correct Answer is B

6. Solution:

The length of the shorter leg in 30° -60° -90° degrees triangle can be found using the ratio

Shorter leg: Hypotenuse = 1: 2

Given that the hypotenuse measures $12\sqrt{3}$ units,

we can determine the length of the shorter leg:

Shorter leg = $\dfrac{1}{2}$ • Hypotenuse

Shorter leg = $\dfrac{1}{2}\cdot 12\sqrt{3}$

Shorter leg = $6\sqrt{3}$ units

Correct Answer is B

7. Solution:

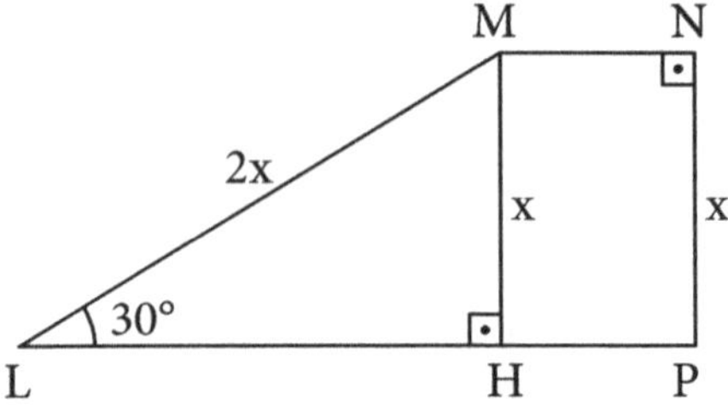

Since NP = MH = x, then LM = 2x

From above special angle (30° -60° -90°)

Angle L = 30°

Correct Answer is A

8 Solution:

In a 45°-45°-90° degrees triangle, the ratios of the side lengths are as follows:

Leg: Leg: Hypotenuse = 1: 1: $\sqrt{2}$

Given that the hypotenuse measures 10 units,

we can find the lengths of the legs:

$\text{Leg} = \left(\dfrac{1}{\sqrt{2}}\right) \cdot \text{Hypotenuse}$

$\text{Leg} = \left(\dfrac{1}{\sqrt{2}}\right) \cdot 10$

$\text{Leg} = \left(\dfrac{10}{\sqrt{2}}\right) \text{ units}$

Simplifying the radical in the leg:

$\text{Leg} = \left(\dfrac{10}{\sqrt{2}}\right) \cdot \left(\dfrac{\sqrt{2}}{\sqrt{2}}\right)$

$\text{Leg} = \left(\dfrac{10\sqrt{2}}{2}\right) \text{ units}$

$\text{Leg} = 5\sqrt{2} \text{ units}$

Correct Answer is B

9. Solution:

Given that the longer leg is 9 units, we can determine the length of the hypotenuse as follows:

Shorter leg = $\dfrac{9}{\sqrt{3}}$ units (since the longer leg is $\sqrt{3}$ times the length of the shorter leg)

Hypotenuse = $2 \cdot \left(\dfrac{9}{\sqrt{3}}\right)$ units = $\dfrac{18}{\sqrt{3}}$ units (since the hypotenuse is twice the length of the shorter leg)

To rationalize the denominator, we multiply the numerator and denominator by $\sqrt{3}$:

$\text{Hypotenuse} = \left(\dfrac{18}{\sqrt{3}}\right) \cdot \left(\dfrac{\sqrt{3}}{\sqrt{3}}\right)$

$= \dfrac{18\sqrt{3}}{3}$

$= 6\sqrt{3}$ units

Therefore, the length of the hypotenuse is $6\sqrt{3}$ units.

Correct Answer is D

10 Solution:

In a 45 - 45 - 90 triangle, the two legs are congruent, which means they have the same length. In this case, if one leg has a length of 10 units, the other leg will also have a length of 10 units

Correct Answer is B

11. Solution:

In a 30 - 60 - 90 triangle, the ratio of the sides is $1:\sqrt{3}:2$.

The hypotenuse is twice the length of the shorter leg, and the longer leg is $\sqrt{3}$ times the length of the shorter leg.

Given that the hypotenuse has a length of 24 units, we can determine the length of the longer leg as follows:

Shorter leg = $\dfrac{24}{2} = 12$ units

Longer leg = $\sqrt{3} \cdot 12 = 12\sqrt{3}$ units

Correct Answer is C

12. Solution:

In a 45 - 45 - 90 triangle, the ratio of the sides is $1:1:\sqrt{2}$.

This means that the length of each leg is equal to the hypotenuse divided by $\sqrt{2}$.

Given that the hypotenuse has a length of $20\sqrt{2}$ units, we can determine the length of each leg as follows:

Length of each leg = $\dfrac{(20\sqrt{2})}{\sqrt{2}} = 20$ units

Therefore, the length of each leg is 20 units.

Correct Answer is C

Similar Triangles

- **Similar triangles:** Triangles with corresponding angles equal and proportional side lengths.

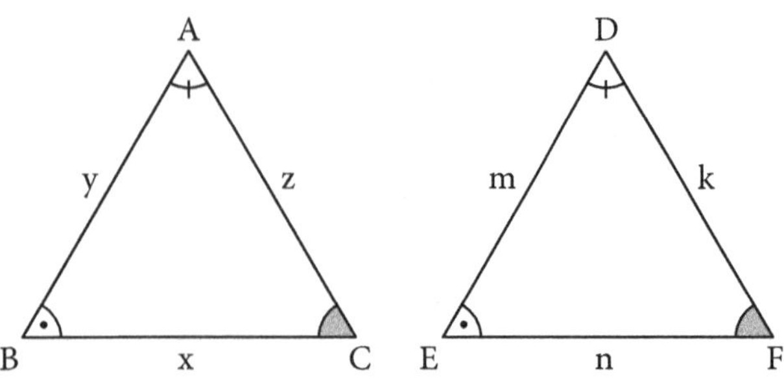

When two figures are similar, the ratios of the lengths of their corresponding sides

If $\widehat{ABC} \sim \widehat{DEF}$ then $\angle A = \angle D$ and
$$\angle B = \angle E$$
$$\angle C = \angle F$$

$$\frac{|AB|}{|DE|} = \frac{|AC|}{|DF|} = \frac{|BC|}{|EF|}$$

$$\frac{x}{n} = \frac{y}{m} = \frac{z}{k}$$

Note :

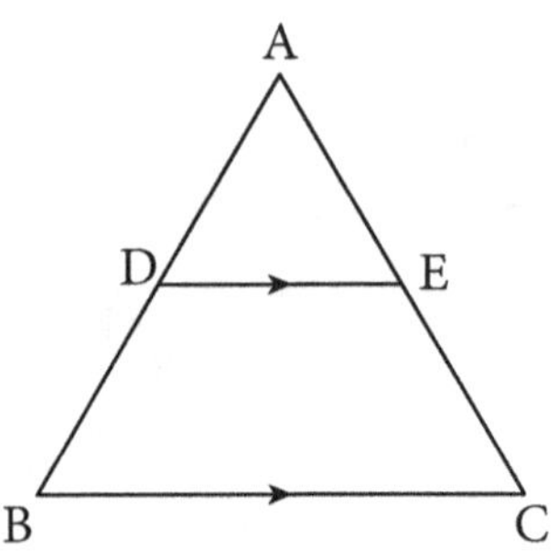

If [DE] // [BC], then

$$\frac{|AD|}{|AB|} = \frac{|DE|}{|BC|} = \frac{|AE|}{|AC|}$$

Digital SAT Sample Question:

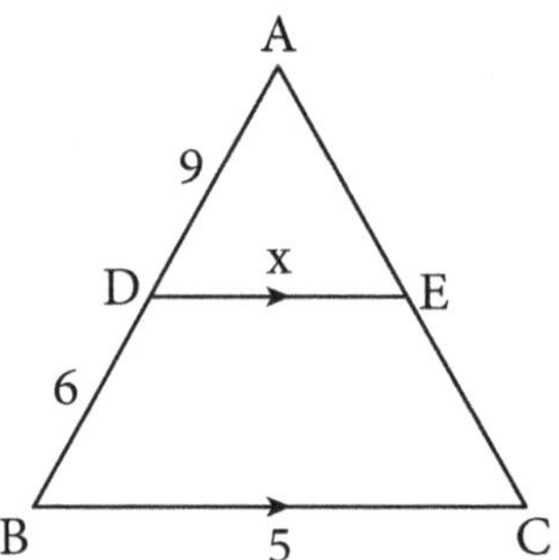

If DE // BC in the figure above, what is the value of x?

A) 3

B) 4

C) 5

D) 6

Solution:

From similarity theorem:

$$\frac{9}{9+6} = \frac{x}{5}, \frac{\overset{3}{\cancel{9}}}{\underset{5}{\cancel{15}}} = \frac{x}{5}, \frac{3}{5} = \frac{x}{5}$$

$$5x = 15$$
$$x = 3$$

Correct Answer is A

AMERICAN MATH
ACADEMY

Similar Triangles Test

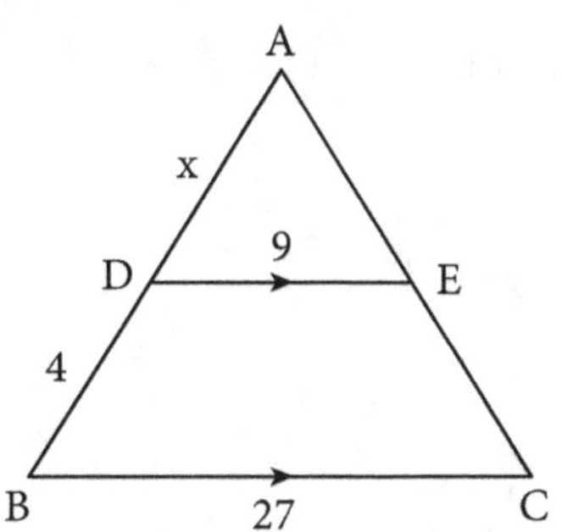

If DE // BC in the figure above, what is the value of x?

A) 2

B) 4

C) 6

D) 8

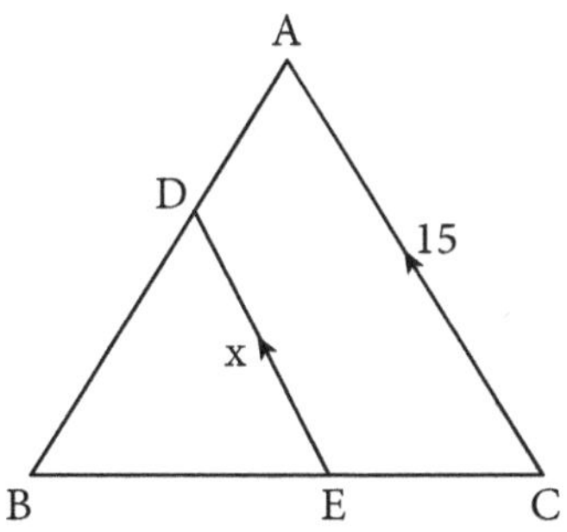

If DE // AC and $3|AD| = 2|BD|$ in the figure above, what is the value of x?

A) 3

B) 6

C) 9

D) 12

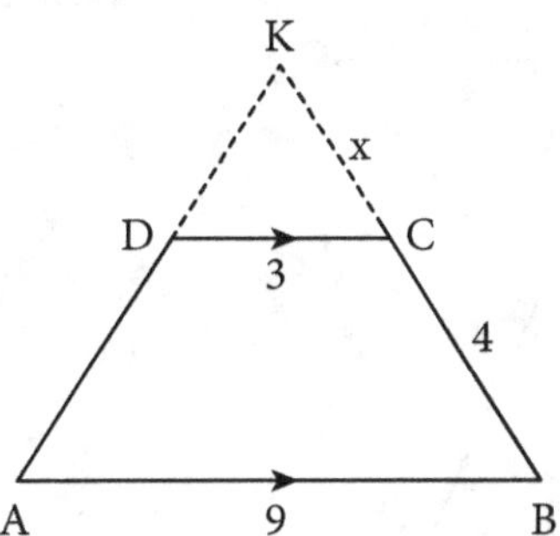

If DC // AB in the figure above, what is the value of x?

A) 2

B) 4

C) 6

D) 8

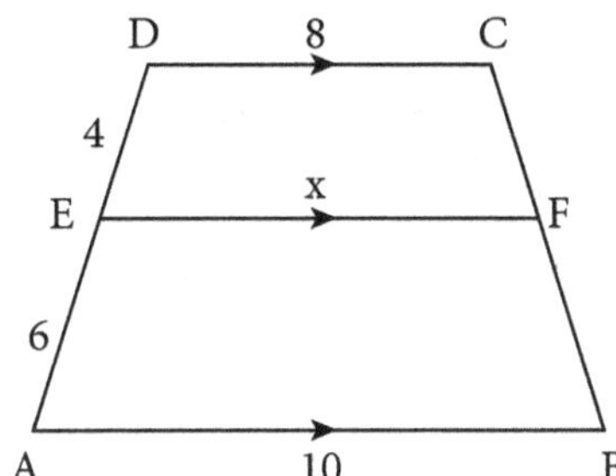

If DC // EF // AB in the trapezoid ABCD above, DC = 8, EF = x, and AB = 10. What is the value of x?

A) 2.2

B) 4.4

C) 8.8

D) 9.8

Similar Triangles Test

Easy

5

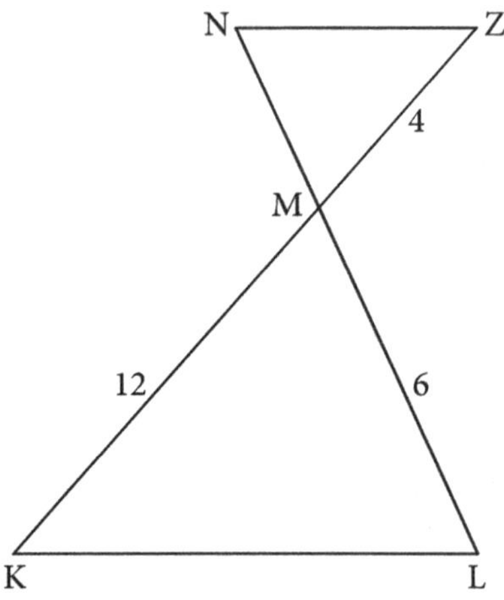

In the figure above, $\overline{KL} \parallel \overline{NZ}$ and segment, KZ intersects segment NL at M. What is the length of segment NM?

A) 1

B) 2

C) 3

D) 4

Hard

6

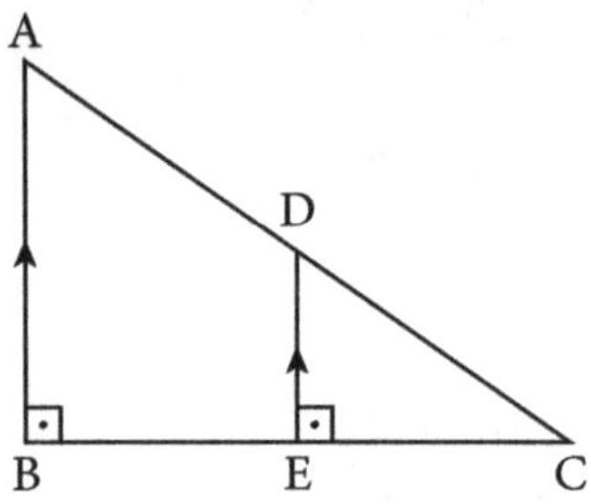

If AB // DE and |AB| = 8, |BC| = 6 and |DE| = 4 then find |DC| + |EC|?

A) 5

B) 6

C) 7

D) 8

Medium

7

JK is the angle bisector of m $\angle$ LJM

m $\angle$ LJK $= \dfrac{x}{2} - 10°$, and

m $\angle$ KJM $= \dfrac{3x}{2} - 24°$. Find x

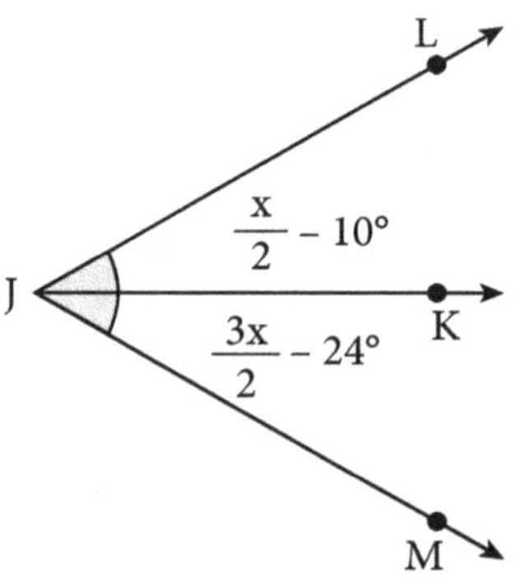

A) 14°

B) 28°

C) 32°

D) 48°

Similar Triangles Test

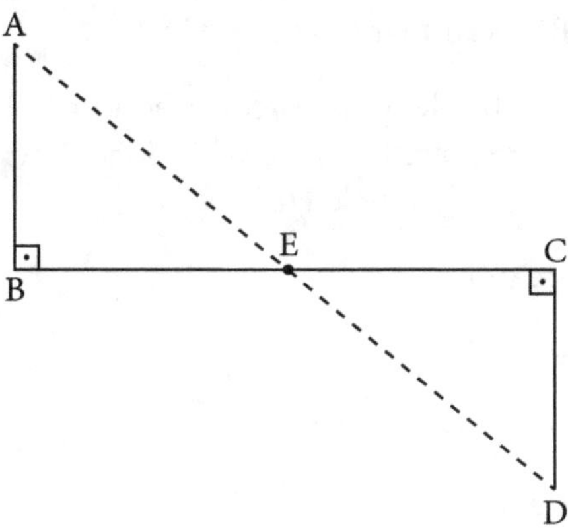

If AB // CD and

$\overline{AB} = \overline{BE}$

$\overline{EC} = \overline{CD}$

$\overline{AB} = 4\,\text{m}$

$|CD| = 8\,\text{m}$

$|BC| = 12\,\text{m}$

What is the value of $|\overline{AD}| = ?$

A) $8\sqrt{2}$

B) $12\sqrt{2}$

C) $16\sqrt{2}$

D) $18\sqrt{2}$

Triangle ABC is similar to triangle DEF.

If the ratio of the corresponding sides is 2:3, what is the ratio of their perimeters?

A) 2:3

B) 3:2

C) 4:9

D) 9:4

In triangle ABC, angle A is 60 degrees and angle B is 30 degrees.

If triangle DEF is similar to triangle ABC, what is the measure of angle D?

A) 30 degrees

B) 45 degrees

C) 60 degrees

D) 90 degrees

Triangle ABC is similar to triangle DEF.

If the length of side AB is 12 units and the length of side DE is 6 units, what is the ratio of their areas?

A) 1:4

B) 2:1

C) 4:1

D) 1:2

Triangle ABC is similar to triangle DEF.

If the ratio of the lengths of corresponding sides is 4:3, and the area of triangle ABC is 48 square units, what is the area of triangle DEF?

A) 21 square units

B) 24 square units

C) 27 square units

D) 36 square units

| 1. | A | 2. | C | 3. | A | 4. | C | 5. | B | 6. | D | 7. | A | 8. | B | 9. | A | 10. | C | 11. | C | 12. | C |

1. Solution:

From similarity theorem:

$$\frac{x}{x+4} = \frac{\overset{1}{\cancel{9}}}{\underset{27}{\cancel{3}}}, \qquad \frac{x}{x+4} = \frac{1}{3}$$

$$3x = x + 4$$
$$2x = 4$$
$$x = 2$$

Correct Answer is A

2. Solution:

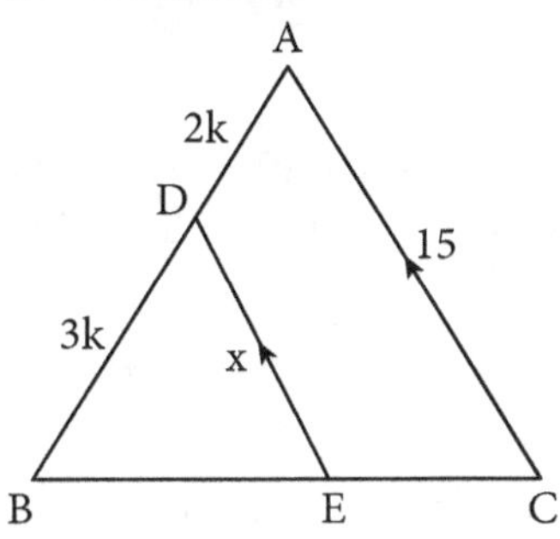

$$3|AD| = 2|BD| \qquad \frac{x}{15} = \frac{3k}{5k}$$

$$BD = 3k \qquad \frac{x}{15} = \frac{3}{5}$$

$$|AB| = 2k \qquad 5x = 45, \quad x = 9$$

Correct Answer is C

3. Solution:

From similarity theorem $\dfrac{DC}{AB} = \dfrac{KC}{KB}$

$$\frac{\overset{1}{\cancel{3}}}{\underset{9}{\cancel{3}}} = \frac{x}{x+4}, \; \frac{1}{3} = \frac{x}{x+4} \; \text{(Cross multiply)}$$

$$3x = x + 4$$
$$2x = 4$$
$$x = 2$$

Correct Answer is A

4. Solution:

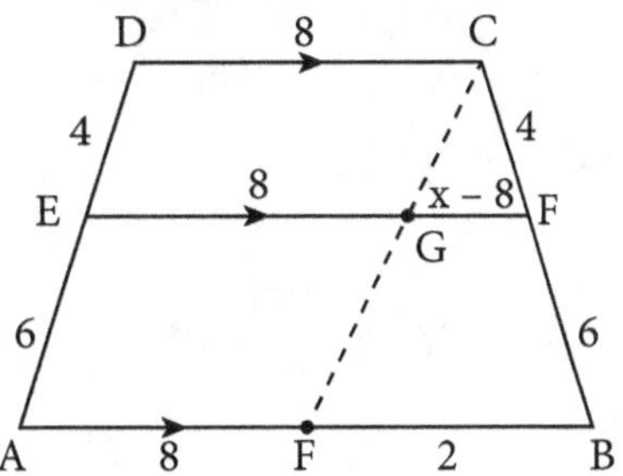

From similerity theorem:

$$\frac{GF}{FB} = \frac{CF}{CB}$$

$$\frac{x-8}{2} = \frac{4}{10}, \; \frac{x-8}{2} = \frac{2}{5}$$

$$5(x-8) = 2 \cdot 2$$
$$5x - 40 = 4$$
$$5x = 44$$
$$x = 8.8$$

Correct Answer is C

5. Solution:

Segment KZ intersects segment NL at M.

First, let's observe triangle KLM and triangle MNZ.

Triangle KLM and triangle MNZ are similar triangles because KL is parallel to NZ, and segment KZ intersects segment NL at M.

Similarity of the triangles:

$$\frac{KM}{ML} = \frac{MZ}{MN}$$

Plugging in the given values, we have:

$$\frac{12}{6} = \frac{4}{MN}$$

$$2 = MN$$

Correct Answer is B

6. Solution:

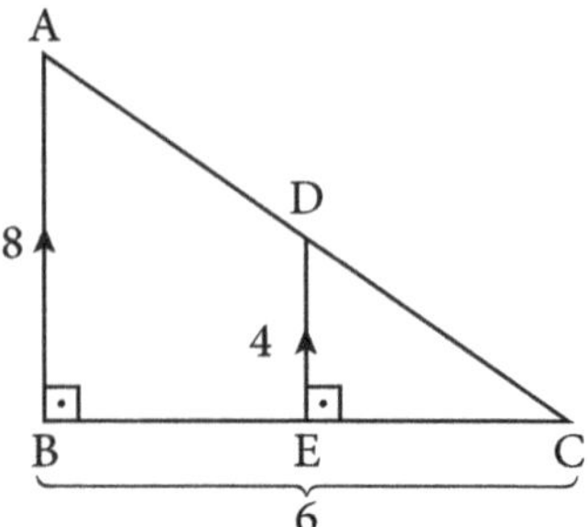

From pythagorean theorem:

$$|AC|^2 = 6^2 + 8^2 = 10^2$$
$$\sqrt{|AC|} = \sqrt{100}, \text{ then } |AC| = 10$$
$$\frac{4}{8} = \frac{|DC|}{|AC|}, \frac{1}{2} = \frac{|DC|}{10}$$
$$|DC| = 5$$
$$\frac{1}{2} = \frac{|EC|}{|BC|}, \frac{1}{2} = \frac{|EC|}{6}$$
$$|EC| = 3$$
$$|DC| + |EC| = 5 + 3 = 8$$

Correct Answer is D

7. Solution:

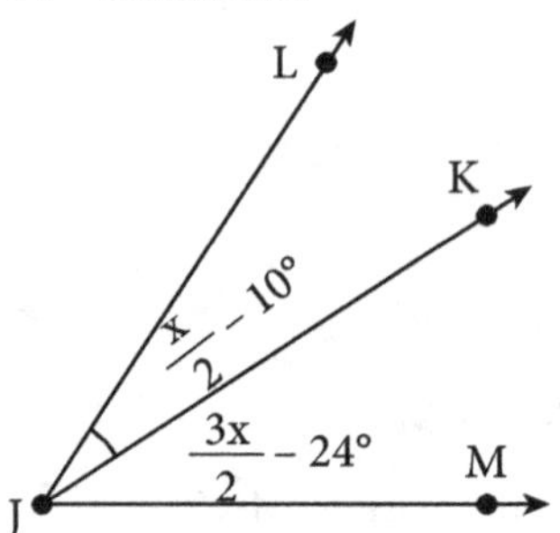

Since JK is bisector of $m \angle LJM$

then $m \angle LJK = m \angle KJM$

$$\frac{x}{2} - 10° = \frac{3x}{2} - 24°$$
$$+ \quad \frac{-x}{2} \qquad \frac{-x}{2}$$
$$\overline{\qquad\qquad\qquad\qquad}$$
$$-10° = \frac{3x}{2} - \frac{x}{2} - 24°$$
$$-10 = x - 24° \qquad 14° = x$$

Correct Answer is A

8. Solution:

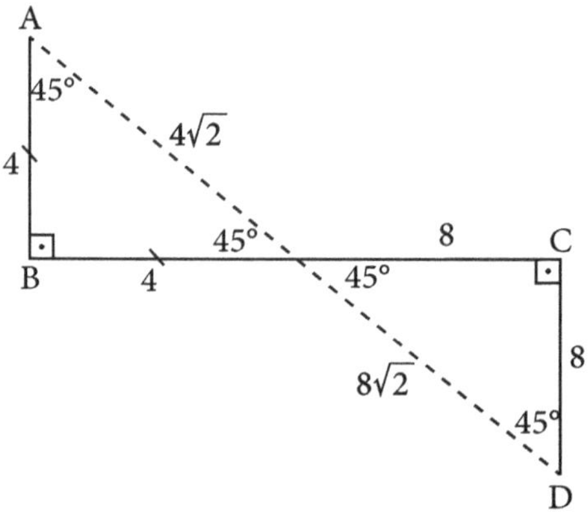

$$|AD| = 4\sqrt{2} + 8\sqrt{2}$$
$$= 12\sqrt{2}$$

Correct Answer is B

9. Solution:

Since the triangles are similar, the ratio of their perimeters will be the same as the ratio of their corresponding side lengths.

Correct Answer is A

10. Solution:

Since the triangles are similar, the corresponding angles will be equal.

Therefore, angle D in triangle DEF is also 60 degrees.

Correct Answer is C

11. Solution:

The ratio of the areas of similar triangles is equal to the square of the ratio of their corresponding side lengths.

Therefore, the correct answer is

$$\left(\frac{12}{6}\right)^2 = 4:1$$

Correct Answer is C

12. Solution:

Since the ratio of the lengths of corresponding sides is 4:3, the ratio of their areas will be the square of this ratio.

Therefore, the area of triangle DEF is

$$\left(\frac{4}{3}\right)^2 = \frac{48}{x}$$
$$\frac{16}{9} = \frac{48}{x}, \text{ then } x = 27 \text{ square units.}$$

Correct Answer is C

Parallelogram:

Area = base · height

$P = 2(h + b)$

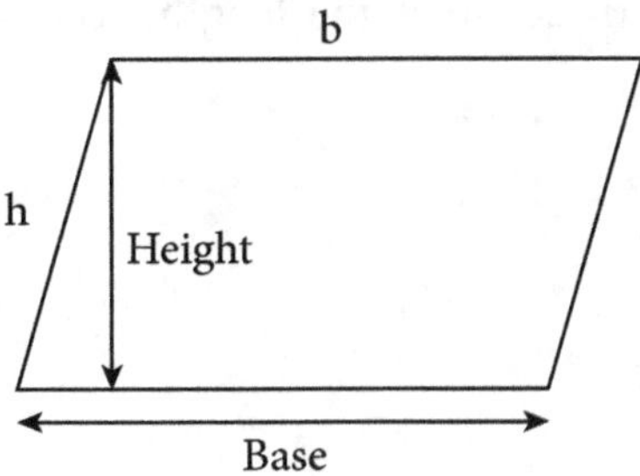

Rectangular:

Area = base · height = b · h

$P = 2(h + b)$

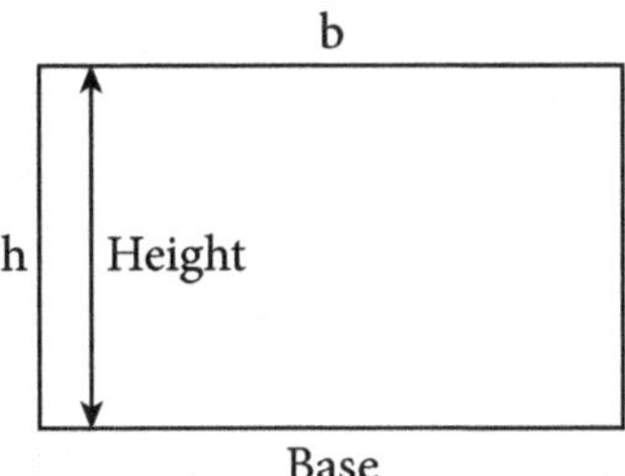

Square:

Area = width · length = s · s = s^2

$P = 4s$

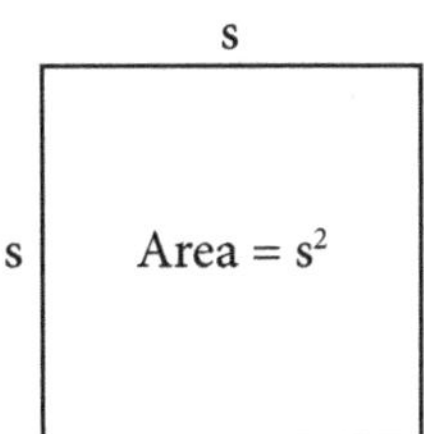

Trapezoid:

$$\text{Area} = \frac{(b_1 + b_2)}{2} \cdot h$$

$P = m + n + b_1 + b_2$

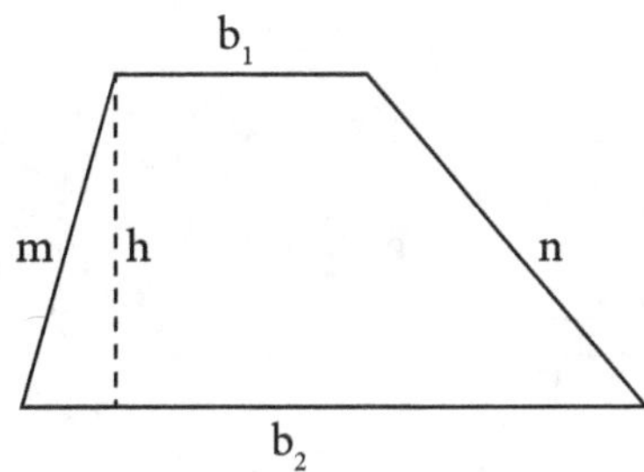

Medium

1

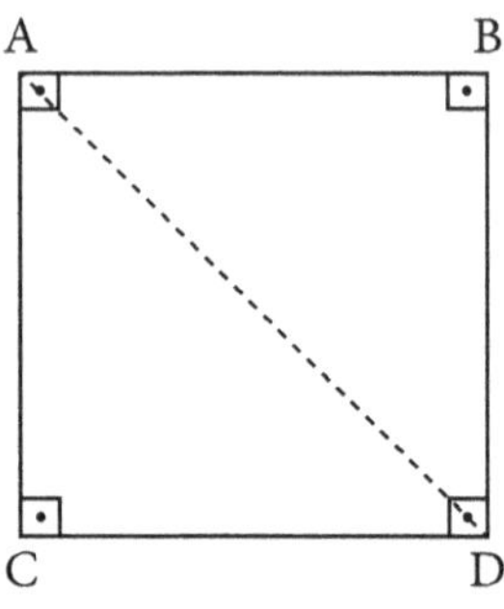

What is the area of the above square if the length of AD is $6\sqrt{2}$?

A) 16

B) 25

C) 36

D) 47

Easy

2

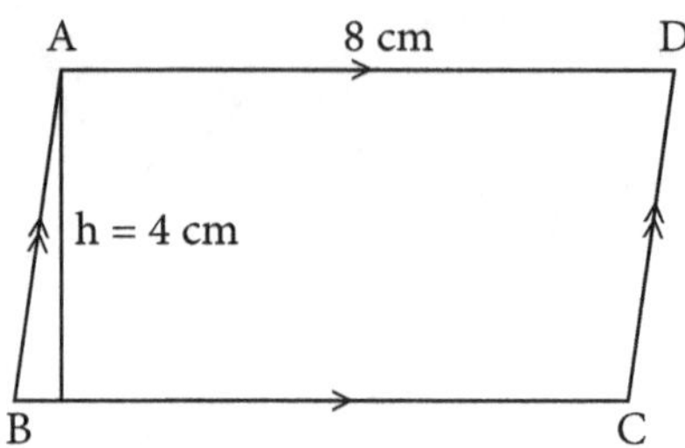

What is the area of parallelogram ABCD?

A) 32 cm^2

B) 48 cm^2

C) 52 cm^2

D) 64 cm^2

Medium

3

The perimeter of a rectangle is 48 m. If the width of the rectangle is three times the length, what is the width?

A) 6 cm

B) 9 cm

C) 15 cm

D) 18 cm

Medium

4

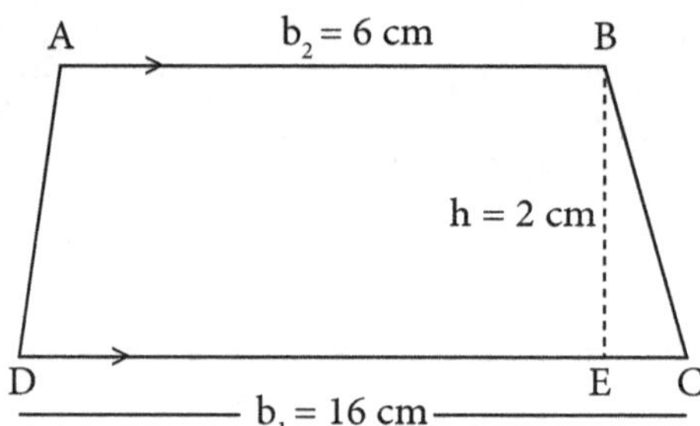

What is the area of trapezoid ABCD?

A) 11 cm^2

B) 22 cm^2

C) 33 cm^2

D) 42 cm^2

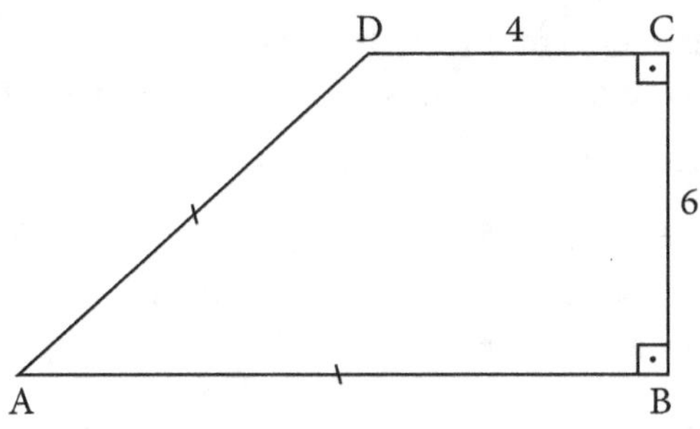

In the above trapezoid ABCD, DC = 4, BC = 6, and AD = AB. What is the value of |AB|?

A) $\dfrac{13}{4}$

B) $\dfrac{13}{2}$

C) 13

D) 41

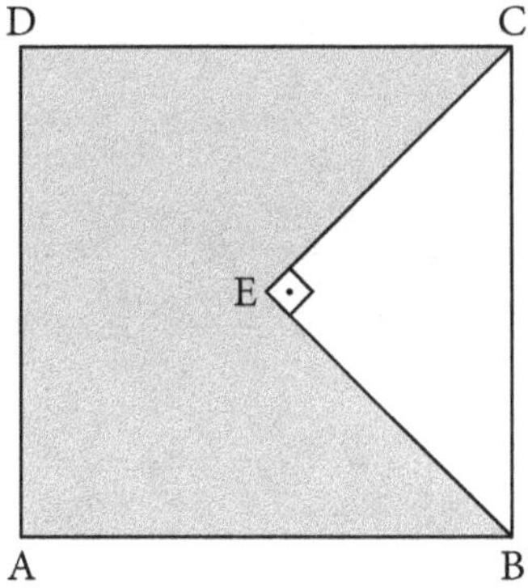

Square ABCD has a perimeter of 32m, and the perimeter of the triangle EBC is 18m.

Find the area of the shaded part.

A) 18 m^2

B) 52 m^2

C) 55 m^2

D) 64 m^2

What is the area of ABCD?

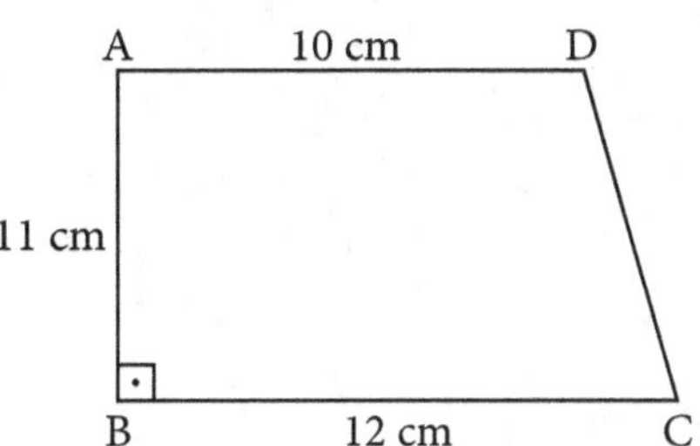

A) 22 cm^2

B) 44 cm^2

C) 108 cm^2

D) 121 cm^2

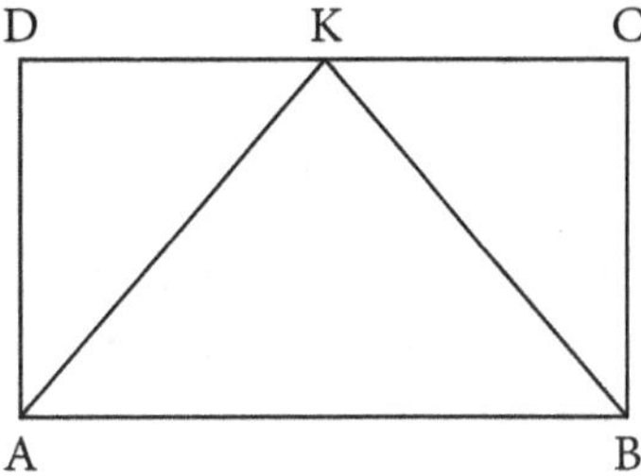

The figure ABCD is a rectangle and AKB is an equilateral triangle. If the area of the rectangle is $8\sqrt{3}$, then find the length of AB.

A) 2

B) 4

C) 8

D) 12

Medium

9

The diagonal of a rectangle is 10 units, and the length of one side is 6 units.

What is the area of the rectangle?

A) 18 square units

B) 24 square units

C) 36 square units

D) 48 square units

Medium

10

The area of a trapezoid is 50 square units. If the bases have lengths of 7 units and 9 units, what is the height?

A) 4.25 units

B) 5.5 units

C) 6.25 units

D) 8 units

Hard

11

The perimeter of a rhombus is 60 units. If each side length is 15 units, what is the length of each diagonal?

A) $15\sqrt{2}$ units

B) $20\sqrt{2}$ units

C) 25 units

D) 30 units

Hard

12

The area of a square is numerically equal to its perimeter. What is the length of each side?

A) 1 unit

B) 2 units

C) 3 units

D) 4 units

Area and Perimeter of Quadrilaterals Test Solution

| 1. | C | 2. | A | 3. | D | 4. | B | 5. | B | 6. | C | 7. | D | 8. | B | 9. | D | 10. | C | 11. | A | 12. | D |

1. Solution:

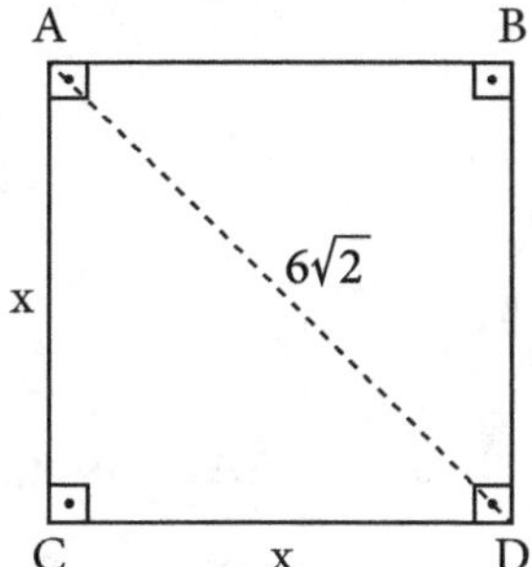

From pythagorean theorem:

$x^2 + x^2 = \left(6\sqrt{2}\right)^2$

$2x^2 = 72$

$x^2 = 36$

$x = 6$

Area $= x^2 = 36$

Correct Answer is C

2. Solution:

Area of ABCD parallelogram $= b \cdot h$

$\qquad\qquad = 4\,\text{cm} \cdot 8\,\text{cm}$

$\qquad\qquad = 32\,\text{cm}^2$

Correct Answer is A

3. Solution:

If perimeter of rectangle is 48, and $w = 3\ell$ then

$2\ell + 2w = 48\,\text{m},\ \ell + w = 24\,\text{m}$

$\qquad\qquad \ell + 3\ell = 24\,\text{m}$

$\qquad\qquad\quad 4\ell = 24\,\text{m}$

$\qquad\qquad\quad\ \ \ell = 6\,\text{m}$

$\qquad\quad w = 3\ell = 3 \cdot 6 = 18\,\text{m}$

Correct Answer is D

4. Solution:

Area of ABCD trapezoid $= \dfrac{(b_1 + b_2) \cdot h}{2}$

Area $= \dfrac{(6\,\text{cm} + 16\,\text{cm}) \cdot 2\,\text{cm}}{2} = \dfrac{22\,\text{cm} \cdot 2\,\text{cm}}{2}$

Area $= 22\,\text{cm}^2$

Correct Answer is B

5. Solution:

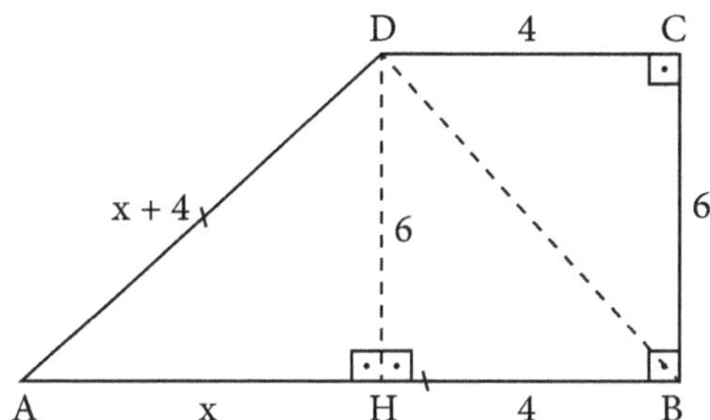

From pythagorean theorem:

$(x + 4)^2 = x^2 + 6^2$

$x^2 + 8x + 16 = x^2 + 36$

$8x + 16 = 36$

$8x = 20 \quad x = \dfrac{5}{2}$

$AB = x + 4 = \dfrac{5}{2} + 4 = \dfrac{13}{2}$

Correct Answer is B

6. Solution:

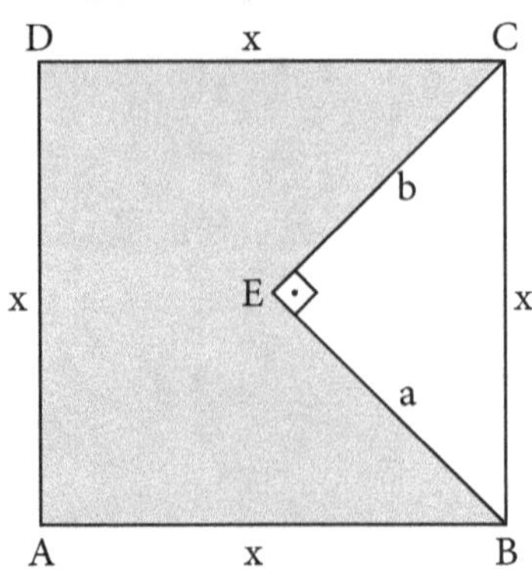

Perimeter of ABCD = 32 m

40 = 32 m   x = 8 m

Perimeter of $\triangle$BEC = 32 m = a + b + x = 18 m

From pythagorean theorem:

$a^2 + b^2 = x^2$ $a^2 + b^2 = 64$ cm^2

$(a + b)^2 - 2ab = 64$, since a + b = 10, then

$100 - 2ab = 64$ cm^2, ab = 18 cm^2

$$A(BEC) = \frac{18\,m^2}{2} = 9\,m^2$$

Shaded Area = 64 m^2 – 9 m^2

= 55 m^2

Correct Answer is C

7. Solution:

$$\text{Area of ABCD trapezoid} = \frac{(b_1 + b_2)\cdot h}{2}$$

$$\text{Area} = \frac{(10\,cm + 12\,cm)\cdot 11\,cm}{2}$$

$$= \frac{22\,cm \cdot 11\,cm}{2} = 121\,cm^2$$

Correct Answer is D

8. Solution:

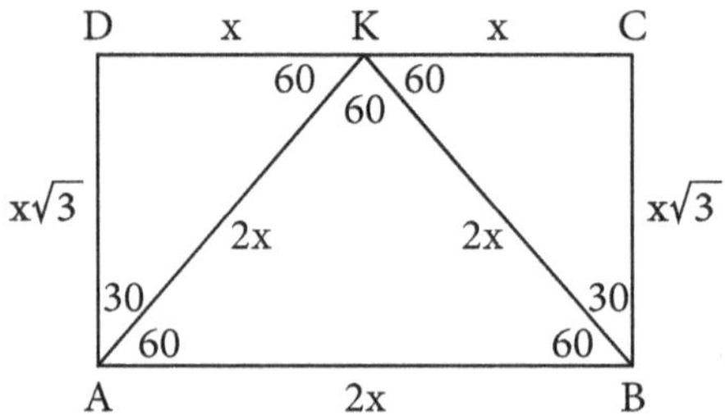

Since the area of rectangle ABCD is $8\sqrt{3}$ and $\triangle$AKB is an iquilateral triangle,

$$A(ABCD) = 8\sqrt{3}$$
$$x\sqrt{3}\cdot 2x = 8\sqrt{3}$$
$$2x^2 = 8$$
$$x^2 = 4$$

x = 2, AB = 2x

AB = 2 · 2 = 4

Correct Answer is B

9. Solution:

In a rectangle, the diagonal forms a right triangle with the sides of the rectangle.

Using the Pythagorean theorem, we can find the width of the rectangle: width

$$= \sqrt{(10^2 - 6^2)} = \sqrt{(100 - 36)} = \sqrt{64} = 8 \text{ units.}$$

The area of a rectangle is given by length times width, so the area is 6 · 8 = 48 square units.

Correct Answer is D

10. Solution:

The area of a trapezoid is given by

$A = (a + b) \cdot \dfrac{h}{2}$, where a and b are the lengths of the bases,

and h is the height.

Substituting the values, we have

$50 = (7 + 9) \cdot \dfrac{h}{2}$.

Solving the equation 16h = 100,

we find h = 6.25 units.

Correct Answer is C

11. Solution:

The perimeter of a rhombus is the sum of all its four side lengths.

In this case, the perimeter is given as 60 units, and each side length is 15 units.

Perimeter = 4 · Side Length

60 = 4 · 15

To find the length of each diagonal, we can use the formula for the length of the diagonals in a rhombus:

Length of Diagonal = $\sqrt{\left(\text{Side Length}_1^2 + \text{Side Lingth}_2^2 \right)}$

Since all sides of a rhombus are congruent, the length of both diagonals is the same. Let's calculate it:

Length of Diagonal = $\sqrt{\left(15^2 + 15^2 \right)}$

Length of Diagonal = $\sqrt{\left(225 + 225 \right)}$ $\sqrt{(225 + 225)}$

Length of Diagonal = $\sqrt{450}$

Length of Diagonal = $15\sqrt{2}$

The length of each diagonal is approximately $15\sqrt{2}$ units

Correct Answer is A

12. Solution:

To solve this question, let's assume that the length of each side of the square is s units.

According to the given information, the area of the square is equal to its perimeter.

The area of a square is given by the formula $A = s^2$,

and the perimeter is given by the formula P = 4s.

Setting the area equal to the perimeter, we have:

$s^2 = 4s$

Rearranging the equation, we get:

$s^2 - 4s = 0$

Factoring out an s, we have:

s(s - 4) = 0

This equation will hold true if either s = 0 or s - 4 = 0.

However, the length of a side cannot be zero, so we disregard s = 0.

Solving s - 4 = 0, we find:

s = 4

Therefore, the length of each side of the square is 4 units.

Correct Answer is D

Circle and Circle Equations

Area of a Circle:

$A = \pi r^2$

Area of the Sector:

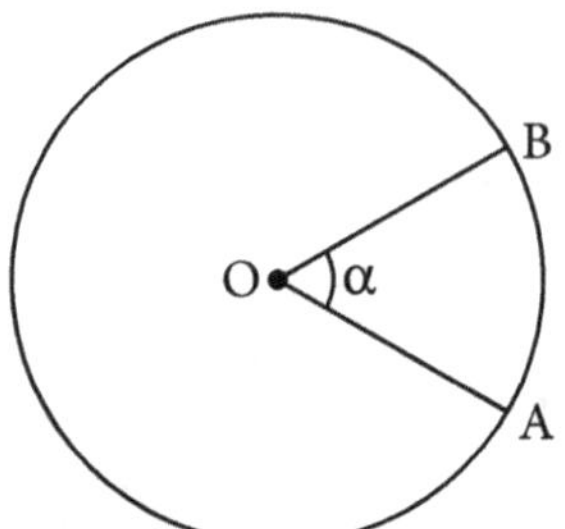

$A = \dfrac{n^\circ}{360^\circ} \pi r^2$

Central Angle:

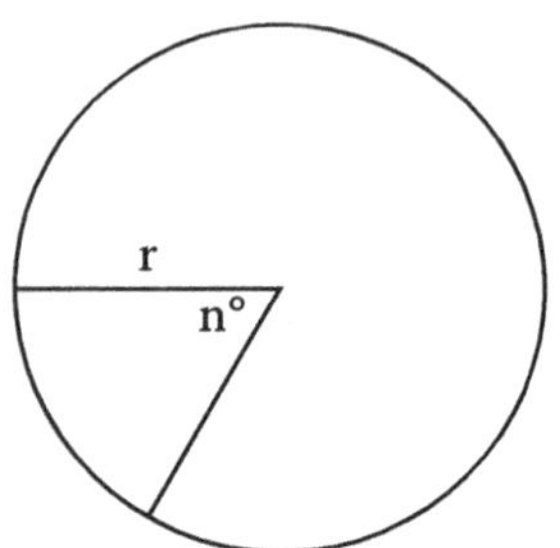

$\angle AOB = \angle arcAB$

Circumference:

$C = 2\pi r$

Equations of a Circle:

$(x - h)^2 + (y - k)^2 = r^2$

Inscription of a Circle:

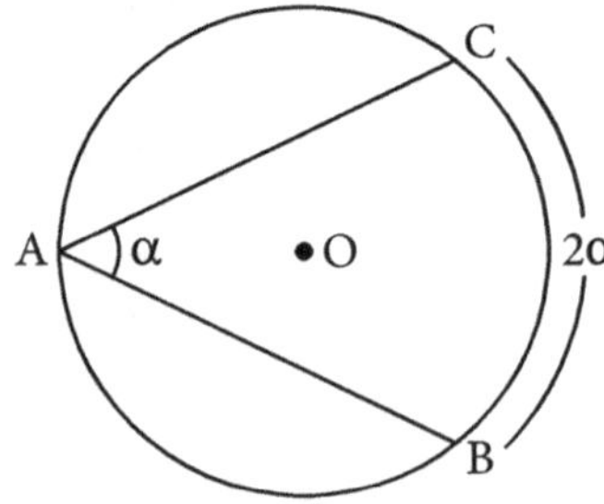

$\angle BAC = \dfrac{arcBC}{2}$

Semi-Circle:

$A = \dfrac{1}{2} \pi r^2$

Tangent Chord Angle:

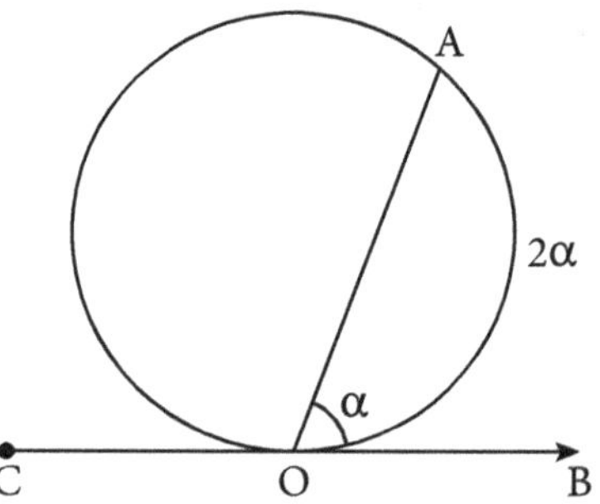

$\angle AOB = \dfrac{\angle arcAO}{2}$

Angle formed by two Intersecting Chords:

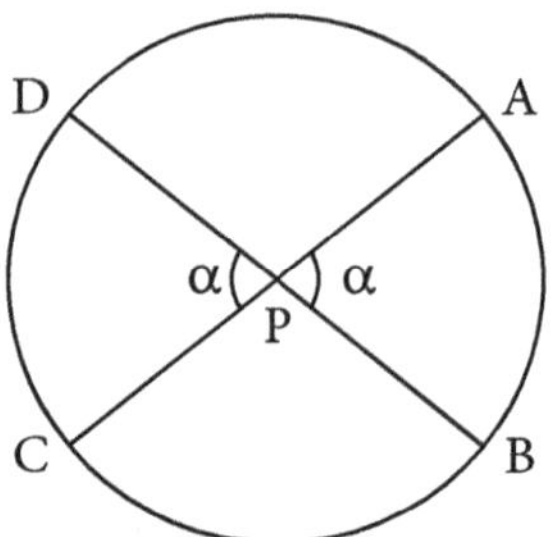

$a = \angle DPC = (APB) = \dfrac{m(BA) + m(DC)}{2}$

Angle formed outside of circle by Intersection:

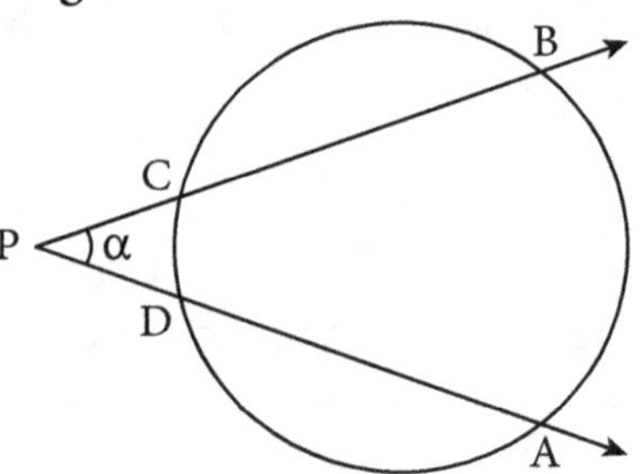

$\angle BPA = \alpha = \dfrac{m(AB) - m(DC)}{2}$

Length of an Arc formula:

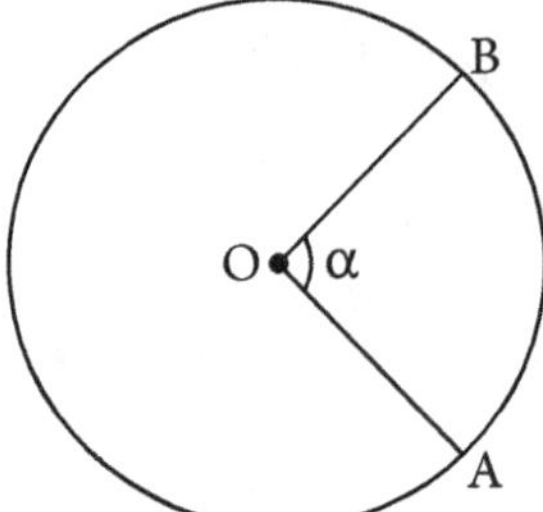

$ArcAB = 2\pi r \dfrac{\alpha}{360^\circ}$

1

Find the circumference of the following circle.

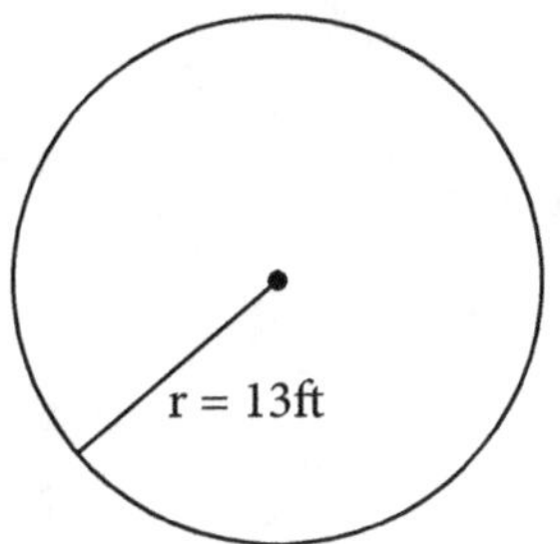

A) 13π ft

B) 26π ft

C) 36π ft

D) 42π ft

2

Find the area of the following circle.

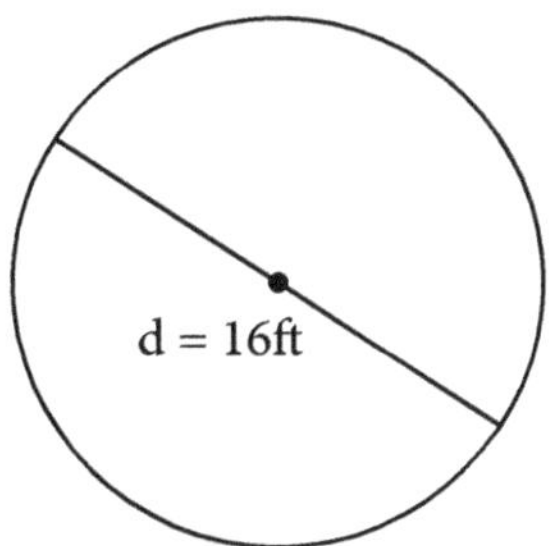

A) 6π ft^2

B) 32π ft^2

C) 48π ft^2

D) 64π ft^2

3

Using the two circles shown below, what is

$$\frac{\text{area of circle A}}{\text{area of circle B}}?$$

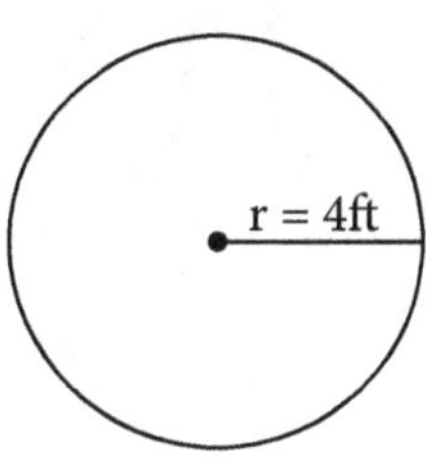 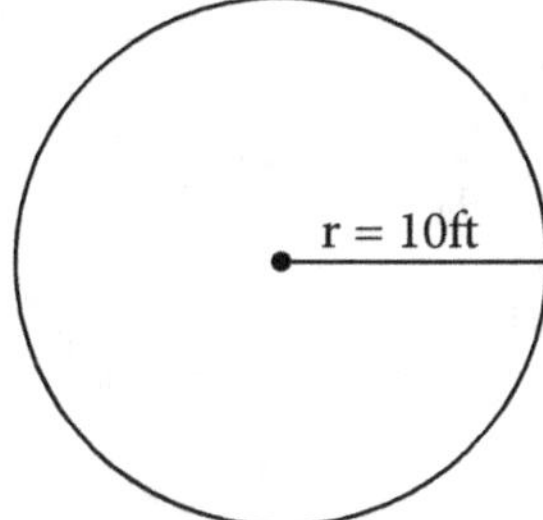

Circle A   **Circle B**

A) $\dfrac{4}{25}$

B) $\dfrac{1}{5}$

C) $\dfrac{3}{4}$

D) $\dfrac{4}{5}$

4

In the following figure, O is the center of the circle and the radius is 4 cm. Find the area of the shaded part.

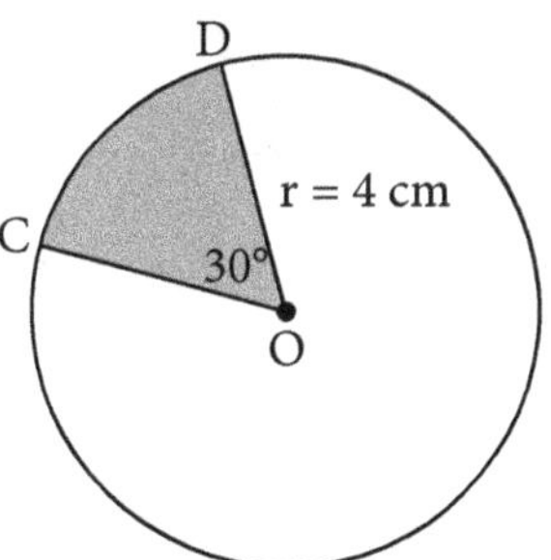

A) $\dfrac{3}{4}\pi$ cm^2

B) $\dfrac{4}{3}\pi$ cm^2

C) 4π cm^2

D) 16π cm^2

Hard

5

If the ratio of the circumference to the area of the circle is 4 to 6, what is the radius of the circle?

A) 1

B) 3

C) 4

D) 6

Medium

6

Using the two circles shown below, what is

$$\frac{\text{circumference of circle X}}{\text{circumference of circle Y}}?$$

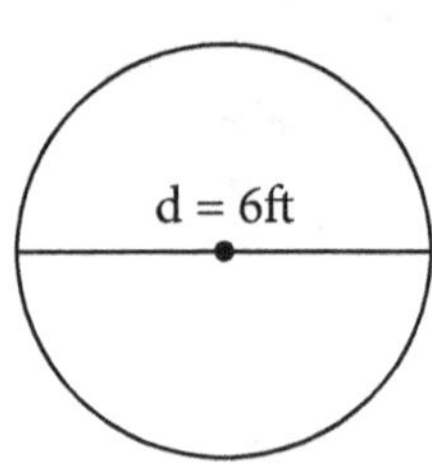

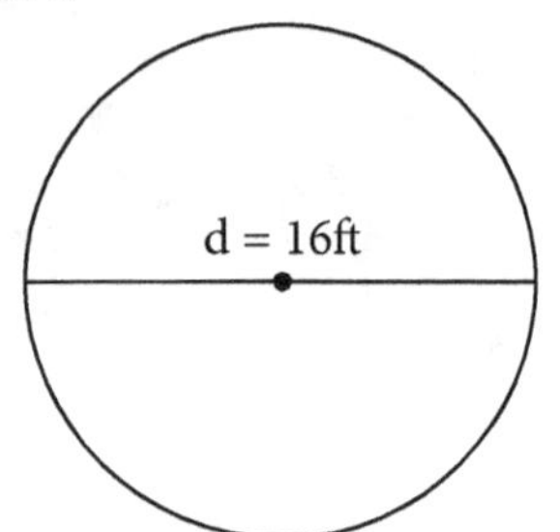

Circle X   **Circle Y**

A) $\frac{3}{8}$

B) $\frac{3}{4}$

C) $\frac{3}{2}$

D) 3

Medium

7

In the following figure, what is the measure of a?

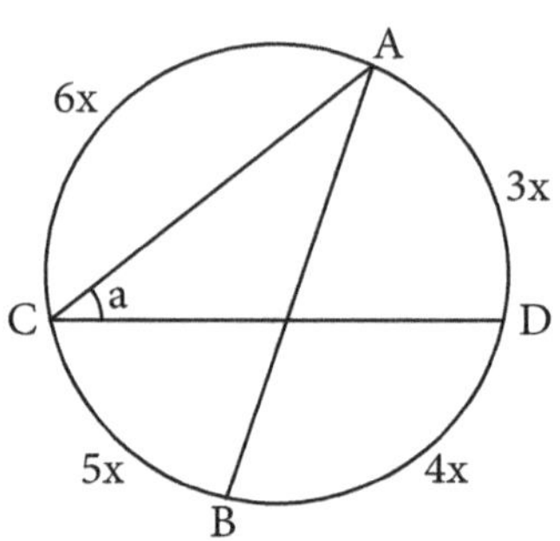

A) 15°

B) 25°

C) 30°

D) 45°

Hard

8

In the figure below, AB and CE are the diameters of the circles. What is the measure of x?

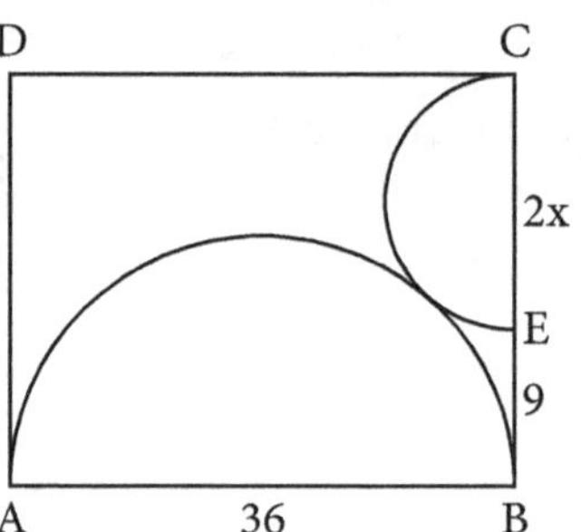

A) 1

B) 3

C) 4.5

D) 5

Circle and Circle Equations Test

Hard

9

$$x^2 + y^2 - 6x + 4y = 9$$

The equation of a circle in the xy-plane is shown above.

What is the radius of the circle?

A) $\sqrt{11}$

B) $\sqrt{22}$

C) $\sqrt{33}$

D) $\sqrt{43}$

Medium

10

In a circle with center O, the central angle AOC measures $\dfrac{3\pi}{4}$ radians.

The area of the sector formed by central angle AOC is what fraction of the area of the circle?

A) $\dfrac{1}{4}$

B) $\dfrac{3}{8}$

C) $\dfrac{1}{2}$

D) $\dfrac{3}{4}$

Medium

11

$$x^2 + 12x + y^2 - 6y = 25$$

The equation above defines a circle in the xy-plane.

What are the coordinates of the center of the circle?

A) (-6, 3)

B) (-6, -3)

C) (-12, 6)

D) (-12, -6)

Hard

12

In a circle with center O, the central angle AOB measures 60 degrees.

If the circumference of the circle is 20π units, what is the length of the arc formed by the central angle AOB?

A) $\dfrac{10\pi}{3}$ units

B) $\dfrac{10\pi}{6}$ units

C) $\dfrac{5\pi}{3}$ units

D) $\dfrac{6\pi}{6}$ units

Circle and Circle Equations Test Solution

1. Solution:

$r = 13\,\text{ft} \qquad C = 2\pi r$

$\qquad\qquad C = 2\pi \cdot 13\,\text{ft} = 26\pi\ \text{ft}$

Correct Answer is B

2. Solution:

$\text{Area} = \pi r^2 \qquad$ If $d = 16\,\text{ft}$, then $r = 8\,\text{ft}$

$\text{Area} = \pi(8\,\text{ft})^2$

$\qquad = 64\pi\ \text{ft}^2$

Correct Answer is D

3. Solution:

Area of circle A $= \pi r^2 = \pi(4\,\text{ft})^2 = 16\pi\,\text{ft}^2$

Area of circle B $= \pi r^2 = \pi(10\,\text{ft})^2 = 100\pi\,\text{ft}^2$

$$\frac{\text{Area of circle A}}{\text{Area of circle B}} = \frac{16\pi\,\text{ft}^2}{100\pi\,\text{ft}^2} = \frac{16}{100}$$

$$= \frac{4}{25}$$

Correct Answer is A

4. Solution:

Area of shaded circle

$$\frac{a \cdot \pi \cdot r^2}{360^\circ} \qquad a^\circ = 30^\circ$$

$$r = 4\,\text{cm}$$

Area of shaded part

$$= \frac{30^\circ \cdot \pi \cdot 16\,\text{cm}^2}{360^\circ} = \frac{16\pi}{12}\,\text{cm}^2$$

$$= \frac{4}{3}\pi\,\text{cm}^2$$

Correct Answer is B

5. Solution:

$$\frac{\text{Circumference}}{\text{Area}} = \frac{2\pi r}{\pi r^2}, \text{ then } \frac{2}{r} = \frac{4}{6}$$

$$4r = 12$$

$$r = 3$$

Correct Answer is B

6. Solution:

$$\frac{\text{Circumference of circle X}}{\text{Circumference of circle Y}}$$

$$= \frac{2\pi \cdot 3\,\text{ft}}{2\pi \cdot 8\,\text{ft}} = \frac{3}{8}$$

Correct Answer is A

7. Solution:

$6x + 3x + 5x + 4x = 360^\circ$

$18x = 360^\circ$

$x = 20^\circ, a = \dfrac{3x}{2} = \dfrac{3 \times 20^\circ}{2} = 30^\circ$

Correct Answer is C

8. Solution:

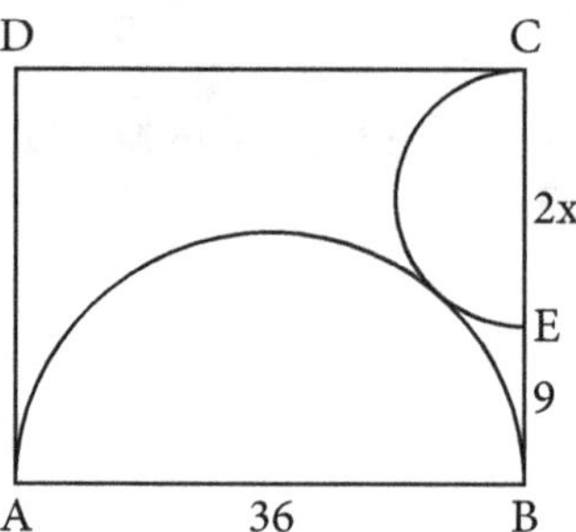

From pythagorean theorem:

$(x + 9)^2 + 18^2 = (x + 18)^2$

$x^2 + 18x + 81 + 324 = x^2 + 36x + 81 = 18x$

$$\frac{81}{18} = x$$

$$\frac{9}{2} = x, \ 4.5 = x$$

Correct Answer is C

9. Solution:

Let's rewrite the equation in the standard form of a circle:

$x^2 + y^2 - 6x + 4y = 9$

To complete the square for the x terms, we add

$\left(\frac{6}{2}\right)^2 = 9$ to both sides: $x^2 - 6x + 9 + y^2 + 4y = 9 + 9$

Simplifying further: $(x - 3)^2 + y^2 + 4y = 18$

Now, we need to complete the square for the y terms. To do that, we add $\left(\frac{4}{2}\right)^2 = 4$ to both sides:

$(x - 3)^2 + y^2 + 4y + 4 = 18 + 4$

$(x - 3)^2 + (y + 2)^2 = 22$

The center of the circle is (3, -2), and the radius squared is 22.

Therefore, the radius of the circle is $\sqrt{22}$

Correct Answer is B

10. Solution:

The formula to calculate the area of a sector is:

$$\text{Area of Sector} = \frac{\theta}{2\pi} \cdot \pi r^2$$

where θ is the central angle and r is the radius of the circle.

In this case, the central angle AOC measures $\theta = \frac{3\pi}{4}$ radians.

Let's assume the radius of the circle is 'r'.

The area of the sector formed by the central angle AOC can be calculated as:

$$\text{Area of Sector} = \frac{\frac{3\pi}{4}}{2\pi} \cdot \pi r^2 = \frac{3}{8}\pi r^2$$

The area of the entire circle is:

$\text{Area of Circle} = \pi r^2$

The fraction of the area of the sector to the area of the circle is then: $\text{Fraction} = \dfrac{\text{Area of Sector}}{\text{Area of Circle}} = \dfrac{\frac{3}{8}\pi r^2}{\pi r^2} = \dfrac{3}{8}$

Therefore, the area of the sector formed by central angle AOC is $\frac{3}{8}$

Correct Answer is B

11. Solution:

Equation in the standard form of a circle:

$(x - h)^2 + (y - k)^2 = r^2$

where (h, k) represents the center of the circle, and r represents the radius.

Let's rearrange the given equation to match the standard form: $x^2 + 12x + y^2 - 6y = 25$

To complete the square for the x terms,

we add $\left(\frac{12}{2}\right)^2 = 36$ to both sides:

$x^2 + 12x + 36 + y^2 - 6y = 25 + 36$

Simplifying further: $(x + 6)^2 + y^2 - 6y = 61$

Now, we need to complete the square for the y terms. To do that, we add $\left(\frac{6}{2}\right)^2 = 9$ to both sides:

$(x + 6)^2 + y^2 - 6y + 9 = 61 + 9$

Simplifying further: $(x + 6)^2 + (y - 3)^2 = 70$

Now, the equation is in the standard form of a circle.

The center of the circle is (-6, 3).

Correct Answer is A

12. Solution:

The formula to calculate the length of an arc is given by:

$\text{Arc Length} = \dfrac{\theta}{360°} \cdot \text{Circumference}$ where θ is the central angle and Circumference is the total circumference of the circle. In this case, the central angle AOB measures 60 degrees, and the circumference of the circle is 20π units.

The length of the arc formed by the central angle AOB can be calculated as: $\text{Arc Length} = \dfrac{60}{360°} \cdot (20\pi) = \dfrac{10\pi}{3}$ units

Therefore, the length of the arc formed by the central angle AOB is $\dfrac{10\pi}{3}$ units

Correct Answer is A

Volume

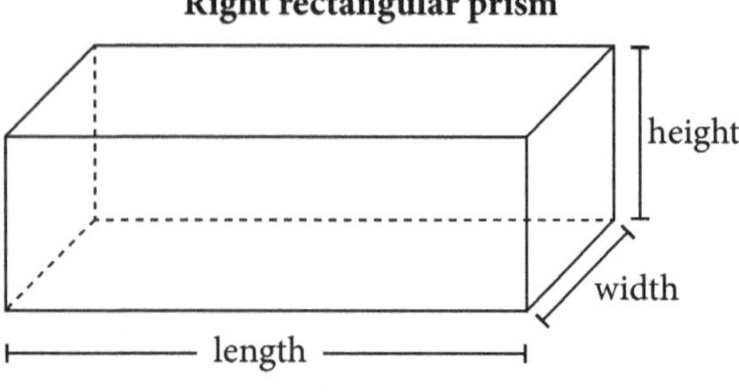

Right rectangular prism

$$V = l \cdot w \cdot h$$

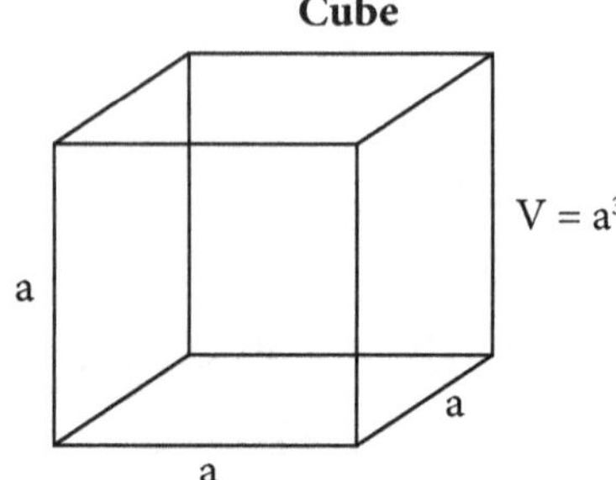

Cube

$$V = a^3$$

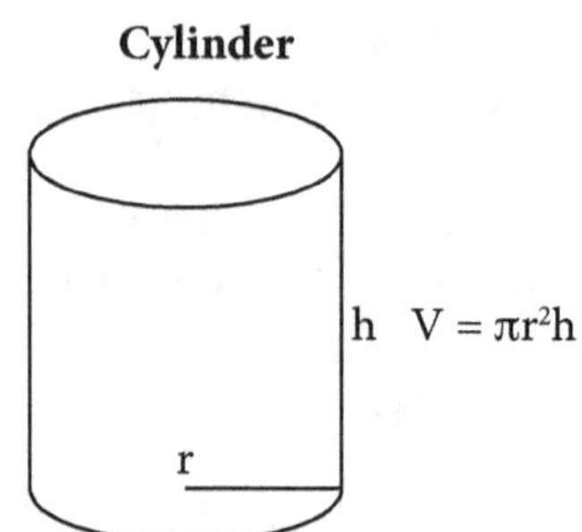

Cylinder

$$V = \pi r^2 h$$

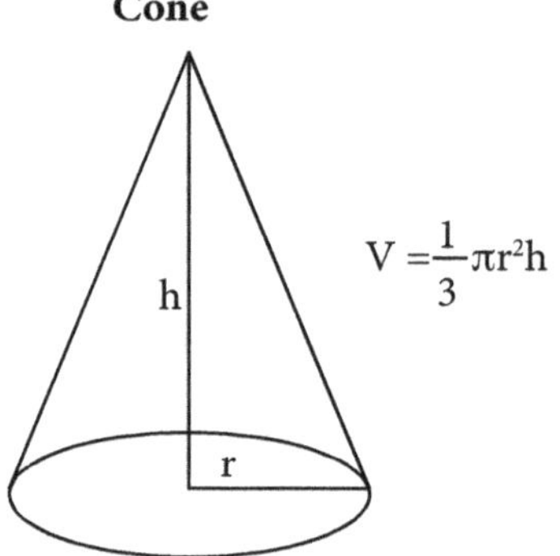

Cone

$$V = \frac{1}{3}\pi r^2 h$$

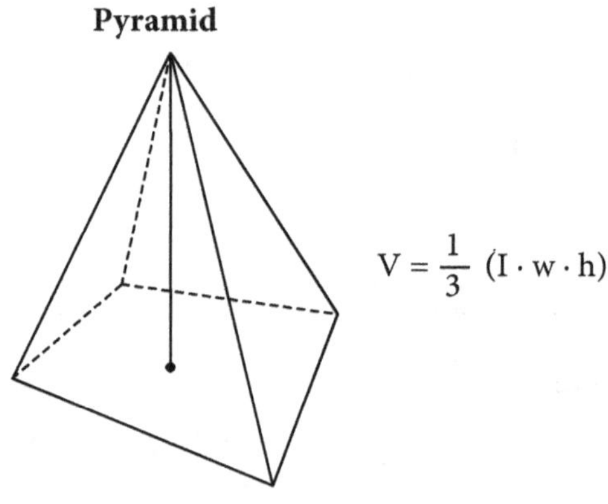

Pyramid

$$V = \frac{1}{3}(l \cdot w \cdot h)$$

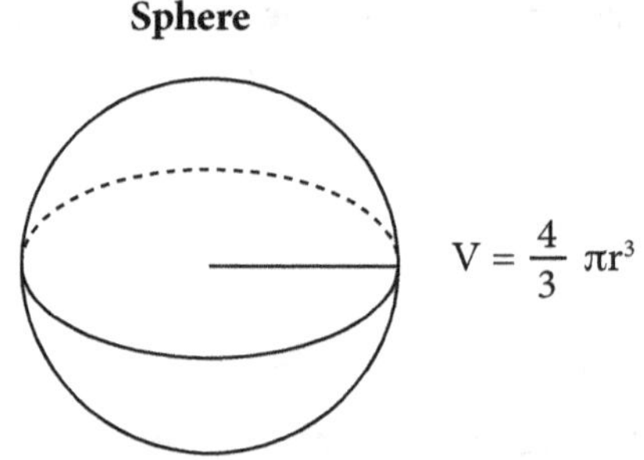

Sphere

$$V = \frac{4}{3}\pi r^3$$

Volume Test

A cone and a sphere have the same radius and volume. Find the radius r in terms of the height h.

A) n

B) 2h

C) $\dfrac{h}{2}$

D) $\dfrac{h}{4}$

The radius of a cylinder is increased by 25% and its height is decreased by 20%. What is the effect on the volume of cylinder?

A) It is decreased by 50%

B) It is decreased by 25%

C) It is increased by 25%

D) It is increased by 50%

If the volume of the cylinder is 72π cm^3, find the radius of the cylinder.

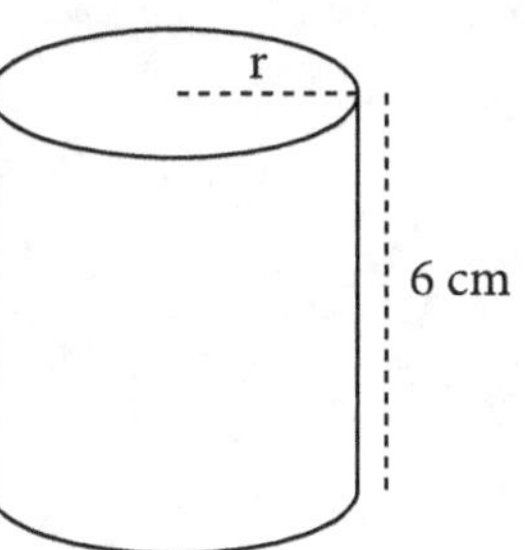

A) $\sqrt{3}$ cm

B) $2\sqrt{3}$ cm

C) $4\sqrt{3}$ cm

D) 6 cm

Find the volume of the following pyramid.

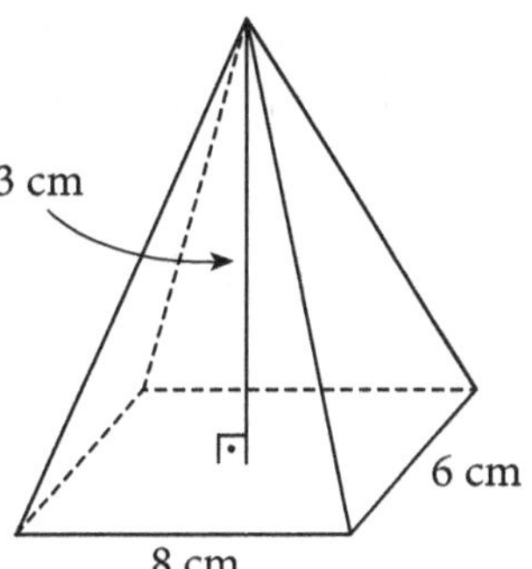

A) 12 cm^3

B) 24 cm^3

C) 48 cm^3

D) 60 cm^3

The volume of the following rectangular prism is 96 cm³. What is value of h?

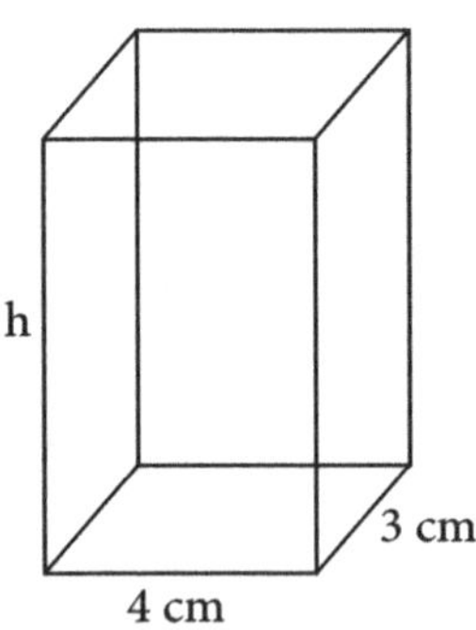

A) 4 cm

B) 8 cm

C) 12 cm

D) 16 cm

In the following figures, the volume of the cone and the cylinder are equal. What is the value of a?

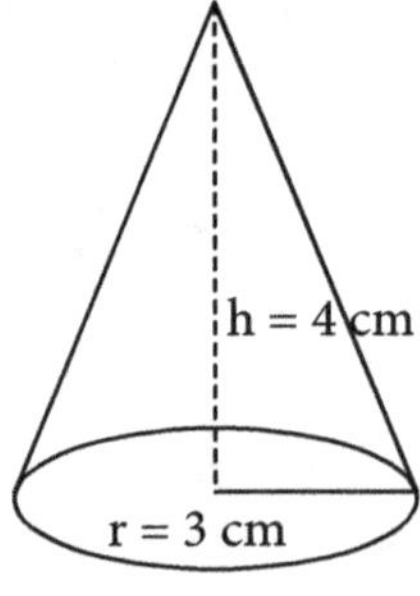

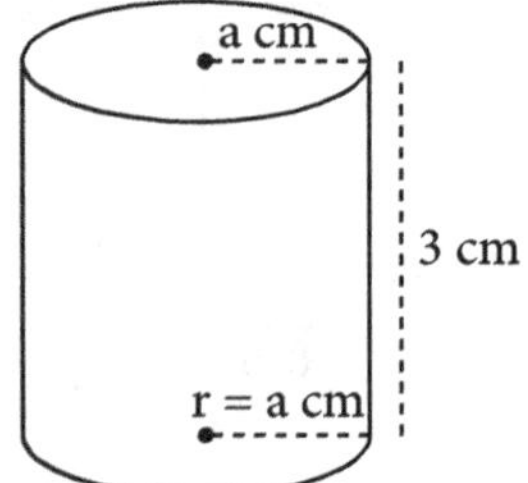

A) 1 cm

B) 2 cm

C) 3 cm

D) 4 cm

A cylindrical tank has a diameter of 10 meters and a height of 6 meters.

It is filled to 80% of its capacity. What is the volume of the water in the tank, in cubic meters?

A) 18π cubic meters

B) 30π cubic meters

C) 36π cubic meters

D) 120π cubic meters

A rectangular prism has dimensions of length 12 cm, width 8 cm, and height 5 cm.

What is the volume of the rectangular prism?

A) 160π cm³

B) 36π cm³

C) 480π cm³

D) 520π cm

Volume Test

The volume of a rectangular prism is 810 cubic units. If its dimensions are in the ratio 2:3:5, what is its height?

A) 4 units

B) 5 units

C) 8 units

D) 15 units

A solid figure is formed by placing a hemisphere on top of a cylinder. The cylinder has a radius of 3 units and a height of 10 units. The hemisphere has the same radius as the cylinder. What is the total volume of the solid figure?

A) 108π cubic units

B) 240π cubic units

C) 300π cubic units

D) 360π cubic units

A cylinder has a radius of 3 units and a height of 6 units.

If both the radius and height are doubled, how does the volume change?

A) The volume becomes 4 times larger.

B) The volume becomes 6 times larger.

C) The volume becomes 7 times larger.

D) The volume becomes 12 times larger.

A cylinder has a radius of 4 units and a height of 6 units.

If the radius is increased by 50%, how does the volume change?

A) The volume becomes 50% larger.

B) The volume becomes 75% larger.

C) The volume becomes 100% larger.

D) The volume becomes 125% larger.

1.	D	2.	C	3.	B	4.	C	5.	B	6.	B	7.	D	8.	C	9.	D	10.	A	11.	C	12.	D

1. Solution:

$$V_{cone} = \frac{1}{3}\pi r^2 h \left.\begin{matrix} \end{matrix}\right\} \begin{matrix} V_{cone} = V_{sphere} \\ \frac{1}{3}\pi r^2 h = \frac{4}{3}\pi r^3 \end{matrix}$$

$$V_s = \frac{4}{3}\pi r^3$$

$$\frac{1}{4}h = r$$

Correct Answer is D

2. Solution:

Suppose $r = 4$ $V = \pi r^2$

$h = 5$ $V = \pi \cdot 16 \cdot 5 = 80\pi$

$r \rightarrow 25\%$ increase $r = 5$

$r \rightarrow 20\%$ decrease $h = 4$

$v = \pi r^2 = 25 \cdot 4 \cdot \pi = 100\pi$

$$\frac{100\pi - 80\pi}{80\pi} = \frac{1}{4} = 25\% \text{ increase}$$

Correct Answer is C

3. Solution:

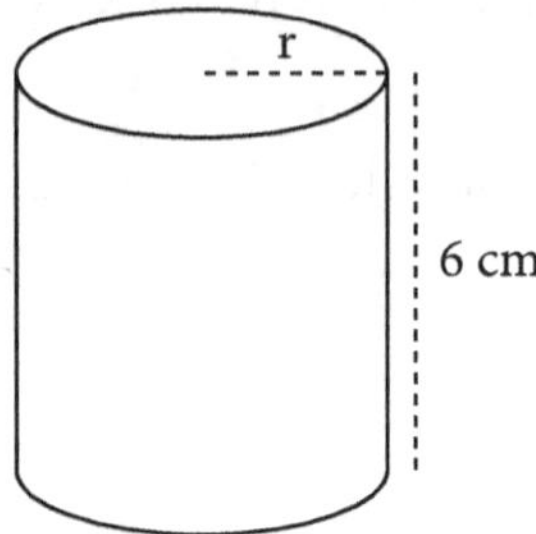

Volume of cylinder $= \pi r^2 h$

$$\pi r^2 \cdot 6cm = 72\pi \, cm^3$$
$$r^2 \cdot 6cm = 72 \, cm^3$$
$$r^2 = \frac{72 \, cm^3}{6 \, cm}, r^2 = 12 \, cm$$
$$r = 2\sqrt{3} \, cm$$

Correct Answer is B

4. Solution:

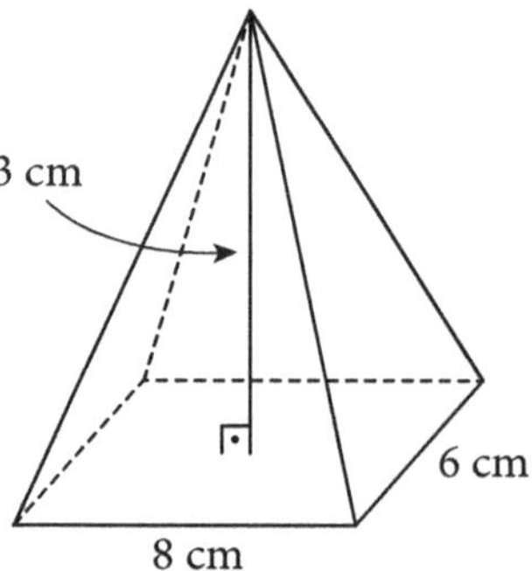

$$V_{pyramid} = \frac{l \cdot w \cdot h}{3}$$

$$V = \frac{3\,cm \cdot 6\,cm \cdot 8\,cm}{3}$$

$$V = 48 \, cm^3$$

Correct Answer is C

5. Solution:

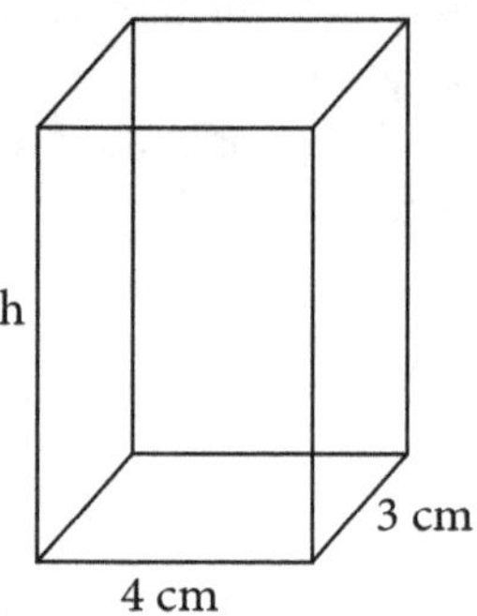

Vrectangular $= l \cdot w \cdot h$

$$h \cdot 4 \, cm \cdot 3 \, cm = 96 \, cm^3$$

$$h = \frac{96 \, cm^3}{12 \, cm^3}$$

$$h = 8 \, cm$$

Correct Answer is B

6. Solution:

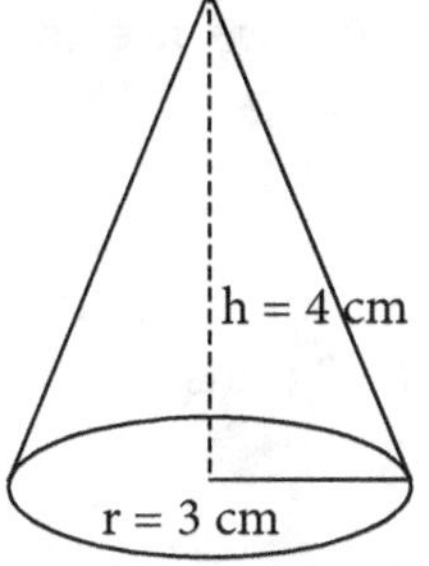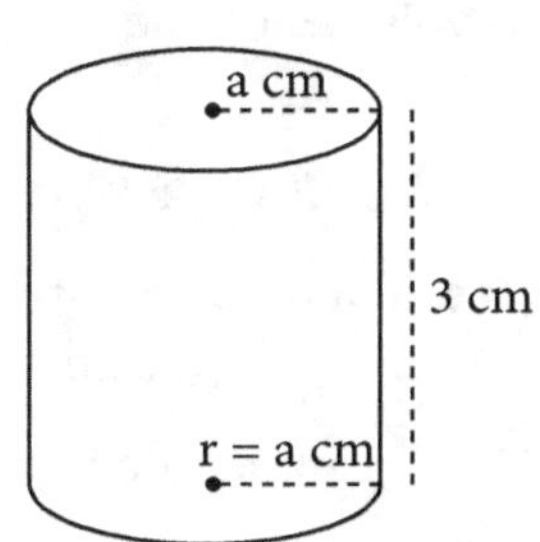

$$V_{cone} = \frac{1}{3}\pi r^2 h = \frac{1}{3\pi} \cdot 9 \cdot 4 = 12\pi$$

$$V_{cylinder} = \pi r^2 h = \pi \cdot a^2 \cdot 3$$

$$= \pi \cdot a^2 \cdot 3$$

$$V_{cone} = V_{cylinder}$$

$$12\pi = \pi \cdot a^2 \cdot 3$$

$$\frac{12}{3} = a^2, \ a^2 = 4, \ a = 2 \text{ cm}$$

Correct Answer is B

7. Solution:

The formula to calculate the volume of a cylinder is given by:

Volume $= \pi \cdot r^2 \cdot h$

In this case, the diameter of the cylinder is given as 10 meters, which means the radius r is half of that 5meters.

The height (h) of the cylinder is 6 meters.

Let's calculate the volume of the cylinder:

Volume $= \pi \cdot 5^2 \cdot h = 25\pi \cdot 6 = 150\pi$ cubic meters

Now, to find the volume of the water in the tank, we multiply the volume of the cylinder by the percentage filled, which is 80% or 0.8:

Volume of water $= 150\pi \cdot 0.8 = 120\pi$ cubic meters

Therefore, the volume of the water in the tank is 120π cubic meters.

Correct Answer is D

8. Solution:

The formula for the volume of a rectangular prism is given by:

Volume of Prism = length • width • height

Given the dimensions of the prism as length = 12 cm, width = 8 cm, and height = 5 cm, we can calculate the volume of the prism as:

Volume of Prism = 12 cm • 8 cm • 5 cm = 480 cm^3

Correct Answer is C

9. Solution:

Let's assign the dimensions of the rectangular prism as 2x, 3x, and 5x, where x is a common factor. According to the problem, the volume is given as 810 cubic units, so we can set up the equation:

$$V = l \cdot w \cdot h = 810$$

$$V = (2x)(3x)(5x) = 810$$

$$30x^3 = 810$$

$$x^3 = 27, \text{ then } x = 3$$

Now that we have the value of x, we can find the height of the rectangular prism by substituting it into the expression for the height:

Height = 5x

$$= 5 \cdot 3 = 15$$

Therefore, the height of the rectangular prism is 15 units

Correct Answer is D

10. Solution:

To solve this question, we need to calculate the volume of the cylinder and the volume of the hemisphere separately, and then add them together.

The volume of the cylinder is given by $V_{cylinder} = \pi r^2 h$, where r is the radius of the cylinder and h is its height.

$V_{cylinder} = \pi \cdot (3^2) \cdot 10 = 90\pi$ cubic units.

The volume of the hemisphere is half the volume of a full sphere with the same radius, which is given by

$V_{sphere} = \left(\frac{2}{3}\right)\pi r^3$.

$V_{sphere} = \left(\frac{2}{3}\right)\pi(3^3) = \left(\frac{2}{3}\right)\pi(27) = 18\pi$ cubic units.

To find the total volume of the solid figure, we add the volume of the cylinder and the volume of the hemisphere:

Total volume $= V_{cylinder} + V_{sphere}$

$= 90\pi + 18\pi$

$= 108\pi$ cubic units.

Therefore, the total volume of the solid figure is 108π cubic units,

Correct Answer is A

11. Solution:

To find the volume of the original cylinder, we use the formula

$V = \pi r^2 h$: $V = \pi(3^2)(6) = 54\pi$ cubic units.

If both the radius and height are doubled, the new cylinder will have a radius of 6 units and a height of 12 units.

The new volume can be calculated as follows:

New $V = \pi(6^2)(12) = 432\pi$ cubic units.

To determine how the volume changed, we divide the new volume by the original volume:

$$\text{Change} = \frac{\text{Diffreance}}{\text{Original V}}$$
$$= \frac{432\pi - 54\pi}{54\pi} = \frac{378\pi}{54\pi} = 7.$$

Therefore, the volume becomes 7 times larger,

Correct Answer is C

12. Solution:

To find the volume of the original cylinder, we use the formula

$V = \pi r^2 h$: $V = \pi(4^2)(6) = 96\pi$ cubic units.

If the radius is increased by 50%, it becomes $(1 + 0.5)$ times the original radius:

New radius $= 4 + (0.5)(4) = 6$ units.

The new volume can be calculated using the new radius:

New $V = \pi(6^2)(6) = 216\pi$ cubic units.

To determine how the volume changed, we divide the new volume by the original volume:

$$\text{Change} = \frac{\text{Differance}}{\text{Original V}}$$
$$\frac{216\pi - 96\pi}{96\pi} = \frac{120\pi}{96\pi} = 1.25$$

Therefore, the volume becomes 1.25 times larger, which corresponds to an increase of 125%.

Correct Answer is D

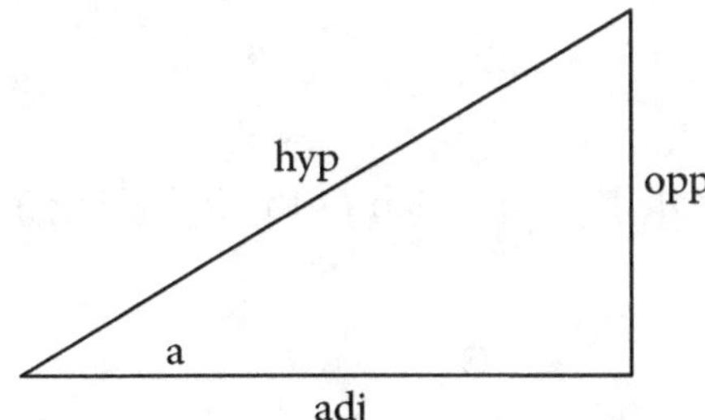

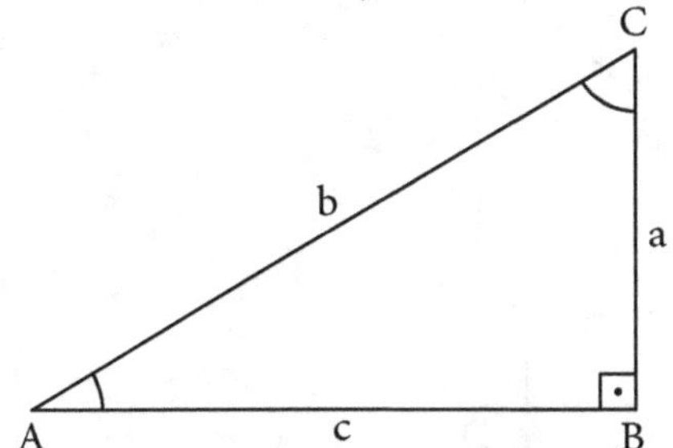

Convert Radians to Degrees

D: Degrees

R: Radians

$$\frac{D}{180} = \frac{R}{\pi}$$

Example:

Convert 150 degrees to radians.

Solution:

From $\frac{D}{180°} = \frac{R}{\pi}$, then $\frac{150}{180°} = \frac{R}{\pi}$ (cross-multiply)

$$R = \frac{150\pi}{180°} = \frac{15\pi}{18} = \frac{5\pi}{6}$$

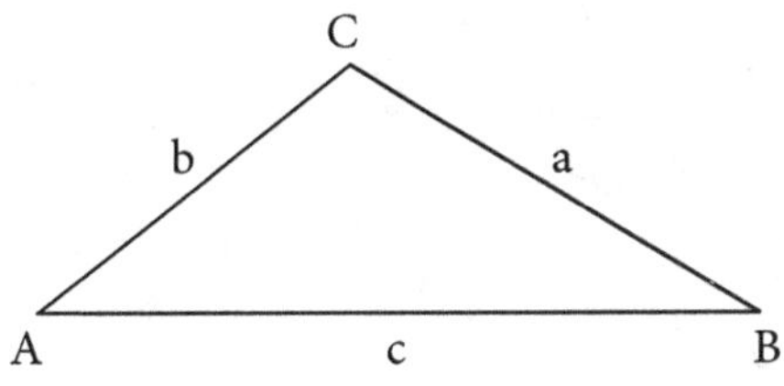

Law Of Cosines

$$c^2 = a^2 + b^2 - 2 \cdot a \cdot b \cdot \text{Cosine } C$$

Law Of Sines

$$\frac{\sin A}{a} = \frac{\sin B}{b} = \frac{\sin C}{c}$$

$$\sin \alpha = \frac{\text{opposite}}{\text{hypotenuse}}$$

$$\sin \widehat{A} = \frac{\left| BC \right|}{\left| AC \right|} = \frac{a}{b}$$

$$\sin \widehat{C} = \frac{\left| AB \right|}{\left| AC \right|} = \frac{c}{b}$$

$$\cos \alpha = \frac{\text{adjacent}}{\text{hypotenuse}}$$

$$\cos \widehat{A} = \frac{\left| AB \right|}{\left| AC \right|} = \frac{c}{b}$$

$$\cos \widehat{C} = \frac{\left| BC \right|}{\left| AB \right|} = \frac{a}{b}$$

$$\tan \alpha = \frac{\text{opposite}}{\text{adjacent}}$$

$$\tan \widehat{A} = \frac{\left| BC \right|}{\left| AB \right|} = \frac{a}{c}$$

$$\tan \widehat{C} = \frac{\left| AB \right|}{\left| BC \right|} = \frac{c}{a}$$

$$\cot \alpha = \frac{\text{adjacent}}{\text{opposite}}$$

$$\cot \widehat{A} = \frac{\left| AB \right|}{\left| BC \right|} = \frac{c}{a}$$

$$\cot \widehat{C} = \frac{\left| BC \right|}{\left| AB \right|} = \frac{a}{c}$$

In the two right triangles below, if tanA = CotD, find the value of EF.

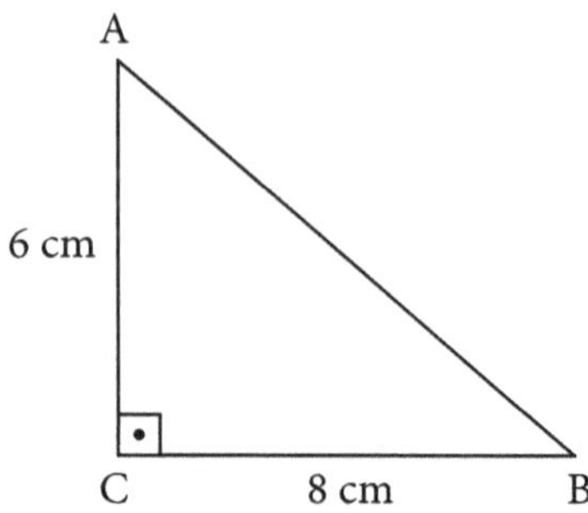

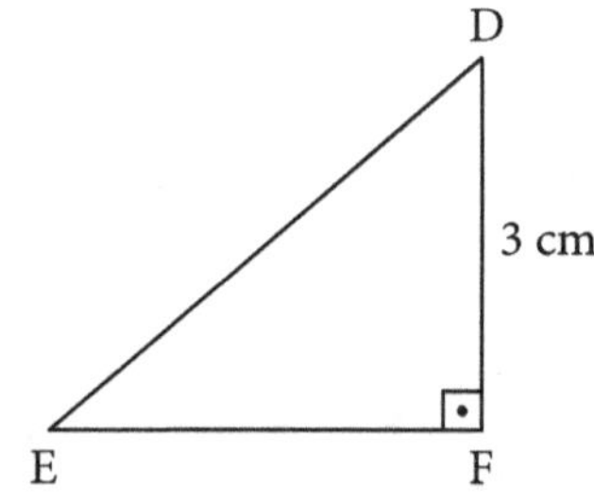

A) 4

B) 10

C) $\frac{9}{2}$

D) $\frac{9}{4}$

In the right triangle below, which of the following is correct?

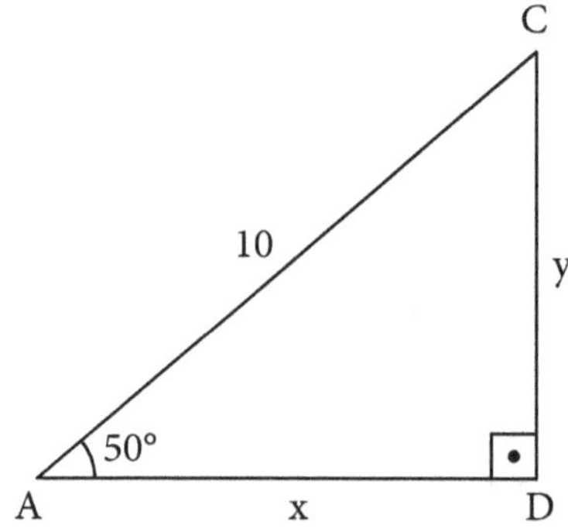

A) $Sin50° = \dfrac{x}{y}$

B) $Tan50° = \dfrac{y}{x}$

C) $Cos50° = \dfrac{10}{x}$

D) $Cot50° = \dfrac{10}{y}$

Convert 60° into radians measure.

(Give your answer in terms of π)

A) $\frac{1}{3}\pi$

B) 3π

C) 2π

D) $\frac{1}{2}\pi$

If $0° \, x < 90°$ and $sin\, x = \frac{3}{5}$, then find cotx.

A) $\frac{3}{4}$

B) $\frac{4}{3}$

C) $\frac{4}{5}$

D) 5

Trigonometry Test

Find $\cos 30° \cdot \sin 60° \cdot \tan 60°$.

A) $\dfrac{\sqrt{3}}{3}$

B) $\dfrac{3}{4}$

C) $\sqrt{3}$

D) $\dfrac{3\sqrt{3}}{4}$

In a right triangle, one angle measures $x°$, where $\cos x° = \dfrac{5}{13}$.

What is $\tan (90° - x°)$?

A) $\dfrac{12}{13}$

B) $\dfrac{5}{12}$

C) $\dfrac{7}{12}$

D) $\dfrac{13}{12}$

$\tan x + \dfrac{\cos x}{1 + \sin x}$ what is the simplest form of the given equation?

A) $\sec x$

B) $\csc x$

C) $\cot x$

D) $\sin 2x$

In a right triangle, the length of one leg is 8 units and the length of the hypotenuse is 10 units.

What is the cosine of one of the acute angles?

A) $\dfrac{3}{5}$

B) $\dfrac{5}{8}$

C) $\dfrac{3}{4}$

D) $\dfrac{5}{4}$

Hard

9

Given that $\sin\theta = \frac{4}{5}$, what is the value of $\cos\theta$?

A) $\frac{3}{5}$

B) $\frac{4}{5}$

C) $\frac{5}{4}$

D) $\frac{\sqrt{3}}{2}$

Medium

10

Given that $\tan\theta = \frac{3}{4}$, what is the value of $\cos\theta$?

A) $\frac{3}{4}$

B) $\frac{4}{3}$

C) $\frac{3}{5}$

D) $\frac{4}{5}$

Medium

11

In a right triangle, the length of one leg is 7 units, and the length of the hypotenuse is 13 units.

What is the value of $\sin\theta$, where θ is one of the acute angles?

A) $\frac{7}{13}$

B) $\frac{7}{12}$

C) $\frac{12}{13}$

D) $\frac{5}{12}$

Medium

12

Given that $\sin\theta = 0.6$ and $\cos\theta = 0.8$, what is the value of $\tan\theta$?

A) 0.5

B) 0.6

C) 0.75

D) 1.25

| 1. | D | 2. | A | 3. | B | 4. | B | 5. | D | 6. | A | 7. | B | 8. | A | 9. | A | 10. | D | 11. | C | 12. | C |

1. Solution:

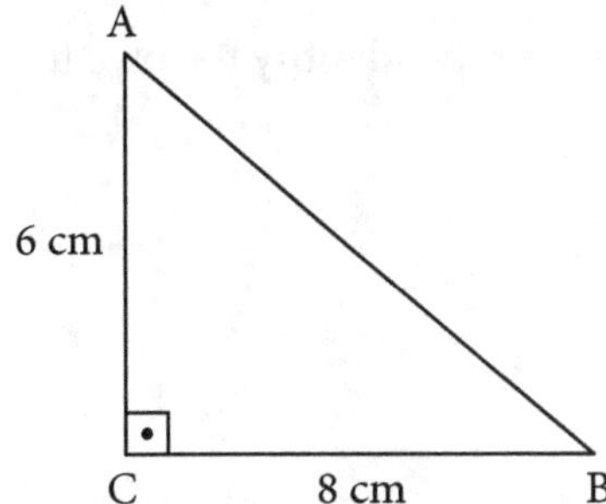

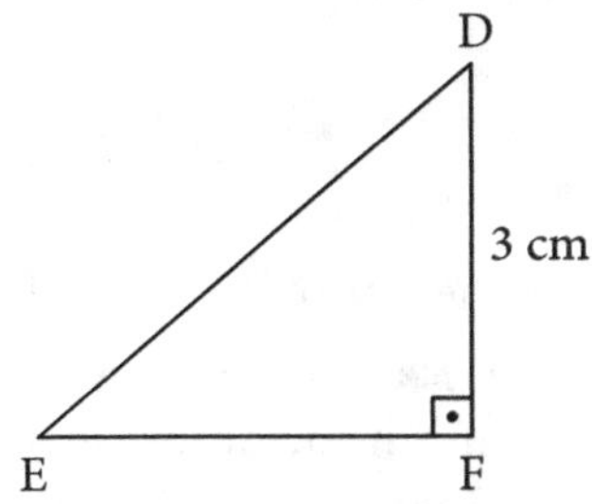

If $\tan A = \cot D$

$$\left.\begin{array}{l} \tan A = \dfrac{8}{6} \\[2mm] \cot D = \dfrac{3}{EF} \end{array}\right\} \dfrac{8}{6} = \dfrac{3}{EF}, EF = \dfrac{18}{8} = \dfrac{9}{4}$$

Correct Answer is D

2. Solution:

$$\dfrac{60°}{180°} = \dfrac{R}{\pi}, R = \dfrac{1}{3}\pi$$

Correct Answer is A

3. Solution:

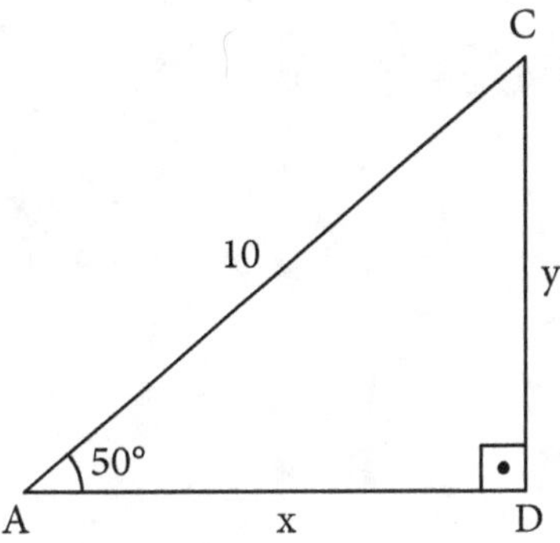

$$\tan 50° = \dfrac{\sin 50°}{\cos 50°} = \dfrac{y}{x}$$

Correct Answer is B

4. Solution:

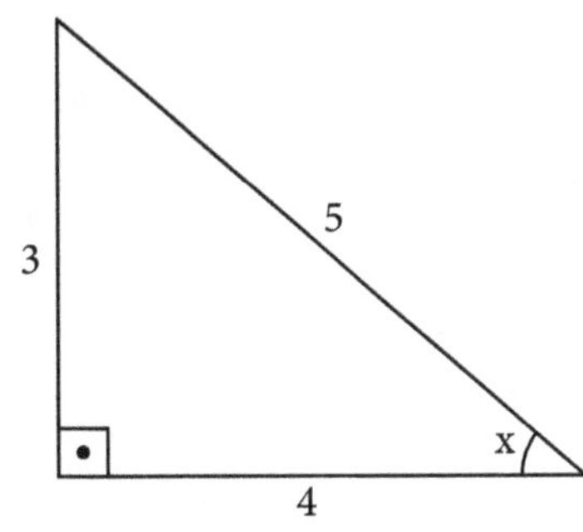

$$\cot x = \dfrac{Adj}{Opposite}$$

$$\cot x = \dfrac{4}{3}$$

Correct Answer is B

5. Solution:

$$\cos 30° \cdot \sin 60° \cdot \tan 60°$$

$$= \dfrac{\sqrt{3}}{2} \cdot \dfrac{\sqrt{3}}{2} \cdot \sqrt{3}$$

$$= \dfrac{3\sqrt{3}}{4}$$

Correct Answer is D

6. Solution:

$$\frac{\sin x}{\cos x} + \frac{\cos x}{1 + \sin x} = \frac{\sin x + \sin^2 x + \cos^2 x}{\cos x\,(1 + \sin x)}$$

$$= \frac{1 + \sin x}{\cos x\,(1 + \sin x)} = \frac{1}{\cos x} = \sec x$$

Correct Answer is A

7. Solution:

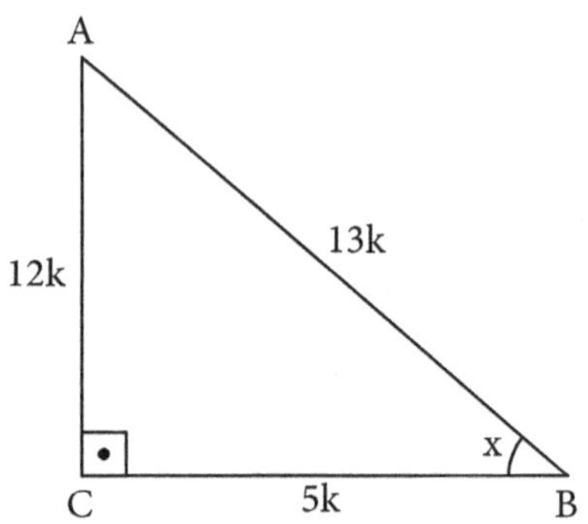

$$\tan(90 - x°) = \cot x° = \frac{5k}{12k} = \frac{5}{12}$$

Correct Answer is B

8. Solution:

In a right triangle, the cosine of an acute angle is equal to the length of the adjacent side divided by the length of the hypotenuse. If one leg has length 8 units and the hypotenuse has length 10 units, then the other leg (adjacent side) has length $\sqrt{(10^2 - 8^2)} = \sqrt{(100 - 64)} = \sqrt{36} = 6$ units.

Therefore, $\cos\theta = \dfrac{\text{adjacen}}{\text{hypotenuse}} = \dfrac{6}{10} = \dfrac{3}{5}$

Correct Answer is A

9. Solution:

The Pythagorean identity states that $\sin^2\theta + \cos^2\theta = 1$. Since $\sin\theta = \dfrac{4}{5}$, we can substitute it into the identity to solve for $\cos\theta$. We have $\left(\dfrac{4}{5}\right)^2 + \cos^2\theta = 1$.

Simplifying, we get $\dfrac{16}{25} + \cos^2\theta = 1$.

Rearranging, $\cos^2\theta = 1 - \dfrac{16}{25} = \dfrac{9}{25}$.

Taking the square root of both sides, we get $\cos\theta = \pm\dfrac{3}{5}$.

Since cosine is positive in the given quadrant,

Correct Answer is A

10. Solution:

The tangent of an angle is defined as the ratio of the opposite side to the adjacent side. In this case, $\tan\theta = \dfrac{3}{4}$, which means the opposite side is 3 units and the adjacent side is 4 units. To find $\cos\theta$, we can use the Pythagorean theorem, which states that the square of the hypotenuse is equal to the sum of the squares of the other two sides. Using this, we have $h^2 = (4^2) + (3^2) = 16 + 9 = 25$. Taking the square root, we get $h = 5$ units. Therefore, $\cos\theta = \dfrac{\text{adjacent}}{\text{hypotenuse}} = \dfrac{4}{5}$.

Correct Answer is D

11. Solution:

In a right triangle, $\sin\theta = \dfrac{\text{opposite}}{\text{hypotenuse}}$. In this case, the opposite side is 7units and the hypotenuse is 13 units. Therefore, $\sin\theta = \dfrac{7}{13}$.

Correct Answer is C

12. Solution:

The tangent of an angle is defined as the ratio of the sine of the angle to the cosine of the angle.

In this case, $\tan\theta = \dfrac{\sin\theta}{\cos\theta} = \dfrac{0.6}{0.8} = 0.75$.

Correct Answer is C

CHAPTER 5
Review Tests

1. If $3x - (4x + 2) = 7$, what is the value of $2(3x + 1)$?

A) 9

B) 14

C) -28

D) -52

2. In a chemistry experiment, Mia will mix x grams of a 20% by weight solution with y grams of a 30% by weight solution to create a 25% by weight solution. The equation below represents this situation:

$$0.2x + 0.3y = 0.25(x + y)$$

If Mia uses 120 grams of the 30% by weight solution, how many grams of the 20% by weight solution must she use?

A) 80 grams

B) 100 grams

C) 120 grams

D) 140 grams

3. A gym membership costs a joining fee of $100 and a monthly fee of $30.

Let's represent the number of months as x and the total cost as T(x).

Which of the following equations represents the total cost T(x) in terms of the number of months?

A) $T(x) = 100x + 30$

B) $T(x) = 100 + 30x$

C) $T(x) = 30x - 100$

D) $T(x) = 30 - 100x$

4. A shipping company charges a base fee of $20 plus $2.50 per pound for shipping packages.

Let's represent the weight of the package in pounds as x and the total cost as C(x).

Which of the following inequalities represents the condition where the total cost of shipping a package is at most $50?

A) $20x + 2.50 > 50$

B) $20 + 2.50x \leq 50$

C) $20x + 2.50x \leq 50$

D) $20 + 2.50x \geq 50$

5. Which of the following expressions is equivalent to $3(2x - 5) - 4(3x + 2) + 2(4x - 1)$?

A) $12x - 29$

B) $2x - 25$

C) $12x - 15$

D) $6x + 1$

6. In a right triangle, one angle measures x degrees, where $\sin(x°) = \frac{3}{4}$.

What is $\cos(90° - x°)$?

A) $\frac{3}{4}$

B) $\frac{1}{3}$

C) $\frac{4}{3}$

D) $\frac{1}{4}$

7. Line p contains the point $(3, -4)$ and $(2, k)$. If line p is parallel to line q, whose equation is $2x + 3y = 7$, what is the value of k?

A) $k = -\frac{7}{3}$

B) $k = -\frac{10}{3}$

C) $k = \frac{5}{2}$

D) $k = \frac{7}{3}$

8. In a 45°-45°-90° special triangle, if the hypotenuse measures 10 units, what are the lengths of the other two sides?

A) Shorter leg: 5 units, longer leg: 5 units, hypotenuse: $10\sqrt{2}$ units

B) Shorter leg: 5 units, longer leg: $10\sqrt{2}$ units, hypotenuse: 10 units

C) Shorter leg: 10 units, longer leg: 5 units, hypotenuse: $5\sqrt{2}$ units

D) Shorter leg: $5\sqrt{2}$ units, longer leg: $5\sqrt{2}$ units, hypotenuse: 10 units

9. $x^2 + 10x + y^2 - 8y = 16$

The equation above defines a circle in the xy-plane.

What are the coordinates of the center of the circle?

A) (-5, 4)

B) (-5, -4)

C) (-10, 8)

D) (-10, -8)

10. A cylindrical container has a diameter of 8 meters and a height of 12 meters.

It is filled to 60% of its capacity. What is the volume of the liquid in the container, in cubic meters?

A) 45π cubic meters

B) 64π cubic meters

C) 92π cubic meters

D) 115.2π cubic meters

11. Which of the following represents all the possible values of x that satisfy the equation:

$$2x + 3 = 5\left(x - \frac{1}{2}\right) - 1?$$

A) $x = -\frac{27}{2}$

B) $x = 2$

C) $x = 27$

D) $x = \frac{13}{6}$

12. If $\dfrac{3 + 2i}{1 - i} = a + bi,$

what is the value of $a + b$?

A) 2

B) -2

C) 3

D) -5

Mixed Review Test I Solution

1. Solution:

To find the value of 2(3x + 1), we can simplify the given equation step by step:

Given equation: 3x - (4x + 2) = 7 First, distribute the negative sign inside the parentheses: 3x - 4x - 2 = 7

Combine like terms: -x - 2 = 7

Add 2 to both sides of the equation: -x = 7 + 2,

-x = 9

Multiply both sides by -1 (to isolate x): x = -9

Now, substitute the value of x into the expression

2(3x + 1): 2(3(-9) + 1) = 2(-27 + 1) = 2(-26) = -52

Therefore, the value of 2(3x + 1) is -52.

Correct answer is D

2. Solution:

To find the value of x, we'll substitute the given values into the equation and solve for x.

0.2x + 0.3y = 0.25(x + y)

Given that Mia uses 120 grams of the 30% by weight solution, we can substitute y = 120 into the equation:

0.2x + 0.3(120) = 0.25(x + 120)

Simplifying:

0.2x + 36 = 0.25x + 30

Now, let's isolate the x term:

0.2x - 0.25x = 30 - 36

-0.05x = -6

Dividing both sides by -0.05:

$$x = \frac{-6}{-0.05}$$

x = 120

Correct answer is C

3. Solution:

According to the given information, the joining fee for the gym membership is $100, which is a one-time cost. The monthly fee is $30, multiplied by the number of months, represented by x.

Therefore, the total cost T(x) is the sum of the joining fee and the monthly fee multiplied by the number of months:

T(x) = 100 + 30x

Correct answer is B

4. Solution:

According to the given information, the base fee for shipping a package is $20, which is a constant value. The additional cost per pound is $2.50, multiplied by the weight of the package in pounds, represented by x. To represent the condition where the total cost is at most $50, we use the less than or equal to symbol (≤).

Therefore, the correct inequality is 20 + 2.50x ≤ 50

Correct answer is B

5. Solution:

To find the equivalent expression, we need to simplify the given expression by combining like terms.

Expanding each term:

3(2x - 5) - 4(3x + 2) + 2(4x - 1)

Multiplying within each set of parentheses:

6x - 15 - 12x - 8 + 8x - 2

Combining like terms:

(6x - 12x + 8x) + (-15 - 8 - 2)

Simplifying further:

2x − 25

Correct answer is B

6. Solution:

To find $\cos(90° - x°)$, we can use the trigonometric identity: $\cos(90° - x°) = \sin(x°)$. Given $\sin(x°) = \frac{3}{4}$, we can determine the value of $\cos(90° - x°)$ as $\sin(x°) = \frac{3}{4}$.

Therefore, $\cos(90° - x°) = \sin(x°) = \frac{3}{4}$. Hence, the value of $\cos(90° - x°)$ is $\frac{3}{4}$

Correct answer is A

7. Solution:

To determine the value of k, we need to use the fact that line p is parallel to line q. Parallel lines have the same slope.

The equation of line q is 2x + 3y = 7.

To find the slope of line q, we can rearrange the equation into slope-intercept form (y = mx + b):

$$3y = -2x + 7 \quad y = \left(-\frac{2}{3}\right)x + \frac{7}{3}$$

The slope of line q is $-\frac{2}{3}$.

Since line p is parallel to line q, it must have the same slope.

We can calculate the slope of line p using the coordinates (3, -4) and (2, k):

$$\text{Slope}(m) = \frac{\text{change in y}}{\text{change in x}}$$

$$m = \frac{k - (-4)}{2 - 3} \quad m = \frac{k + 4}{-1}$$

Since the slope of line p is equal to $-\frac{2}{3}$, we have the equation: $\frac{k + 4}{-1} = -\frac{2}{3}$

To solve for k, we can cross-multiply and solve the resulting equation:

-3(k + 4) = -2

-3k - 12 = -2

-3k = 10

$k = -\frac{10}{3}$

Therefore, the value of k is $-\frac{10}{3}$.

Correct answer is B

8. Solution:

In a 45°-45°-90° special triangle, the ratios of the sides are as follows:

- The shorter leg is opposite the 45° angles and has a length of x.

- The longer leg is opposite the other 45° angle and has a length of x.

- The hypotenuse is opposite the 90° angle and has a length of $x\sqrt{2}$.

Given that the hypotenuse measures 10 units, we can determine the lengths of the other two sides. The lengths of the sides in the triangle are as follows:

- Shorter leg: $x = \frac{10}{\sqrt{2}} = \frac{10\sqrt{2}}{2} = 5\sqrt{2}$ units

- Longer leg: $x = \frac{10}{\sqrt{2}} = \frac{10\sqrt{2}}{2} = 5\sqrt{2}$ units

- Hypotenuse: $x\sqrt{2} = (5\sqrt{2})\sqrt{2} = 10$ units

Therefore, the lengths of the sides are:

Shorter leg: $5\sqrt{2}$ units

Longer leg: $5\sqrt{2}$ units

Hypotenuse: 10 units

Correct answer is D

9. Solution:

To find the coordinates of the center of the circle, we need to rewrite the given equation in the standard form of a circle equation:

$$(x-h)^2 + (y-k)^2 = r^2, \text{where} (h,k)$$

represents the coordinates of the center and r represents the radius.

Given equation: $x^2 + 10x + y^2 - 8y = 16$

To complete the square for x, we add $\left(\frac{10}{2}\right)^2 = 25$

to both sides: $x^2 + 10x + 25 + y^2 - 8y = 16 + 25$

To complete the square for y, we add $\left(-\frac{8}{2}\right)^2 = 16$ to both sides:

$x^2 + 10x + 25 + y^2 - 8y + 16 = 16 + 25 + 16$

Simplifying both sides: $(x + 5)^2 + (y - 4)^2 = 57$

Comparing this equation to the standard form, we can see that the center of the circle is (-5, 4).

Correct answer is A

10. Solution:

To find the volume of the liquid in the cylindrical container, we can use the formula for the volume of a cylinder:

$V = \pi r^2 h,$

where V represents the volume, r represents the radius, and h represents the height. Given that the diameter of the container is 8 meters, we can calculate the radius by dividing the diameter by 2: $r = \frac{8}{2} = 4$ meters.

The height of the container is given as 12 meters.

To find the volume of the liquid in the container, we need to calculate 60% of the total volume of the container.

The total volume of the container is given by $V_{total} = \pi r^2 h$.

Substituting the values, we have

$V_{total} = \pi(4^2)(12) = 16\pi(12) = 192\pi$ cubic meters.

To find 60% of the total volume, we multiply by 0.6:

$V_{liquid} = 0.6 \cdot 192\pi = 115.2\pi$ cubic meters.

Correct answer is D

11. Solution:

To solve the equation, we'll simplify and solve for x: Let's simplify the equation step by step: $2x + 3 = 5\left(x - \frac{1}{2}\right) - 1$

Distribute 5 to the terms inside the parentheses:

$2x + 3 = 5x - \frac{5}{2} - 1$

Combine like terms:

$2x + 3 = 5x - \frac{5}{2} - \frac{2}{2}$

$2x + 3 = 5x - \frac{7}{2}$

Move the x term to one side and the constant terms to the other side: $2x - 5x = -\frac{7}{2} - 3$

Combine like terms:

$-3x = -\frac{7}{2} - \frac{6}{2}$

$-3x = -\frac{13}{2}$

To solve for x, divide both sides by -3:

$$= \frac{-\frac{13}{2}}{-3}$$

Simplifying further:

$x = \frac{13}{6}$

Correct answer is D

12. Solution:

To find the value of a + b, we need to simplify the expression $\frac{3 + 2i}{1 - i}$ and rewrite it in the form a + bi. To simplify the expression, we'll multiply the numerator and denominator by the conjugate of the denominator, which is

$$1 + i : \left(\frac{3 + 2i}{1 - i} \right) \left(\frac{1 + i}{1 + i} \right)$$

Expanding and simplifying:

$$\frac{(3 + 2i)(1 + i)}{(1 - i)(1 + i)}$$

$$\frac{(3 + 3i + 2i + 2i^2)}{1 - i^2}$$

$$\frac{(3 + 5i + 2i^2)}{1 - (-1)}$$

$$\frac{(3 + 5i + 2(-1))}{1 + 1}$$

$$\frac{(3 + 5i - 2)}{2}$$

$$\frac{(1 + 5i)}{2} = \frac{1}{2} + \frac{5}{2}i$$

Now, we can separate the real and imaginary parts:

$$a = \frac{1}{2}$$

$$b = \frac{5}{2}$$

Therefore, the value of a + b is:

$$a + b = \left(\frac{1}{2} \right) + \left(\frac{5}{2} \right) = \frac{6}{2} = 3$$

Correct answer is C

1. What is the solution to the equation $2x + 5 = 3x - 1$?

A) $x = 6$

B) $x = 4$

C) $x = 2$

D) $x = -2$

2. In a triangle with angles measuring 30°, 60°, and 90°, what is the length of the hypotenuse if the shorter leg measures 5 units?

A) 5 units

B) 10 units

C) $5\sqrt{3}$ units

D) $10\sqrt{3}$ units

3. The equation of a line is given as $y = 2x - 3$.

What is the y-intercept of this line?

A) -3

B) 2

C) 3

D) -2

4. Solve the equation $3(2x - 1) + 2 = 5x + 4$.

A) $x = 5$

B) $x = -5$

C) $x = 10$

D) $x = -10$

5. What is the value of y in the equation $2y + 4 = 3y - 1$?

A) $y = 5$

B) $y = -5$

C) $y = 1$

D) $y = -1$

6. If $f(x) = 2x^2 + 3x - 4$, what is $f(2)$?

A) $f(2) = 10$

B) $f(2) = 12$

C) $f(2) = 14$

D) $f(2) = -14$

7. Solve the equation $\sqrt{(x+2)} = 3$.

A) $x = 7$

B) $x = 9$

C) $x = 1$

D) $x = -1$

8. In a right triangle, the longer leg measures 8 units and the hypotenuse measures 10 units.

What is the length of the shorter leg?

A) 4 units

B) 6 units

C) 2 units

D) 5 units

9. Solve the equation $4x - 7 = 3 - 2x$.

A) $x = \dfrac{5}{3}$

B) $x = -\dfrac{1}{2}$

C) $x = 1$

D) $x = -1$

10. What is the solution to the equation $2(x - 1) + 3 = 4x - 2$?

A) $x = 1$

B) $x = 2$

C) $x = \dfrac{3}{2}$

D) $x = 4$

11. Solve the equation $|3x - 2| = 5$.

A) $x = 1, -1$

B) $x = 2, -1$

C) $x = -1, \dfrac{7}{3}$

D) $x = -3, -1$

12. If $2y - 3 = 5y - 7$, what is the value of y?

A) $y = 1$

B) $y = \dfrac{4}{3}$

C) $y = 6$

D) $y = 8$

1.	A	2.	B	3.	A	4.	A	5.	A	6.	A	7.	A	8.	B	9.	A	10.	C	11.	C	12.	B

1. Solution:

To solve the equation, we'll subtract 2x from both sides and add 1 to both sides. Simplifying, we find x = 6.

Correct answer is A

2. Solution:

In a 30°-60°-90° triangle, the hypotenuse is twice the length of the shorter leg.

Therefore, the length of the hypotenuse is 2 · 5 = 10 units.

Correct answer is B

3. Solution:

The y-intercept is the value of y when x = 0.

Substituting x = 0 into the equation, we find y = -3.

Correct answer is A

4. Solution:

Expanding and simplifying both sides of the equation, we get 6x - 3 + 2 = 5x + 4.

Combining like terms, we find 6x - 1 = 5x + 4.

Subtracting 5x from both sides and adding 1 to both sides, we find x = 5.

Correct answer is A

5. Solution:

Subtracting 2y from both sides and adding 1 to both sides, we find 5 = y.

Correct answer is A

6. Solution:

Substituting x = 2 into the function, we find

$f(2) = 2(2)^2 + 3(2) - 4 = 10$.

Correct answer is A

7. Solution:

Squaring both sides of the equation,

we find x + 2 = 9.

Subtracting 2 from both sides,

we find x = 7.

Correct answer is A

8. Solution:

In a right triangle, the length of the shorter leg can be found using the Pythagorean theorem.

Let the length of the shorter leg be x.

Then, we have $x^2 + 8^2 = 10^2$. Simplifying,

we find $x^2 + 64 = 100$.

Subtracting 64 from both sides, we find $x^2 = 36$.

Taking the square root, we find x = 6.

Correct answer is B

Mixed Review Test II Solution

9. Solution:

Combining like terms, we find $6x - 7 = 3$. Adding 7 to both sides, we find $6x = 10$.

Dividing both sides by 6, we find $x = \frac{5}{3}$.

Correct answer is A

10. Solution:

Expanding and simplifying both sides of the equation, we get $2x - 2 + 3 = 4x - 2$.

Combining like terms, we find $2x + 1 = 4x - 2$.

Subtracting $2x$ from both sides, we find $1 = 2x - 2$.

Adding 2 to both sides, we find $3 = 2x$.

Dividing both sides by 2, we find $x = \frac{3}{2}$.

Correct answer is C

11. Solution:

We can write the equation as two separate equations:

$3x - 2 = 5$ and $3x - 2 = -5$.

Solving the first equation, we find $3x = 7$,

which gives $x = \frac{7}{3}$.

Solving the second equation, we find $3x = -3$,

which gives $x = -1$.

Correct answer is C

12. Solution:

Subtracting $2y$ from both sides and adding 7 to both sides, we find $-3 + 7 = 5y - 2y$.

Simplifying, we find $4 = 3y$.

Dividing both sides by 3,

we find $y = \frac{4}{3}$. Therefore,

Correct answer is B

1. If $\dfrac{1}{4} = m^n$, then $\dfrac{4^{-1}}{m} = ?$

   A) m^n

   B) m^{n-1}

   C) m^{n+1}

   D) 4

2. $\dfrac{a^{2m}}{a^{10}} = a^6$ and $a^{3n} = a^{30}$, then $m \cdot n = ?$

   A) 50

   B) 60

   C) 70

   D) 80

3. If $10^{m-2} = n$, then $10^{-m} = ?$

   A) 10

   B) $100n$

   C) $\dfrac{1}{10n}$

   D) $\dfrac{1}{100n}$

4. If $3^4 \cdot 81^3 = 3^{4x}$, then $x = ?$

   A) 3

   B) 4

   C) 8

   D) 12

5. If $\dfrac{m}{n} = 3$, what is the value of $\dfrac{6n}{m}$?

   A) 1

   B) 2

   C) 3

   D) $\dfrac{1}{2}$

6. If $2x + 10 = 20$, what is the value of 2^{-x}?

   A) 8

   B) 32

   C) $\dfrac{1}{8}$

   D) $\dfrac{1}{32}$

7. If $\frac{a}{3} = \frac{28-a}{4}$, what is the value of $\frac{32}{a} = ?$

A) 4

B) 8

C) 32

D) $\frac{8}{3}$

8. Which value of n satisfies the equation below?

$$\frac{3}{4}(n^2) = \frac{27}{64}$$

A) $\frac{3}{4}$

B) 3

C) 4

D) $\frac{4}{3}$

9. If $\frac{1}{2}a \cdot \frac{1}{2}a \cdot \frac{1}{2}a = \frac{1}{64}$, then a = ?

A) 1

B) 2

C) $\frac{1}{2}$

D) 4

10. If $\frac{a}{4} = 3$, then $\frac{a^{-1}}{12} = ?$

A) 12

B) 144

C) $\frac{1}{12}$

D) $\frac{1}{144}$

11. If $A = \frac{1}{2}tv^2$, what is v in terms of A and t?

A) $\frac{2A}{t}$

B) $\frac{A}{2t}$

C) $\sqrt{\frac{2A}{t}}$

D) $\sqrt{\frac{t}{2A}}$

12. If $a = \frac{3m+n}{k}$, then m = ?

A) $\frac{ak}{3n}$

B) $\frac{ak+n}{3}$

C) $\frac{ak-n}{3}$

D) $\frac{n}{ak-3}$

13. $\dfrac{m-n}{n} = \dfrac{4}{5}$, what is the value of $\dfrac{m}{n}$

A) $\dfrac{9}{5}$

B) $\dfrac{5}{9}$

C) 5

D) 9

14. If $(a + b)^2 = 36$ and $ab = 12$, what is the value of $a^2 + b^2$?

A) 6

B) 8

C) 12

D) 16

15. If $x = 7y$ and $x - 4y = 24$, then $x = ?$

A) 8

B) 12

C) 24

D) 56

16. After a 30% decrease, the new price of a shirt is \$140. What was the original price?

A) \$100

B) \$150

C) \$200

D) \$210

17. If $16^x = 64^y$, what is the ratio of y to x?

A) $\dfrac{3}{2}$

B) $\dfrac{2}{3}$

C) 2

D) 3

18. A new copy machine can print 120 pages per hour, and an older copy machine can print 80 pages per hour. How many minutes will two copy machines working together take to copy a total of 360 pages?

A) 72

B) 96

C) 108

D) 120

19. If $3-y = 6$ and $2x + 3y = 4$, what is the average of x and y?

A) 1

B) 2

C) 3

D) 4

20. If $2^a \cdot 2^a \cdot 2^a \cdot 2^a = 8^{4b}$, then $a = ?$

A) b

B) 2b

C) 3b

D) 8b

21. If $2^a + 2^a + 2^a + 2^a = 8^{4b}$, then $a = ?$

A) 12b

B) 12-b

C) b-12

D) 12b-2

Mixed Review Test III Solution

1. Solution

$$\frac{1}{4} = m^n$$

$$4^{-1} = m^n$$

$$\frac{4^{-1}}{m^1} = \frac{m^n}{m^1} = m^{n-1}$$

Correct answer is B

2. Solution

$$\frac{a^{2m}}{a^{10}} = a^6$$

$$a^{2m-10} = a^6$$

$$2m-10 = 6$$

$$m = 8$$

$$a^{3n} = a^{30}, \quad 3n = 30 \quad n = 10$$

$$m \cdot n = 8 \cdot 10 = 80$$

Correct answer is D

3. Solution

$$10^{m-2} = n$$

$$\frac{10^m}{100} = n \quad 10m = 100n$$

$$10^{-m} = \frac{1}{10^m} = \frac{1}{100n}$$

Correct answer is D

4. Solution

$$3^4 \cdot 81^3 = 3^{4x}$$

$$3^4 \cdot (3^4)^3 = 3^{4x}$$

$$3^4 \cdot 3^{12} = 3^{4x}$$

$$3^{16} = 3^{4x}, \quad 4x = 16, \quad x = 4$$

Correct answer is B

5. Solution

$$m = 3n$$

$$\frac{6n}{m} = 6 \cdot \frac{n}{m}$$

$$6 \cdot \frac{n}{3n} = 6 \cdot \frac{1}{3} = 2$$

Correct answer is B

6. Solution

$$2x + 10 = 20$$

$$2x = 10$$

$$x = 5$$

$$2^{-x} = \frac{1}{2^x} = \frac{1}{2^5} = \frac{1}{32}$$

Correct answer is D

7. Solution

$$\frac{a}{3} = \frac{28-a}{4}$$

$$4a = 84-3a$$

$$7a = 84$$

$$a = 12$$

$$\frac{32}{a} = \frac{32}{12} = \frac{8}{3}$$

Correct answer is D

8. Solution

$$\frac{3}{4}n^2 = \frac{27}{64}$$

$$n^2 = \frac{27}{64} \cdot \frac{4}{3}$$

$$n^2 = \frac{9}{16}$$

$$n = \frac{3}{4}$$

Correct answer is A

9. Solution

$$\frac{1}{2}a \cdot \frac{1}{2}a \cdot \frac{1}{2}a = \frac{1}{64}$$

$$\frac{1}{8}a^3 = \frac{1}{64}$$

$$a^3 = \frac{1}{8}$$

$$a = \frac{1}{2}$$

Correct answer is C

10. Solution

$$\frac{a}{4} = 3, \text{ then } \frac{a^{-1}}{12}$$

$$a = 12, \quad \frac{1}{a^1 \cdot 12} = \frac{1}{12 \cdot 12} = \frac{1}{144}$$

Correct answer is D

11. Solution

$$A = \frac{1}{2}tV^2$$

$$2A = tV^2$$

$$\sqrt{\frac{2A}{t}} = \sqrt{V^2}$$

$$\sqrt{\frac{2A}{t}} = V$$

Correct answer is C

12. Solution

$$a = \frac{3m + n}{k}$$

$$ak = 3m + n$$

$$\frac{ak - n}{3} = m$$

Correct answer is C

13. Solution

$$\frac{m-n}{n} = \frac{4}{5}$$

$$5m - 5n = 4n$$

$$5m = 9n$$

$$\frac{m}{n} = \frac{9}{5}$$

Correct answer is A

14. Solution

$$ab = 12$$

$$(a + b)^2 = 36$$

$$a^2 + b^2 + 2ab = 36$$

$$a^2 + b^2 + 2.12 = 36$$

$$a^2 + b^2 = 36 - 24 = 12$$

Correct answer is C

15. Solution

$$x = 7y$$

$$x - 4y = 24$$

$$7y = 4y = 24$$

$$3y = 24$$

$$y = 8$$

$$x = 7y = 7 \cdot 8 = 56$$

Correct answer is D

16. Solution

Original Price = 100x

30% decrease 100x - 30x = 70x

70x = \$140 x = \$2

Original Price = 100x

$= 100 \cdot 2$

$= 200$

Correct answer is C

17. Solution

$16^x = 64^y$

$2^{4x} = 2^{6y}$

$4x = 6y$

$\dfrac{y}{x} = \dfrac{2}{3}$

Correct answer is B

18. Solution

$\left(\dfrac{120}{60} + \dfrac{80}{60} \right) t = 360$

$\left(\dfrac{200}{60} \right) t = 360$

$\dfrac{10\,t}{3} = 360$

$\dfrac{t}{3} = 36, \quad t = 108$

Correct answer is C

19. Solution

$3/3x - y = 6$

$2x + 3y = 4$

$9x - 3y = 18$

$2x + 3y = 4$

$+\ \overline{11x = 22}$

$x = 2, y = 0$

Average of x and $y = \dfrac{x + y}{2}$

$= \dfrac{2 + 0}{2} = 1$

Correct answer is A

20. Solution

$2^a \cdot 2^a \cdot 2^a \cdot 2^a = 8^{4b}$

$2^{a+a+a+a} = \left(2^3 \right)^{4b}$

$2^{4a} = 2^{12b}$

$4a = 12b$

$a = 3b$

Correct answer is C

21. Solution

$2^a + 2^a + 2^a + 2^a = 8^{4b}$

$2^a (1 + 1 + 1 + 1) = (2^3)^{4b}$

$2^a \cdot 4 = 2^{12b}$

$2^a \cdot 2^2 = 2^{12b}$

$a + 2 = 12b$

$a = 12b - 2$

Correct answer is D

1. $f(x) = x^3 - 2x^2 + 2x - 1$. Find $f(x + 1)$.

A) $x^3 + x^2 + x$

B) $x^3 - x^2 - x$

C) $2x^3 + x^2 - x$

D) $3x^3 + x^2 - x$

2. What is the sum of $(4i + 3) + (3 - 3i)$? $(i = \sqrt{-1})$?

A) $i+3$

B) $i-3$

C) $i+6$

D) $i-6$

3. If $\dfrac{x-1}{4} = y$ and $y = 6$, what is the value of x?

A) 20

B) 23

C) 25

D) 27

4. Which of the following is equivalent to theexpression below?

$$(x^2y - 2x^2 + 6xy) - (xy^2 - 2x^2 + 4xy)$$

A) $x^2y - xy^2 + 2xy$

B) $x^2y - xy^2 - 2xy$

C) $x^2y + xy^2 + 2xy$

D) $-x^2y - xy^2 - 2xy$

5. If $\dfrac{x}{y} = 3$, what is the value of $\dfrac{5y}{x}$?

A) 3

B) 5

C) $\dfrac{3}{5}$

D) $\dfrac{5}{3}$

6. What is the solution (x, y) to the system of equations below?

$$x + 4y = -23$$
$$y - x = 18$$

A) $(-1,19)$

B) $(-19,-1)$

C) $(-19,1)$

D) $(1,-19)$

7. A line in the xy plane passes through the origin and has a slope of $\frac{1}{3}$. Which of the following points lies on the line?

A) $(0, 3)$

B) $(3, 0)$

C) $(1, 3)$

D) $(3, 1)$

8. $f(x) = ax^3 + 8$

For the function f defined above, a is a constant and $f(2) = 6$. What is the value of $f(-2)$?

A) 4

B) 8

C) 10

D) 24

9. If $2x - y = 3$, what is the value of $\dfrac{4^x}{2^y} = ?$

A) 4

B) 6

C) 8

D) 12

10. If $x > 0$ and $x^2 - 25 = 0$, what is the value of x?

A) 0

B) -5

C) 5

D) 25

11. According to the system of equations below, what is the value of x?

$$x + y = 10$$
$$x + 2y = 6$$

A) 4

B) 6

C) 8

D) 14

12. If $a = 2\sqrt{3}$ and $3a = \sqrt{3x}$, what is the value of x?

A) 18

B) 24

C) 36

D) 72

13. For what value of x is $|x-3| - 2x$ equal to 0?

A) 0

B) 1

C) -1

D) -2

16. If, $\frac{6}{5}x = \frac{4}{9}$, what is the value of x?

A) 10

B) 2

C) $\frac{10}{27}$

D) $\frac{27}{16}$

14. What is the solutions to $x^2 + 2x + 3 = 0$?

A) -1

B) -2

C) $1 \pm \sqrt{2}i$

D) $-1 \pm \sqrt{2}i$

17. Which of the following equations passes through the coordinates (1,2) and (-1, -2)?

A) $y = x$

B) $y = 2x$

C) $y = \frac{1}{2}x + 1$

D) $y = 2x - 1$

15. If $\frac{3}{4}x - \frac{1}{8}x = \frac{1}{12} + \frac{2}{3}$, what is the value of x?

A) 6

B) 7

C) $\frac{6}{7}$

D) $\frac{6}{5}$

18. What is the value of k in the equation shown below?

$$2k - 3 + 3k = 6(k - 4)$$

A) 11

B) 14

C) 19

D) 21

19.

$$2(x - 3) > 3(x - 6)$$

Which of the following numbers is NOT a solution of the above inequality?

A) 12

B) 11

C) 10

D) 9

20. If x and y are positive integers and x-4y=3, then find $\dfrac{3^x}{81^y}$.

A) 3

B) 6

C) 9

D) 27

Mixed Review Test IV Solution

1. Solution

$F(x) = x^3 - 2x^2 + 2x - 1$

$F(x + 1) = (x + 1)^3 - 2(x + 1)^2 + 2(x + 1) - 1$

$= x^3 + 2x^2 + x + x^2 + 2x + 1 - 2x^2 - 4x - 2 + 2x + 2 - 1$

$= x^3 + x^2 + x$

Correct answer is A

2. Solution

Sum of $(4i + 3) + (3 - 3i)$

$= 4i - 3i + 3 + 3$

$= i + 6$

Correct answer is C

3. Solution

$\dfrac{x-1}{4} = y$

$x - 1 = 4y$

$x = 4y + 1$

Since $y = 6$

$x = 4 \cdot 6 + 1$

$x = 24 + 1 = 25$

Correct answer is C

4. Solution

$(x^2y - 2x^2 + 6xy) - (xy^2 - 2x^2 + 4xy)$

$= x^2y - 2x^2 + 6xy - xy^2 + 2x^2 - 4xy$

$= x^2y - xy^2 + 2xy$

Correct answer is A

5. Solution

$\dfrac{x}{y} = 3, \quad x = 3y$

$\dfrac{5y}{x} = \dfrac{5y}{3y} = \dfrac{5}{3}$

Correct answer is D

6. Solution

$x + 4y = -23$

$+ \quad y - x = 18$

$\overline{}$

$5y = -5 \quad y = -1$

$x = -19$

Correct answer is B

7. Solution

xy plane passes through the origin

$(0, 0)$ and has a slope of $\dfrac{1}{3}$.

$(0, 0)$ and (x, y)

$\dfrac{1}{3} = \dfrac{y}{x} \Rightarrow x = 3y$

$y = 1 \quad x = 3 \quad (3, 1)$

Correct answer is D

8. Solution

$F(x) = ax^3 + 8$

$F(2) = 6$

$F(2) = a \cdot 2^3 + 8$

$6 = 8a + 8$

$-2 = 8a$

$\dfrac{-1}{4} = a$

$F(x) = \dfrac{-1}{4}x^3 + 8$

$F(-2) = \dfrac{-1}{4}(-2)^3 + 8$

$= \dfrac{8}{4} + 8 = 2 + 8 = 10$

Correct answer is C

9. Solution

$2x - y = 3$

$\dfrac{4^x}{2^y} = \dfrac{2^{2x}}{2^y} = 2^{2x-y}$

$= 2^3 = 8$

Correct answer is C

10. Solution

$x > 0$ and $x^2 - 25 = 0$

$(x - 5)(x + 5) = 0$

$x = 5$ or $x = -5$

since $x > 0$, then $x = 5$

Correct answer is C

11. Solution

$- \;/x + y = 10$

$x + 2y = 6$

$-x - y = -10$

$+ \;x + 2y = 6$

$\overline{y = -4,\ x = 14}$

Correct answer is D

12. Solution

$a = 2\sqrt{3}$

$3a = \sqrt{3x}$

$6\sqrt{3} = \sqrt{3x}$

$\sqrt{36 \cdot 3} = \sqrt{3x}$

$\left(\sqrt{108}\right)^2 = \left(\sqrt{3x}\right)^2$

$108 = 3x$

$36 = x$

Correct answer is C

13. Solution

$|x - 3| - 2x = 0$

$x - 3 - 2x = 0 \,,\ x = -3 \,,\ (x \text{ can not be } -3)$

or

$-x + 3 - 2x = 0 \,,\ x = 1$

Correct answer is B

14. Solution

$x^2 + 2x = -3$

$(x + 1)^2 - 1 = -3$

$(x + 1)^2 = -2$

$x + 1 = \mp i\sqrt{2}$

$x = -1 \mp i\sqrt{2}$

Correct answer is D

15. Solution

$\dfrac{3}{4}x - \dfrac{1}{8}x = \dfrac{1}{12} + \dfrac{2}{3}$

$\dfrac{6x - x}{8} = \dfrac{9}{12}$

$\dfrac{5x}{8} = \dfrac{3}{4} \qquad x = \dfrac{6}{5}$

Correct answer is D

16. Solution

$\dfrac{6}{5}x = \dfrac{4}{9}$

$x = \dfrac{4}{9} \cdot \dfrac{5}{6}$

$x = \dfrac{20}{54} = \dfrac{10}{27}$

Correct answer is C

17. Solution

$(1, 2)$ and $(-1, -2)$

$\text{Slope} = \dfrac{y_2 - y_1}{x_2 - x_1} = \dfrac{-2-2}{-1-1}$

$\text{Slope} = \dfrac{-4}{-2} = 2$

$y = mx + b$

$y = 2x + b, \ (1, 2)$

$2 = 2 + b$

$0 = b$

$y = 2x$

Correct answer is B

18. Solution

$2k - 3 + 3k = 6(k - 4)$

$2k - 3 + 3k = 6k - 24$

$5k - 3 = 6k - 24$

$24 - 3 = k$

$21 = k$

Correct answer is D

19. Solution

$2(x - 3) > 3(x - 6)$

$2x - 6 > 3x - 18$

$12 > x$

Correct answer is A

20. Solution

$x - 4y = 3$

$\dfrac{3^x}{81^y} = \dfrac{3^x}{3^{4y}}$

$= 3^{x-4y}$

$= 3^3 = 27$

Correct answer is D